MznLnx

Missing Links Exam Preps

Exam Prep for

Financial Markets and Institutions

Mishkin & Eakins, 4th Edition

The MznLnx Exam Prep is your link from the texbook and lecture to your exams.
The MznLnx Exam Preps are unauthorized and comprehensive reviews of your textbooks.

All material provided by MznLnx and Rico Publications (c) 2010
Textbook publishers and textbook authors do not particpate in or contribute to these reviews.

MznLnx

Rico Publications

Exam Prep for Financial Markets and Institutions
4th Edition
Mishkin & Eakins

Publisher: Raymond Houge
Assistant Editor: Michael Rouger
Text and Cover Designer: Lisa Buckner
Marketing Manager: Sara Swagger
Project Manager, Editorial Production: Jerry Emerson
Art Director: Vernon Lowerui

Product Manager: Dave Mason
Editorial Assitant: Rachel Guzmanji
Pedagogy: Debra Long
Cover Image: Jim Reed/Getty Images
Text and Cover Printer: City Printing, Inc.
Compositor: Media Mix, Inc.

(c) 2010 Rico Publications
ALL RIGHTS RESERVED. No part of this work covered by the copyright may be reproduced or used in any form or by an means--graphic, electronic, or mechanical, including photocopying, recording, taping, Web distribution, information storage, and retrieval systems, or in any other manner--without the written permission of the publisher.

Printed in the United States
ISBN:

For more information about our products, contact us at:
Dave.Mason@RicoPublications.com

For permission to use material from this text or product, submit a request online to:
Dave.Mason@RicoPublications.com

Contents

CHAPTER 1
Why Study Financial Markets and Institutions?   1

CHAPTER 2
Overview of the Financial System   6

CHAPTER 3
Understanding Interest Rates   17

CHAPTER 4
The Behavior of Interest Rates   24

CHAPTER 5
The Risk and Term Structure of Interest Rates   31

CHAPTER 6
Structure of Central Banks and the Federal Reserve System   38

CHAPTER 7
Conduct of Monetary Policy: Tools, Goals, and Targets   43

CHAPTER 8
The Money Markets   52

CHAPTER 9
The Capital Markets   60

CHAPTER 10
The Efficient Market Hypothesis   72

CHAPTER 11
The Mortgage Markets   78

CHAPTER 12
The Foreign Exchange Market   88

CHAPTER 13
The International Financial System   92

CHAPTER 14
Theory of Financial Structure   101

CHAPTER 15
The Banking Firm and Bank Management   111

CHAPTER 16
Commercial Banking Industry: Structure and Competition   122

CHAPTER 17
Savings Associations and Credit Unions   129

CHAPTER 18
Banking Regulation   133

CHAPTER 19
Insurance Companies and Pension Funds   139

CHAPTER 20
Venture Capital Firms, Finance Companies, and Financial Conglomerates   144

Contents (Cont.)

CHAPTER 21
  Investment Banks, Brokerage Firms, and Mutual Funds   149
CHAPTER 22
  Risk Management in Financial Institutions   158
CHAPTER 23
  Hedging with Financial Derivatives   160
ANSWER KEY   171

TO THE STUDENT

COMPREHENSIVE

The *MznLnx* Exam Prep series is designed to help you pass your exams. Editors at MznLnx review your textbooks and then prepare these practice exams to help you master the textbook material. Unlike study guides, workbooks, and practice tests provided by the texbook publisher and textbook authors, *MznLnx* gives you **all** of the material in each chapter in exam form, not just samples, so you can be sure to nail your exam.

MECHANICAL

The MznLnx Exam Prep series creates exams that will help you learn the subject matter as well as test you on your understanding. Each question is designed to help you master the concept. Just working through the exams, you gain an understanding of the subject--its a simple mechanical process that produces success.

INTEGRATED STUDY GUIDE AND REVIEW

MznLnx is not just a set of exams designed to test you, its also a comprehensive review of the subject content. Each exam question is also a review of the concept, making sure that you will get the answer correct without having to go to other sources of material. You learn as you go! Its the easiest way to pass an exam.

HUMOR

Studying can be tedious and dry. MznLnx's instructional design includes moderate humor within the exam questions on occassion, to break the tedium and revitalize the brain

Chapter 1. Why Study Financial Markets and Institutions?

1. In economics, a _____ is a mechanism that allows people to easily buy and sell (trade) financial securities (such as stocks and bonds), commodities (such as precious metals or agricultural goods), and other fungible items of value at low transaction costs and at prices that reflect the efficient-market hypothesis.

   _____s have evolved significantly over several hundred years and are undergoing constant innovation to improve liquidity.

   Both general markets (where many commodities are traded) and specialized markets (where only one commodity is traded) exist.

   a. Delta hedging
   b. Cost of carry
   c. Secondary market
   d. Financial market

2. In business and accounting, _____s are everything of value that is owned by a person or company. The balance sheet of a firm records the monetary value of the _____s owned by the firm. The two major _____ classes are tangible _____s and intangible _____s.
   a. Accounts payable
   b. EBITDA
   c. Income
   d. Asset

3. In finance, a _____ is a debt security, in which the authorized issuer owes the holders a debt and, depending on the terms of the _____, is obliged to pay interest (the coupon) and/or to repay the principal at a later date, termed maturity.

   Thus a _____ is a loan: the issuer is the borrower, the _____ holder is the lender, and the coupon is the interest. _____s provide the borrower with external funds to finance long-term investments, or, in the case of government _____s, to finance current expenditure.

   a. Puttable bond
   b. Convertible bond
   c. Catastrophe bonds
   d. Bond

4. The _____ is a financial market where participants buy and sell debt securities, usually in the form of bonds. As of 2006, the size of the international _____ is an estimated $45 trillion, of which the size of the outstanding U.S. _____ debt was $25.2 trillion.

   Nearly all of the $923 billion average daily trading volume in the U.S. _____ takes place between broker-dealers and large institutions in a decentralized, over-the-counter market.

   a. Bond market
   b. 4-4-5 Calendar
   c. Fixed income
   d. 529 plan

5. _____ is that which is owed; usually referencing assets owed, but the term can cover other obligations. In the case of assets, _____ is a means of using future purchasing power in the present before a summation has been earned. Some companies and corporations use _____ as a part of their overall corporate finance strategy.
   a. Partial Payment
   b. Credit cycle
   c. Cross-collateralization
   d. Debt

6. _____ are cash, evidence of an ownership interest in an entity or deliver, cash or another financial instrument.

_____ can be categorized by form depending on whether they are cash instruments or derivative instruments:

- Cash instruments are _____ whose value is determined directly by markets. They can be divided into securities, which are readily transferable, and other cash instruments such as loans and deposits, where both borrower and lender have to agree on a transfer.
- Derivative instruments are _____ which derive their value from the value and characteristics of one or more underlying assets. They can be divided into exchange-traded derivatives and over-the-counter (OTC) derivatives.

Alternatively, _____ can be categorized by 'asset class' depending on whether they are equity based (reflecting ownership of the issuing entity) or debt based (reflecting a loan the investor has made to the issuing entity.) If it is debt, it can be further categorised into short term (less than one year) or long term.

Foreign Exchange instruments and transactions are neither debt nor equity based and belong in their own category.

    a. Cost of carry   b. Secondary market
    c. Financial services   d. Financial instruments

7. A _____ is a fungible, negotiable instrument representing financial value. They are broadly categorized into debt securities (such as banknotes, bonds and debentures), and equity securities; e.g., common stocks. The company or other entity issuing the _____ is called the issuer.

    a. Securities lending   b. Tracking stock
    c. Book entry   d. Security

8. _____ are government bonds issued by the United States Department of the Treasury through the Bureau of the Public Debt. They are the debt financing instruments of the U.S. Federal government, and they are often referred to simply as Treasuries or Treasurys. There are four types of marketable _____: Treasury bills, Treasury notes, Treasury bonds, and Treasury Inflation Protected Securities (TIPS.)

    a. Treasury Inflation-Protected Securities   b. Treasury Inflation Protected Securities
    c. 4-4-5 Calendar   d. Treasury securities

9. _____ is a fee paid on borrowed assets. It is the price paid for the use of borrowed money, or, money earned by deposited funds. Assets that are sometimes lent with _____ include money, shares, consumer goods through hire purchase, major assets such as aircraft, and even entire factories in finance lease arrangements.

    a. A Random Walk Down Wall Street   b. Interest
    c. AAB   d. Insolvency

10. An _____ is the price a borrower pays for the use of money they do not own, and the return a lender receives for deferring the use of funds, by lending it to the borrower. _____s are normally expressed as a percentage rate over the period of one year.

_____s targets are also a vital tool of monetary policy and are used to control variables like investment, inflation, and unemployment.

a. ABN Amro
b. AAB
c. A Random Walk Down Wall Street
d. Interest rate

11. In finance, _____ refers to Monday, October 19, 1987, when stock markets around the world crashed, shedding a huge value in a very short time. The crash began in Hong Kong, spread west through international time zones to Europe, hitting the United States after other markets had already declined by a significant margin. The Dow Jones Industrial Average (DJIA) dropped by 508 points to 1738.74 (22.61%).
a. Black Monday
b. 529 plan
c. 4-4-5 Calendar
d. 7-Eleven

12. The _____ is one of several stock market indices, created by nineteenth-century Wall Street Journal editor and Dow Jones ' Company co-founder Charles Dow. Dow compiled the index to gauge the performance of the industrial sector of the American stock market. It is the second-oldest U.S. market index, after the Dow Jones Transportation Average, which Dow also created.
a. 7-Eleven
b. 529 plan
c. 4-4-5 Calendar
d. Dow Jones Industrial Average

13. The _____ was a worldwide economic downturn starting in most places in 1929 and ending at different times in the 1930s or early 1940s for different countries. It was the largest and most important economic depression in the 20th century, and is used in the 21st century as an example of how far the world's economy can fall. The _____ originated in the United States; historians most often use as a starting date the stock market crash on October 29, 1929, known as Black Tuesday.
a. 7-Eleven
b. 4-4-5 Calendar
c. 529 plan
d. Great Depression

14. A _____ is a private or public market for the trading of company stock and derivatives of company stock at an agreed price; these are securities listed on a stock exchange as well as those only traded privately.

The size of the world _____ is estimated at about $36.6 trillion US at the beginning of October 2008 . The world derivatives market has been estimated at about $480 trillion face or nominal value, 12 times the size of the entire world economy.

a. Andrew Tobias
b. Anton Gelonkin
c. Stock market
d. Adolph Coors

15. A _____ is a sudden dramatic decline of stock prices across a significant cross-section of a stock market. Crashes are driven by panic as much as by underlying economic factors. They often follow speculative stock market bubbles.
a. 529 plan
b. 7-Eleven
c. 4-4-5 Calendar
d. Stock market crash

16. _____ was an arrangement established in 1979 under the Jenkins European Commission where most nations of the European Economic Community (EEC) linked their currencies to prevent large fluctuations relative to one another.

After the collapse of the Bretton Woods system in 1971, most of the EEC countries agreed in 1972 to maintain stable exchange rates by preventing exchange fluctuations of more than 2.25% (the European 'currency snake'.) In March 1979, this system was replaced by the _____, and the European Currency Unit (ECU) was defined.

a. Exchange Rate Mechanism
b. A Random Walk Down Wall Street
c. European Monetary System
d. Euro Interbank Offered Rate

17. The _____ is where currency trading takes place. It is where banks and other official institutions facilitate the buying and selling of foreign currencies. FX transactions typically involve one party purchasing a quantity of one currency in exchange for paying a quantity of another.

a. Floating exchange rate
b. Foreign exchange option
c. Spot market
d. Foreign exchange market

18. A _____ secures the proper functioning of money by regulating economic agents, transaction types, and money supply.

They are traditionally formed by the policy decisions of individual governments and administrated as a domestic economic issue.

The current trend, however, is to use international trade and investment to alter the policy and legislation of individual governments.

a. Pattern day trader
b. Payback period
c. Bond credit rating
d. Monetary System

19. In finance, the _____ between two currencies specifies how much one currency is worth in terms of the other. For example an _____ of 102 Japanese yen to the United States dollar means that JPY 102 is worth the same as USD 1. The foreign exchange market is one of the largest markets in the world.

a. ABN Amro
b. AAB
c. A Random Walk Down Wall Street
d. Exchange rate

20. A _____, reserve bank, or monetary authority is the entity responsible for the monetary policy of a country or of a group of member states. It is a bank that can lend money to other banks in times of need. Its primary responsibility is to maintain the stability of the national currency and money supply, but more active duties include controlling subsidized-loan interest rates, and acting as a lender of last resort to the banking sector during times of financial crisis (private banks often being integral to the national financial system.)

a. Central bank
b. 4-4-5 Calendar
c. 7-Eleven
d. 529 plan

21. A _____ is an institution, firm or individual who mediates between two or more parties in a financial context. Typically the first party is a provider of a product or service and the second party is a consumer or customer.

In the U.S., a _____ is typically an institution that facilitates the channelling of funds between lenders and borrowers indirectly.

a. Savings and loan association   b. Net asset value
c. Mutual fund   d. Financial intermediary

22. _____ is the process by which the government, or monetary authority of a country controls (i) the supply of money central bank (ii) availability of money, and (iii) cost of money or rate of interest, in order to attain a set of objectives oriented towards the growth and stability of the economy. Monetary theory provides insight into how to craft optimal _____.

_____ is referred to as either being an expansionary policy where an expansionary policy increases the total supply of money in the economy, and a contractionary policy decreases the total money supply.

a. Monetary policy   b. Tax exemption
c. Federal Open Market Committee   d. Natural resources consumption tax

23. In economics, _____ is the total amount of money available in an economy at a particular point in time. There are several ways to define 'money', but each includes currency in circulation and demand deposits.

_____ data are recorded and published.

a. 529 plan   b. 7-Eleven
c. 4-4-5 Calendar   d. Money supply

24. In financial accounting, the term _____ is most commonly used to describe any part of shareholders' equity, except for basic share capital. Sometimes, the term is used instead of the term provision; such a use, however, is inconsistent with the terminology suggested by International Accounting Standards Board. For more information about provisions, see provision (accounting.)

a. FIFO and LIFO accounting   b. Closing entries
c. Treasury stock   d. Reserve

25. The _____ is a United States government corporation created by the Glass-Steagall Act of 1933. It provides deposit insurance, which guarantees the safety of checking and savings deposits in member banks, currently up to $250,000 per depositor per bank. Insured deposits are backed by the full faith and credit of the United States.

a. NYSE Group   b. Ford Foundation
c. FASB   d. Federal Deposit Insurance Corporation

26. _____ is the discipline of identifying, monitoring and limiting risks. In some cases the acceptable risk may be near zero. Risks can come from accidents, natural causes and disasters as well as deliberate attacks from an adversary.

a. 4-4-5 Calendar   b. FIFO
c. Penny stock   d. Risk management

Chapter 2. Overview of the Financial System

1. _____ are cash, evidence of an ownership interest in an entity or deliver, cash or another financial instrument.

   _____ can be categorized by form depending on whether they are cash instruments or derivative instruments:

   - Cash instruments are _____ whose value is determined directly by markets. They can be divided into securities, which are readily transferable, and other cash instruments such as loans and deposits, where both borrower and lender have to agree on a transfer.
   - Derivative instruments are _____ which derive their value from the value and characteristics of one or more underlying assets. They can be divided into exchange-traded derivatives and over-the-counter (OTC) derivatives.

   Alternatively, _____ can be categorized by 'asset class' depending on whether they are equity based (reflecting ownership of the issuing entity) or debt based (reflecting a loan the investor has made to the issuing entity.) If it is debt, it can be further categorised into short term (less than one year) or long term.

   Foreign Exchange instruments and transactions are neither debt nor equity based and belong in their own category.

   a. Financial services
   b. Secondary market
   c. Cost of carry
   d. Financial instruments

2. In economics, a _____ is a mechanism that allows people to easily buy and sell (trade) financial securities (such as stocks and bonds), commodities (such as precious metals or agricultural goods), and other fungible items of value at low transaction costs and at prices that reflect the efficient-market hypothesis.

   _____s have evolved significantly over several hundred years and are undergoing constant innovation to improve liquidity.

   Both general markets (where many commodities are traded) and specialized markets (where only one commodity is traded) exist.

   a. Delta hedging
   b. Cost of carry
   c. Financial market
   d. Secondary market

3. A _____ is a fungible, negotiable instrument representing financial value. They are broadly categorized into debt securities (such as banknotes, bonds and debentures), and equity securities; e.g., common stocks. The company or other entity issuing the _____ is called the issuer.
   a. Security
   b. Securities lending
   c. Book entry
   d. Tracking stock

4. In finance, a _____ is a debt security, in which the authorized issuer owes the holders a debt and, depending on the terms of the _____, is obliged to pay interest (the coupon) and/or to repay the principal at a later date, termed maturity.

Chapter 2. Overview of the Financial System

Thus a _____ is a loan: the issuer is the borrower, the _____ holder is the lender, and the coupon is the interest. _____s provide the borrower with external funds to finance long-term investments, or, in the case of government _____s, to finance current expenditure.

a. Catastrophe bonds
b. Bond
c. Convertible bond
d. Puttable bond

5. A _____ is an institution, firm or individual who mediates between two or more parties in a financial context. Typically the first party is a provider of a product or service and the second party is a consumer or customer.

In the U.S., a _____ is typically an institution that facilitates the channelling of funds between lenders and borrowers indirectly.

a. Mutual fund
b. Savings and loan association
c. Net asset value
d. Financial intermediary

6. The _____ is a financial market where participants buy and sell debt securities, usually in the form of bonds. As of 2006, the size of the international _____ is an estimated $45 trillion, of which the size of the outstanding U.S. _____ debt was $25.2 trillion.

Nearly all of the $923 billion average daily trading volume in the U.S. _____ takes place between broker-dealers and large institutions in a decentralized, over-the-counter market.

a. Bond market
b. 529 plan
c. 4-4-5 Calendar
d. Fixed income

7. _____ is that which is owed; usually referencing assets owed, but the term can cover other obligations. In the case of assets, _____ is a means of using future purchasing power in the present before a summation has been earned. Some companies and corporations use _____ as a part of their overall corporate finance strategy.

a. Debt
b. Credit cycle
c. Partial Payment
d. Cross-collateralization

8. A _____ is a payment made by a corporation to its shareholder members. When a corporation earns a profit or surplus, that money can be put to two uses: it can either be re-invested in the business (called retained earnings), or it can be paid to the shareholders as a _____. Many corporations retain a portion of their earnings and pay the remainder as a _____.

a. Dividend puzzle
b. Special dividend
c. Dividend
d. Dividend yield

9. In economic models, the _____ time frame assumes no fixed factors of production. Firms can enter or leave the marketplace, and the cost (and availability) of land, labor, raw materials, and capital goods can be assumed to vary. In contrast, in the short-run time frame, certain factors are assumed to be fixed, because there is not sufficient time for them to change.

Chapter 2. Overview of the Financial System

a. Long-run
c. Short-run
b. 4-4-5 Calendar
d. 529 plan

10. _____ is a life of security. It may also refer to the final payment date of a loan or other financial instrument, at which point all remaining interest and principal is due to be paid.

1, 3, 6 months _____ band can be calculated by using 30-day per month periods.

a. Primary market
c. Replacement cost
b. Maturity
d. False billing

11. The _____ is that part of the capital markets that deals with the issuance of new securities. Companies, governments or public sector institutions can obtain funding through the sale of a new stock or bond issue. This is typically done through a syndicate of securities dealers.

a. Peer group analysis
c. Sector rotation
b. Volatility clustering
d. Primary market

12. The _____ is the financial market where previously issued securities and financial instruments such as stock, bonds, options, and futures are bought and sold. The term '_____' is also used refer to the market for any used goods or assets, or an alternative use for an existing product or asset where the customer base is the second market

With primary issuances of securities or financial instruments, or the primary market, investors purchase these securities directly from issuers such as corporations issuing shares in an IPO or private placement, or directly from the federal government in the case of treasuries.

a. Performance attribution
c. Delta neutral
b. Financial market
d. Secondary market

13. In economics, the concept of the _____ refers to the decision-making time frame of a firm in which at least one factor of production is fixed. Costs which are fixed in the _____ have no impact on a firms decisions. For example a firm can raise output by increasing the amount of labour through overtime.

a. Long-run
c. 4-4-5 Calendar
b. 529 plan
d. Short-run

14. A _____ is a private or public market for the trading of company stock and derivatives of company stock at an agreed price; these are securities listed on a stock exchange as well as those only traded privately.

The size of the world _____ is estimated at about $36.6 trillion US at the beginning of October 2008. The world derivatives market has been estimated at about $480 trillion face or nominal value, 12 times the size of the entire world economy.

a. Stock market
c. Andrew Tobias
b. Adolph Coors
d. Anton Gelonkin

15. _____ is a measure of the ability of a debtor to pay their debts as and when they fall due. It is usually expressed as a ratio or a percentage of current liabilities.

Chapter 2. Overview of the Financial System

For a corporation with a published balance sheet there are various ratios used to calculate a measure of liquidity.

- a. Operating leverage
- b. Accounting liquidity
- c. Operating profit margin
- d. Invested capital

16. The _____ is a stock exchange based in New York City, New York. It is the largest stock exchange in the world by dollar value of its listed companies securities. As of October 2008, the combined capitalization of all domestic _____ listed companies was $10.1 trillion.
    - a. 4-4-5 Calendar
    - b. 7-Eleven
    - c. 529 plan
    - d. New York Stock Exchange

17. A _____, securities exchange or (in Europe) bourse is a corporation or mutual organization which provides 'trading' facilities for stock brokers and traders, to trade stocks and other securities. _____s also provide facilities for the issue and redemption of securities as well as other financial instruments and capital events including the payment of income and dividends. The securities traded on a _____ include: shares issued by companies, unit trusts and other pooled investment products and bonds.
    - a. 4-4-5 Calendar
    - b. 529 plan
    - c. 7-Eleven
    - d. Stock Exchange

18. A _____ is a financial contract whose value is derived from the value of something else (known as the underlying.) The underlying on which a _____ is based can be an asset, weather conditions bonds or other forms of credit.
    - a. 529 plan
    - b. 7-Eleven
    - c. 4-4-5 Calendar
    - d. Derivative

19. The _____ is the market for securities, where companies and governments can raise longterm funds. The _____ includes the stock market and the bond market. Financial regulators, such as the U.S. Securities and Exchange Commission, oversee the _____s in their designated countries to ensure that investors are protected against fraud.
    - a. Forward market
    - b. Spot rate
    - c. Delta neutral
    - d. Capital market

20. _____ is the removal or simplification of government rules and regulations that constrain the operation of market forces. _____ does not mean elimination of laws against fraud, but eliminating or reducing government control of how business is done, thereby moving toward a more free market.

The stated rationale for '_____' is often that fewer and simpler regulations will lead to a raised level of competitiveness, therefore higher productivity, more efficiency and lower prices overall.

- a. Value added
- b. Demand shock
- c. Deregulation
- d. Supply shock

21. In finance, the _____ is the global financial market for short-term borrowing and lending. It provides short-term liquidity funding for the global financial system. The _____ is where short-term obligations such as Treasury bills, commercial paper and bankers' acceptances are bought and sold.

Chapter 2. Overview of the Financial System

a. Cramdown
b. Consumer debt
c. Debt-for-equity swap
d. Money market

22. In economics, business, and accounting, a _____ is the value of money that has been used up to produce something, and hence is not available for use anymore. In business, the _____ may be one of acquisition, in which case the amount of money expended to acquire it is counted as _____. In this case, money is the input that is gone in order to acquire the thing.
   a. Sliding scale fees
   b. Cost
   c. Marginal cost
   d. Fixed costs

23. _____ has been viewed as a process of increasing involvement of enterprises in international markets, although there is no agreed definition of _____ or international entrepreneurship. There are several _____ theories which try to explain why there are international activities.

Adam Smith claimed that a country should specialise in, and export, commodities in which it had an absolute advantage.

   a. A Random Walk Down Wall Street
   b. ABN Amro
   c. Internationalization
   d. AAB

24. A _____ is an international bond that is denominated in a currency not native to the country where it is issued. It can be categorised according to the currency in which it is issued. London is one of the centers of the _____ market, but _____s may be traded throughout the world - for example in Singapore or Tokyo.
   a. Education production function
   b. Economic entity
   c. Eurobond
   d. Interest rate option

25. _____s are deposits denominated in United States dollars at banks outside the United States, and thus are not under the jurisdiction of the Federal Reserve. Consequently, such deposits are subject to much less regulation than similar deposits within the United States, allowing for higher margins. There is nothing 'European' about _____ deposits; a US dollar-denominated deposit in Tokyo or Caracas would likewise be deemed _____ deposits.
   a. AAB
   b. ABN Amro
   c. A Random Walk Down Wall Street
   d. Eurodollar

26. A _____ is a method of measuring a section of the stock market. Many indices are cited by news or financial services firms and are used to benchmark the performance of portfolios such as mutual funds.
   a. Trading curb
   b. Program trading
   c. Stock market index
   d. Stop order

27. A _____ is a financial crisis that occurs when many banks suffer runs at the same time. A systemic banking crisis is one where all or almost all of the banking capital in a country is wiped out. The resulting chain of bankruptcies can cause a long economic recession. Much of the Great Depression's economic damage was caused directly by bank runs. The cost of cleaning up a systemic banking crisis can be huge, with fiscal costs averaging 13% of GDP and economic output losses averaging 20% of GDP for important crises from 1970 to 2007.
   a. Probability of default
   b. Credit bureau
   c. Deposit insurance
   d. Banking panic

Chapter 2. Overview of the Financial System

28. _____ or financing is to provide capital (funds), which means money for a project, a person, a business or any other private or public institutions.

Those funds can be allocated for either short term or long term purposes. The health fund is a new way of _____ private healthcare centers.

a. Product life cycle
c. Proxy fight
b. Funding
d. Synthetic CDO

29. In economics and related disciplines, a _____ is a cost incurred in making an economic exchange. For example, most people, when buying or selling a stock, must pay a commission to their broker; that commission is a _____ of doing the stock deal. Or consider buying a banana from a store; to purchase the banana, your costs will be not only the price of the banana itself, but also the energy and effort it requires to find out which of the various banana products you prefer, where to get them and at what price, the cost of traveling from your house to the store and back, the time waiting in line, and the effort of the paying itself; the costs above and beyond the cost of the banana are the _____s.

a. Transaction cost
c. Marginal cost
b. Variable costs
d. Fixed costs

30. _____, in microeconomics, are the cost advantages that a business obtains due to expansion. _____ may be utilized by any size firm expanding its scale of operation.

a. Articles of incorporation
c. Economies of scale
b. Employee Retirement Income Security Act
d. Uniform Commercial Code

31. A _____, reserve bank, or monetary authority is the entity responsible for the monetary policy of a country or of a group of member states. It is a bank that can lend money to other banks in times of need. Its primary responsibility is to maintain the stability of the national currency and money supply, but more active duties include controlling subsidized-loan interest rates, and acting as a lender of last resort to the banking sector during times of financial crisis (private banks often being integral to the national financial system.)

a. Central bank
c. 4-4-5 Calendar
b. 7-Eleven
d. 529 plan

32. In economics and contract theory, _____ deals with the study of decisions in transactions where one party has more or better information than the other. This creates an imbalance of power in transactions which can sometimes cause the transactions to go awry. Examples of this problem are adverse selection and moral hazard.

a. Information asymmetry
c. A Random Walk Down Wall Street
b. ABN Amro
d. AAB

33.

A _____ is a type of financial intermediary and a type of bank. Commercial banking is also known as business banking. It is a bank that provides checking accounts, savings accounts, and money market accounts and that accepts time deposits.

a. 529 plan
c. Commercial bank
b. 7-Eleven
d. 4-4-5 Calendar

Chapter 2. Overview of the Financial System

34. In business and accounting, _____s are everything of value that is owned by a person or company. The balance sheet of a firm records the monetary value of the _____s owned by the firm. The two major _____ classes are tangible _____s and intangible _____s.
    a. EBITDA
    b. Income
    c. Accounts payable
    d. Asset

35. A _____ is a financial institution that specializes in accepting savings deposits and making mortgage and other loans. The S'L or thrift term is mainly used in the United States; similar institutions in the United Kingdom, Ireland and some Commonwealth countries include building societies and trustee savings banks.

    They are often mutually held, meaning that the depositors and borrowers are members with voting rights, and have the ability to direct the financial and managerial goals of the organization, not unlike the poliyholders of a mutual insurance company.

    a. Net asset value
    b. Person-to-person lending
    c. Mutual fund
    d. Savings and loan association

36. _____ is the provision of resources (such as granting a loan) by one party to another party where that second party does not reimburse the first party immediately, thereby generating a debt, and instead arranges either to repay or return those resources (or material(s) of equal value) at a later date. The first party is called a creditor, also known as a lender, while the second party is called a debtor, also known as a borrower.

    Movements of financial capital are normally dependent on either _____ or equity transfers.

    a. Clearing house
    b. Credit
    c. Warrant
    d. Comparable

37. A _____ is a cooperative financial institution that is owned and controlled by its members, and operated for the purpose of promoting thrift, providing credit at reasonable rates, and providing other financial services to its members. Many _____s exist to further community development or sustainable international development on a local level. Worldwide, _____ systems vary significantly in terms of total system assets and average institution asset size since _____s exist in a wide range of sizes, ranging from volunteer operations with a handful of members to institutions with several billion dollars in assets and hundreds of thousands of members.
    a. Credit Union Service Organization
    b. Corporate credit union
    c. Fi-linx
    d. Credit union

38. A _____ is a pool of assets forming an independent legal entity that are bought with the contributions to a pension plan for the exclusive purpose of financing pension plan benefits.

    _____s are important shareholders of listed and private companies. They are especially important to the stock market where large institutional investors like the Ontario Teachers' Pension Plan dominate.

    a. Leveraged buyout
    b. Leverage
    c. Limited liability company
    d. Pension fund

Chapter 2. Overview of the Financial System

39. A _____ is a professionally managed type of collective investment scheme that pools money from many investors and invests it in stocks, bonds, short-term money market instruments, and/or other securities. The _____ will have a fund manager that trades the pooled money on a regular basis. Currently, the worldwide value of all _____s totals more than $26 trillion.

Since 1940, there have been three basic types of investment companies in the United States: open-end funds, also known in the US as _____s; unit investment trusts (UITs); and closed-end funds.

a. Financial intermediary
c. Trust company
b. Net asset value
d. Mutual fund

40. In finance, _____ is the process of estimating the potential market value of a financial asset or liability. they can be done on assets (for example, investments in marketable securities such as stocks, options, business enterprises, or intangible assets such as patents and trademarks) or on liabilities (e.g., Bonds issued by a company.) _____s are required in many contexts including investment analysis, capital budgeting, merger and acquisition transactions, financial reporting, taxable events to determine the proper tax liability, and in litigation.

a. Procter ' Gamble
c. Valuation
b. Margin
d. Share

41. In business, _____ is the total assets minus total outside liabilities of an individual or a company. For a company, this is called shareholders' equity and may be referred to as book value. _____ is stated as at a particular point in time.

a. Certified International Investment Analyst
c. Moneylender
b. Restructuring
d. Net worth

42. Congress enacted the _____, in the aftermath of the stock market crash of 1929 and during the ensuing Great Depression. It requires that any offer or sale of securities using the means and instrumentalities of interstate commerce be registered pursuant to the 1933 Act, unless an exemption from registration exists under the law.

a. 529 plan
c. Securities Act of 1933
b. 4-4-5 Calendar
d. 7-Eleven

43. The U.S. _____ is an independent agency of the United States government which holds primary responsibility for enforcing the federal securities laws and regulating the securities industry, the nation's stock and options exchanges, and other electronic securities markets. The SEC was created by section 4 of the SEC of 1934 (now codified as 15 U.S.C. § 78d and commonly referred to as the 1934 Act.)

a. 529 plan
c. Securities and Exchange Commission
b. 7-Eleven
d. 4-4-5 Calendar

44. A _____ is a sudden dramatic decline of stock prices across a significant cross-section of a stock market. Crashes are driven by panic as much as by underlying economic factors. They often follow speculative stock market bubbles.

a. 4-4-5 Calendar
c. 529 plan
b. 7-Eleven
d. Stock market crash

45. The _____ was the most devastating stock market crash in the history of the United States, taking into consideration the full extent and duration of its fallout.

Chapter 2. Overview of the Financial System

Three phrases--Black Thursday, Black Monday, and Black Tuesday--are commonly used to describe this collapse of stock values. All three are appropriate, for the crash was not a one-day affair. The initial crash occurred on Thursday, October 24, 1929, but the catastrophic downturn of Monday, October 28 and Tuesday, October 29 precipitated widespread alarm and the onset of an unprecedented and long-lasting economic depression for the United States and the world. This stock market collapse continued for a month.

   a. Wall Street Crash of 1929
   c. Securitization
   b. Board of Audit
   d. Legal and regulatory risk

46. The institution most often referenced by the word '_____' is a public or publicly traded _____, the shares of which are traded on a public stock exchange (e.g., the New York Stock Exchange or Nasdaq in the United States) where shares of stock of _____s are bought and sold by and to the general public. Most of the largest businesses in the world are publicly traded _____s. However, the majority of _____s are said to be closely held, privately held or close _____s, meaning that no ready market exists for the trading of shares.
   a. Depository Trust Company
   c. Protect
   b. Corporation
   d. Federal Home Loan Mortgage Corporation

47. Explicit _____ is a measure implemented in many countries to protect bank depositors, in full or in part, from losses caused by a bank's inability to pay its debts when due. _____ systems are one component of a financial system safety net that promotes financial stability.
   a. Time deposit
   c. Banking panic
   b. Reserve requirement
   d. Deposit Insurance

48. The _____ is a United States government corporation created by the Glass-Steagall Act of 1933. It provides deposit insurance, which guarantees the safety of checking and savings deposits in member banks, currently up to $250,000 per depositor per bank. Insured deposits are backed by the full faith and credit of the United States.
   a. Federal Deposit Insurance Corporation
   c. NYSE Group
   b. FASB
   d. Ford Foundation

49. The _____ was a worldwide economic downturn starting in most places in 1929 and ending at different times in the 1930s or early 1940s for different countries. It was the largest and most important economic depression in the 20th century, and is used in the 21st century as an example of how far the world's economy can fall. The _____ originated in the United States; historians most often use as a starting date the stock market crash on October 29, 1929, known as Black Tuesday.
   a. 529 plan
   c. 7-Eleven
   b. 4-4-5 Calendar
   d. Great Depression

50. In business and finance, a _____ (also referred to as equity _____) of stock means a _____ of ownership in a corporation (company.) In the plural, stocks is often used as a synonym for _____s especially in the United States, but it is less commonly used that way outside of North America.

In the United Kingdom, South Africa, and Australia, stock can also refer to completely different financial instruments such as government bonds or, less commonly, to all kinds of marketable securities.

Chapter 2. Overview of the Financial System

a. Bucket shop
c. Margin

b. Procter ' Gamble
d. Share

51. A '_____' is a 'Charge' that is paid to obtain the right to delay a payment. Essentially, the payer purchases the right to make a given payment in the future instead of in the Present. The '_____', or 'Charge' that must be paid to delay the payment, is simply the difference between what the payment amount would be if it were paid in the present and what the payment amount would be paid if it were paid in the future.
  a. Risk aversion
  c. Discount

  b. Value at risk
  d. Risk modeling

52. The _____ , a component of the Federal Reserve System, is charged under United States law with overseeing the nation's open market operations. It is the Federal Reserve Committee that makes key decisions about interest rates and the growth jam of the United States money supply. It is the principal organ of United States national monetary policy.
  a. Fiscal policy
  c. Tax incidence

  b. Federal Open Market Committee
  d. Tax exemption

53. In economics, _____ is the total amount of money available in an economy at a particular point in time. There are several ways to define 'money', but each includes currency in circulation and demand deposits.

_____ data are recorded and published.

  a. 7-Eleven
  c. 529 plan

  b. Money supply
  d. 4-4-5 Calendar

54. _____ is a United States government regulation that put a limit on the interest rates that banks could pay, including a rate of zero on demand deposits (checking accounts.) Section 11 of the Banking Act of 1933 (12 U.S.C. 371a) prohibits member banks from paying interest on demand deposits, which is implemented by _____
  a. Fair Credit Reporting Act
  c. Fair Credit Billing Act

  b. Truth in Lending Act
  d. Regulation Q

55. In financial accounting, the term _____ is most commonly used to describe any part of shareholders' equity, except for basic share capital. Sometimes, the term is used instead of the term provision; such a use, however, is inconsistent with the terminology suggested by International Accounting Standards Board. For more information about provisions, see provision (accounting.)
  a. Closing entries
  c. FIFO and LIFO accounting

  b. Treasury stock
  d. Reserve

56. The _____ is a bank regulation that sets the minimum reserves each bank must hold to customer deposits and notes. These reserves are designed to satisfy withdrawal demands, and would normally be in the form of fiat currency stored in a bank vault (vault cash), or with a central bank.

The reserve ratio is sometimes used as a tool in the monetary policy, influencing the country's economy, borrowing, and interest rates.

a. Prime rate
c. Variable rate mortgage
b. Wall Street Journal prime rate
d. Reserve requirement

57. _____ is a fee paid on borrowed assets. It is the price paid for the use of borrowed money , or, money earned by deposited funds . Assets that are sometimes lent with _____ include money, shares, consumer goods through hire purchase, major assets such as aircraft, and even entire factories in finance lease arrangements.
  a. A Random Walk Down Wall Street
  b. Insolvency
  c. AAB
  d. Interest

Chapter 3. Understanding Interest Rates

1. _____ is a fee paid on borrowed assets. It is the price paid for the use of borrowed money, or, money earned by deposited funds. Assets that are sometimes lent with _____ include money, shares, consumer goods through hire purchase, major assets such as aircraft, and even entire factories in finance lease arrangements.
   a. AAB
   b. A Random Walk Down Wall Street
   c. Insolvency
   d. Interest

2. An _____ is the price a borrower pays for the use of money they do not own, and the return a lender receives for deferring the use of funds, by lending it to the borrower. _____s are normally expressed as a percentage rate over the period of one year.

   _____s targets are also a vital tool of monetary policy and are used to control variables like investment, inflation, and unemployment.

   a. AAB
   b. ABN Amro
   c. Interest rate
   d. A Random Walk Down Wall Street

3. _____ is a life of security. It may also refer to the final payment date of a loan or other financial instrument, at which point all remaining interest and principal is due to be paid.

   1, 3, 6 months _____ band can be calculated by using 30-day per month periods.

   a. Primary market
   b. Replacement cost
   c. False billing
   d. Maturity

4. In finance, the term _____ describes the amount in cash that returns to the owners of a security. Normally it does not include the price variations, at the difference of the total return. _____ applies to various stated rates of return on stocks (common and preferred, and convertible), fixed income instruments (bonds, notes, bills, strips, zero coupon), and some other investment type insurance products (e.g. annuities.)
   a. Yield
   b. Macaulay duration
   c. 4-4-5 Calendar
   d. Yield to maturity

5. The _____ or redemption yield is the yield promised to the bondholder on the assumption that the bond or other fixed-interest security such as gilts will be held to maturity, that all coupon and principal payments will be made and coupon payments are reinvested at the bond's promised yield at the same rate as invested. It is a measure of the return of the bond. This technique in theory allows investors to calculate the fair value of different financial instruments.
   a. Yield
   b. Macaulay duration
   c. 4-4-5 Calendar
   d. Yield to maturity

6. In finance, a _____ is a debt security, in which the authorized issuer owes the holders a debt and, depending on the terms of the _____, is obliged to pay interest (the coupon) and/or to repay the principal at a later date, termed maturity.

   Thus a _____ is a loan: the issuer is the borrower, the _____ holder is the lender, and the coupon is the interest. _____s provide the borrower with external funds to finance long-term investments, or, in the case of government _____s, to finance current expenditure.

a. Catastrophe bonds
b. Puttable bond
c. Convertible bond
d. Bond

7. The coupon or _____ of a bond is the amount of interest paid per year expressed as a percentage of the face value of the bond.

For example if you hold $10,000 nominal of a bond described as a 4.5% loan stock, you will receive $450 in interest each year (probably in two installments of $225 each.)

Not all bonds have coupons.

a. Zero-coupon bond
b. Coupon rate
c. Puttable bond
d. Revenue bonds

8. _____ is that which is owed; usually referencing assets owed, but the term can cover other obligations. In the case of assets, _____ is a means of using future purchasing power in the present before a summation has been earned. Some companies and corporations use _____ as a part of their overall corporate finance strategy.
a. Partial Payment
b. Credit cycle
c. Cross-collateralization
d. Debt

9. A '_____' is a 'Charge' that is paid to obtain the right to delay a payment. Essentially, the payer purchases the right to make a given payment in the future instead of in the Present. The '_____', or 'Charge' that must be paid to delay the payment, is simply the difference between what the payment amount would be if it were paid in the present and what the payment amount would be paid if it were paid in the future.
a. Value at risk
b. Risk aversion
c. Discount
d. Risk modeling

10. A _____ is a bond bought at a price lower than its face value, with the face value repaid at the time of maturity. It does not make periodic interest payments, or so-called 'coupons,' hence the term zero-coupon bond. Investors earn return from the compounded interest all paid at maturity plus the difference between the discounted price of the bond and its par value.
a. Callable bond
b. Bowie bonds
c. Zero coupon bond
d. Municipal bond

11. A _____ is a bond bought at a price lower than its face value, with the face value repaid at the time of maturity. It does not make periodic interest payments, or have so-called 'coupons,' hence the term _____. Investors earn return from the compounded interest all paid at maturity plus the difference between the discounted price of the bond and its par value.
a. Clean price
b. Corporate bond
c. Bond fund
d. Zero-coupon bond

12. A _____ is a bond issued by a corporation. The term is usually applied to longer-term debt instruments, generally with a maturity date falling at least a year after their issue date. (The term 'commercial paper' is sometimes used for instruments with a shorter maturity.)

a. Serial bond
b. Brady bonds
c. Government bond
d. Corporate Bond

13. _____, in finance and accounting, means stated value or face value. From this comes the expressions at par (at the _____), over par (over _____) and under par (under _____.)

The term '_____' has several meanings depending on context and geography.

a. FIDC
b. Sinking fund
c. Global Squeeze
d. Par value

14. _____ is the value on a given date of a future payment or series of future payments, discounted to reflect the time value of money and other factors such as investment risk. _____ calculations are widely used in business and economics to provide a means to compare cash flows at different times on a meaningful 'like to like' basis.

The most commonly applied model of the time value of money is compound interest.

a. Net present value
b. Negative gearing
c. Present value of benefits
d. Present value

15. In economics, business, and accounting, a _____ is the value of money that has been used up to produce something, and hence is not available for use anymore. In business, the _____ may be one of acquisition, in which case the amount of money expended to acquire it is counted as _____. In this case, money is the input that is gone in order to acquire the thing.

a. Marginal cost
b. Sliding scale fees
c. Fixed costs
d. Cost

16. A _____ is an annuity in which the periodic payments begin on a fixed date and continue indefinitely. It is sometimes referred to as a perpetual annuity. Fixed coupon payments on permanently invested (irredeemable) sums of money are prime examples of these. Scholarships paid perpetually from an endowment fit the definition of _____.

a. Current yield
b. Stochastic volatility
c. LIBOR market model
d. Perpetuity

17. The phrase _____ refers to the aspect of corporate strategy, corporate finance and management dealing with the buying, selling and combining of different companies that can aid, finance, or help a growing company in a given industry grow rapidly without having to create another business entity.

An acquisition, also known as a takeover, is the buying of one company (the 'target') by another. An acquisition may be friendly or hostile.

a. 529 plan
b. 7-Eleven
c. 4-4-5 Calendar
d. Mergers and acquisitions

18.

Chapter 3. Understanding Interest Rates

A _____ is a type of financial intermediary and a type of bank. Commercial banking is also known as business banking. It is a bank that provides checking accounts, savings accounts, and money market accounts and that accepts time deposits.

a. 7-Eleven
b. Commercial bank
c. 529 plan
d. 4-4-5 Calendar

19. A _____ is a financial crisis that occurs when many banks suffer runs at the same time. A systemic banking crisis is one where all or almost all of the banking capital in a country is wiped out. The resulting chain of bankruptcies can cause a long economic recession. Much of the Great Depression's economic damage was caused directly by bank runs. The cost of cleaning up a systemic banking crisis can be huge, with fiscal costs averaging 13% of GDP and economic output losses averaging 20% of GDP for important crises from 1970 to 2007.

a. Probability of default
b. Credit bureau
c. Deposit insurance
d. Banking panic

20. The _____, interest yield, income yield, flat yield or running yield is a financial term used in reference to bonds and other fixed-interest securities such as gilts. It is the ratio of the annual interest payment and the bond's current price.

The _____ only therefore refers to the yield of the bond at the current moment. It does not reflect the total return over the life of the bond. In particular, it takes no account of reinvestment risk (the uncertainty about the rate at which future cashflows can be reinvested) or the fact that bonds usually mature at par value, which can be an important component of a bond's return.

a. Perpetuity
b. Current yield
c. Stochastic volatility
d. Modified Internal Rate of Return

21. In the global money market, _____ is an unsecured promissory note with a fixed maturity of one to 270 days. _____ is a money-market security issued (sold) by large banks and corporations to get money to meet short term debt obligations (for example, payroll), and is only backed by an issuing bank or corporation's promise to pay the face amount on the maturity date specified on the note. Since it is not backed by collateral, only firms with excellent credit ratings from a recognized rating agency will be able to sell their _____ at a reasonable price.

a. Financial distress
b. Book building
c. Commercial paper
d. Trade-off theory

22. _____ mature in one year or less. Like zero-coupon bonds, they do not pay interest prior to maturity; instead they are sold at a discount of the par value to create a positive yield to maturity. Many regard _____ as the least risky investment available to U.S. investors.

a. 4-4-5 Calendar
b. Treasury securities
c. Treasury Inflation Protected Securities
d. Treasury bills

23. A _____ is a unit that is equal to 1/100th of a percentage point. It is frequently used to express percentage point changes of less than 1%. It avoids the ambiguity between relative and absolute discussions about rates.

a. 4-4-5 Calendar
b. Bond market
c. 529 plan
d. Basis point

Chapter 3. Understanding Interest Rates

24. The _____ in financial mathematics and economics estimates the relationship between nominal and real interest rates under inflation. It is named after Irving Fisher who was famous for his works on the theory of interest. In finance, the _____ is primarily used in YTM calculations of bonds or IRR calculations of investments.

Letting *r* denote the real interest rate, *i* denote the nominal interest rate, and let >π denote the inflation rate, the _____ is:

a. Treynor-Black model
b. Discount rate
c. Binomial options pricing model
d. Fisher equation

25. In finance and economics _____ refers to the rate of interest before adjustment for inflation (in contrast with the real interest rate); or, for interest balls stated' without adjustment for the full effect of compounding (also referred to as the nominal annual rate.) An interest rate is called nominal if the frequency of compounding (e.g. a month) is not identical to the basic time unit (normally a year.)

The real interest rate includes compensation for the lender's lost value due to inflation, whereas the _____ excludes inflation.

a. Shanghai Interbank Offered Rate
b. Cash accumulation equation
c. Nominal interest rate
d. SIBOR

26. The '_____' is approximately the nominal interest rate minus the inflation rate Since the inflation rate over the course of a loan is not known initially, volatility in inflation represents a risk to both the lender and the borrower.

In economics and finance, an individual who lends money for repayment at a later point in time expects to be compensated for the time value of money, or not having the use of that money while it is lent.

a. Real interest rate
b. 7-Eleven
c. 4-4-5 Calendar
d. 529 plan

27. In finance, the _____ between two currencies specifies how much one currency is worth in terms of the other. For example an _____ of 102 Japanese yen to the United States dollar means that JPY 102 is worth the same as USD 1. The foreign exchange market is one of the largest markets in the world.

a. ABN Amro
b. A Random Walk Down Wall Street
c. AAB
d. Exchange rate

28. In economics, _____ is a rise in the general level of prices of goods and services in an economy over a period of time. The term '_____' once referred to increases in the money supply (monetary _____); however, economic debates about the relationship between money supply and price levels have led to its primary use today in describing price _____.
_____ can also be described as a decline in the real value of money--a loss of purchasing power in the medium of exchange which is also the monetary unit of account.

a. ABN Amro
b. A Random Walk Down Wall Street
c. AAB
d. Inflation

29. A _____ s a time deposit, a financial product commonly offered to consumers by banks, thrift institutions, and credit unions.

They are similar to savings accounts in that they are insured and thus virtually risk-free; they are 'money in the bank'. They are different from savings accounts in that they have a specific, fixed term (often three months, six months, or one to five years), and, usually, a fixed interest rate.

a. Reserve requirement
b. Variable rate mortgage
c. Time deposit
d. Certificate of deposit

30. A _____ is a fungible, negotiable instrument representing financial value. They are broadly categorized into debt securities (such as banknotes, bonds and debentures), and equity securities; e.g., common stocks. The company or other entity issuing the _____ is called the issuer.

a. Book entry
b. Tracking stock
c. Securities lending
d. Security

31. _____ are the inflation-indexed bonds issued by the U.S. Treasury. The principal is adjusted to the Consumer Price Index, the commonly used measure of inflation. The coupon rate is constant, but generates a different amount of interest when multiplied by the inflation-adjusted principal, thus protecting the holder against inflation. _____ are currently offered in 5-year, 10-year and 20-year maturities.

a. 4-4-5 Calendar
b. Treasury securities
c. Treasury Inflation Protected Securities
d. Treasury Inflation-Protected Securities

32. A _____ is a profit that results from investments into a capital asset, such as stocks, bonds or real estate, which exceeds the purchase price. It is the difference between a higher selling price and a lower purchase price, resulting in a financial gain for the seller. Conversely, a capital loss arises if the proceeds from the sale of a capital asset are less than the purchase price.

a. Payroll tax
b. Tax brackets
c. Capital gains tax
d. Capital gain

33. In economic models, the _____ time frame assumes no fixed factors of production. Firms can enter or leave the marketplace, and the cost (and availability) of land, labor, raw materials, and capital goods can be assumed to vary. In contrast, in the short-run time frame, certain factors are assumed to be fixed, because there is not sufficient time for them to change.

a. 4-4-5 Calendar
b. Short-run
c. 529 plan
d. Long-run

34. In economics, the concept of the _____ refers to the decision-making time frame of a firm in which at least one factor of production is fixed. Costs which are fixed in the _____ have no impact on a firms decisions. For example a firm can raise output by increasing the amount of labour through overtime.

a. Short-run
b. 529 plan
c. Long-run
d. 4-4-5 Calendar

35. _____ is one of the main genres of financial risk. The term describes the risk that a particular investment might be canceled or stopped somehow, that one may have to find a new place to invest that money with the risk being there might not be a similarly attractive investment available. This primarily occurs if bonds (which are portions of loans to entities) are paid back earlier then expected.

   a. Reinvestment risk

   b. Biweekly Mortgage

   c. Debt cash flow

   d. Standard of deferred payment

36. In finance, the _____ of a financial asset measures the sensitivity of the asset's price to interest rate movements, expressed as a number of years. The reason for expressing this sensitivity in years is that the time that will elapse until a cash flow is received allows more interest to accumulate. Therefore the price of an asset with long term cashflows has more interest rate sensitivity than an asset with cashflows in the near future.

   a. Macaulay duration

   b. Duration

   c. 4-4-5 Calendar

   d. Yield to maturity

Chapter 4. The Behavior of Interest Rates

1. In business and accounting, _____s are everything of value that is owned by a person or company. The balance sheet of a firm records the monetary value of the _____s owned by the firm. The two major _____ classes are tangible _____s and intangible _____s.

   a. Asset
   b. EBITDA
   c. Income
   d. Accounts payable

2. The _____ is the weighted-average most likely outcome in gambling, probability theory, economics or finance.

   In gambling and probability theory, there is usually a discrete set of possible outcomes. In this case, _____ is a measure of the relative balance of win or loss weighted by their chances of occurring.

   a. ABN Amro
   b. AAB
   c. A Random Walk Down Wall Street
   d. Expected return

3. _____ is a measure of the ability of a debtor to pay their debts as and when they fall due. It is usually expressed as a ratio or a percentage of current liabilities.

   For a corporation with a published balance sheet there are various ratios used to calculate a measure of liquidity.

   a. Operating profit margin
   b. Operating leverage
   c. Invested capital
   d. Accounting liquidity

4. In finance and economics _____ refers to the rate of interest before adjustment for inflation (in contrast with the real interest rate); or, for interest balls stated' without adjustment for the full effect of compounding (also referred to as the nominal annual rate.) An interest rate is called nominal if the frequency of compounding (e.g. a month) is not identical to the basic time unit (normally a year.)

   The real interest rate includes compensation for the lender's lost value due to inflation, whereas the _____ excludes inflation.

   a. Cash accumulation equation
   b. Nominal interest rate
   c. SIBOR
   d. Shanghai Interbank Offered Rate

5. _____ is an economic model based on price, utility and quantity in a market. It predicts that in a competitive market, price will function to equalize the quantity demanded by consumers, and the quantity supplied by producers, resulting in an economic equilibrium of price and quantity. Similarly, an increase in the number of workers tends to result in lower wages and vice-versa.

   a. Supply and demand
   b. Price channel
   c. Rural credit cooperatives
   d. Loan participation

6. In finance, a _____ is a debt security, in which the authorized issuer owes the holders a debt and, depending on the terms of the _____, is obliged to pay interest (the coupon) and/or to repay the principal at a later date, termed maturity.

   Thus a _____ is a loan: the issuer is the borrower, the _____ holder is the lender, and the coupon is the interest. _____s provide the borrower with external funds to finance long-term investments, or, in the case of government _____s, to finance current expenditure.

a. Catastrophe bonds b. Convertible bond
c. Puttable bond d. Bond

7. _____ is a fee paid on borrowed assets. It is the price paid for the use of borrowed money , or, money earned by deposited funds . Assets that are sometimes lent with _____ include money, shares, consumer goods through hire purchase, major assets such as aircraft, and even entire factories in finance lease arrangements.

a. A Random Walk Down Wall Street b. Insolvency
c. AAB d. Interest

8. An _____ is the price a borrower pays for the use of money they do not own, and the return a lender receives for deferring the use of funds, by lending it to the borrower. _____s are normally expressed as a percentage rate over the period of one year.

_____s targets are also a vital tool of monetary policy and are used to control variables like investment, inflation, and unemployment.

a. ABN Amro b. Interest rate
c. A Random Walk Down Wall Street d. AAB

9. In probability and statistics, the _____ of a collection of numbers is a measure of the dispersion of the numbers from their expected (mean) value. It can apply to a probability distribution, a random variable, a population or a data set. The _____ is usually denoted with the letter σ (lowercase sigma.)

a. Sample size b. Mean
c. Kurtosis d. Standard deviation

10. _____ in finance is a risk management technique, related to hedging, that mixes a wide variety of investments within a portfolio. Because the fluctuations of a single security have less impact on a diverse portfolio, _____ minimizes the risk from any one investment.

A simple example of _____ is the following: On a particular island the entire economy consists of two companies: one that sells umbrellas and another that sells sunscreen.

a. 529 plan b. 7-Eleven
c. 4-4-5 Calendar d. Diversification

11. In business and finance, a _____ (also referred to as equity _____) of stock means a _____ of ownership in a corporation (company.) In the plural, stocks is often used as a synonym for _____s especially in the United States, but it is less commonly used that way outside of North America.

In the United Kingdom, South Africa, and Australia, stock can also refer to completely different financial instruments such as government bonds or, less commonly, to all kinds of marketable securities.

a. Procter ' Gamble b. Share
c. Bucket shop d. Margin

12. The _____ is a financial market where participants buy and sell debt securities, usually in the form of bonds. As of 2006, the size of the international _____ is an estimated $45 trillion, of which the size of the outstanding U.S. _____ debt was $25.2 trillion.

Nearly all of the $923 billion average daily trading volume in the U.S. _____ takes place between broker-dealers and large institutions in a decentralized, over-the-counter market.

a. Bond market
b. 4-4-5 Calendar
c. Fixed income
d. 529 plan

13. In economics, _____ is the total amount of money available in an economy at a particular point in time. There are several ways to define 'money', but each includes currency in circulation and demand deposits.

_____ data are recorded and published.

a. 4-4-5 Calendar
b. Money Supply
c. 529 plan
d. 7-Eleven

14. In finance, _____ occurs when a debtor has not met its legal obligations according to the debt contract, e.g. it has not made a scheduled payment, or has violated a loan covenant (condition) of the debt contract. _____ may occur if the debtor is either unwilling or unable to pay their debt. This can occur with all debt obligations including bonds, mortgages, loans, and promissory notes.

a. Debt validation
b. Vendor finance
c. Default
d. Credit crunch

15. A _____ is a bond issued by a national government denominated in the country's own currency. Bonds issued by national governments in foreign currencies are normally referred to as sovereign bonds. The first ever _____ was issued by the British government in 1693 to raise money to fund a war against France.

a. Collateralized debt obligations
b. Zero-coupon bond
c. Municipal bond
d. Government bond

16. In economics, _____ is a rise in the general level of prices of goods and services in an economy over a period of time. The term '_____' once referred to increases in the money supply (monetary _____); however, economic debates about the relationship between money supply and price levels have led to its primary use today in describing price _____.
_____ can also be described as a decline in the real value of money--a loss of purchasing power in the medium of exchange which is also the monetary unit of account.

a. AAB
b. A Random Walk Down Wall Street
c. ABN Amro
d. Inflation

17. In economics, the _____ is the proposition by Irving Fisher that the real interest rate is independent of monetary measures, especially the nominal interest rate. The Fisher equation is

$r_r = r_n >- >\pi^e$.

Chapter 4. The Behavior of Interest Rates

This means, the real interest rate (r_r) equals the nominal interest rate (r_n) minus expected rate of inflation ($>\pi^e$.) Here all the rates are continuously compounded.

a. Fisher hypothesis
b. 7-Eleven
c. 4-4-5 Calendar
d. 529 plan

18. The _____, interest yield, income yield, flat yield or running yield is a financial term used in reference to bonds and other fixed-interest securities such as gilts. It is the ratio of the annual interest payment and the bond's current price.

The _____ only therefore refers to the yield of the bond at the current moment. It does not reflect the total return over the life of the bond. In particular, it takes no account of reinvestment risk (the uncertainty about the rate at which future cashflows can be reinvested) or the fact that bonds usually mature at par value, which can be an important component of a bond's return.

a. Modified Internal Rate of Return
b. Stochastic volatility
c. Current yield
d. Perpetuity

19. In finance, the term _____ describes the amount in cash that returns to the owners of a security. Normally it does not include the price variations, at the difference of the total return. _____ applies to various stated rates of return on stocks (common and preferred, and convertible), fixed income instruments (bonds, notes, bills, strips, zero coupon), and some other investment type insurance products (e.g. annuities.)

a. Yield to maturity
b. Macaulay duration
c. Yield
d. 4-4-5 Calendar

20. The term _____ or economic cycle refers to the fluctuations of economic activity (business fluctuations) around a long-term growth trend. The cycle involves shifts over time between periods of relatively rapid growth of output (recovery and prosperity), and periods of relative stagnation or decline (contraction or recession.) These fluctuations are often measured using the real gross domestic product.

a. Behavioral finance
b. Fixed exchange rate
c. Deflation
d. Business cycle

21. A _____ is a financial crisis that occurs when many banks suffer runs at the same time. A systemic banking crisis is one where all or almost all of the banking capital in a country is wiped out. The resulting chain of bankruptcies can cause a long economic recession. Much of the Great Depression's economic damage was caused directly by bank runs. The cost of cleaning up a systemic banking crisis can be huge, with fiscal costs averaging 13% of GDP and economic output losses averaging 20% of GDP for important crises from 1970 to 2007.

a. Banking panic
b. Deposit insurance
c. Probability of default
d. Credit bureau

22. _____ is the provision of resources (such as granting a loan) by one party to another party where that second party does not reimburse the first party immediately, thereby generating a debt, and instead arranges either to repay or return those resources (or material(s) of equal value) at a later date. The first party is called a creditor, also known as a lender, while the second party is called a debtor, also known as a borrower.

Movements of financial capital are normally dependent on either _____ or equity transfers.

 a. Comparable   b. Credit
 c. Warrant   d. Clearing house

23. John Maynard Keynes developed the _____ of Interest in the General Theory of Employment Interest and Money. The primary consideration of the _____ is the demand for money as an asset, as a means for holding wealth. Interest rates, he argues, cannot be a reward for savings as such because, if a person hoards his savings in cash, keeping it under his mattress say, he will receive no interest, although he has nevertheless, refrained from consuming all his current income.

 a. Liquidity preference   b. 4-4-5 Calendar
 c. 7-Eleven   d. 529 plan

24. _____ or economic opportunity loss is the value of the next best alternative foregone as the result of making a decision. _____ analysis is an important part of a company's decision-making processes but is not treated as an actual cost in any financial statement. The next best thing that a person can engage in is referred to as the _____ of doing the best thing and ignoring the next best thing to be done.

 a. AAB   b. A Random Walk Down Wall Street
 c. ABN Amro   d. Opportunity cost

25. In economics, business, and accounting, a _____ is the value of money that has been used up to produce something, and hence is not available for use anymore. In business, the _____ may be one of acquisition, in which case the amount of money expended to acquire it is counted as _____. In this case, money is the input that is gone in order to acquire the thing.

 a. Sliding scale fees   b. Marginal cost
 c. Fixed costs   d. Cost

26. _____, refers to consumption opportunity gained by an entity within a specified time frame, which is generally expressed in monetary terms. However, for households and individuals, '_____ is the sum of all the wages, salaries, profits, interests payments, rents and other forms of earnings received... in a given period of time.' For firms, _____ generally refers to net-profit: what remains of revenue after expenses have been subtracted.

 a. Accrual   b. Annual report
 c. OIBDA   d. Income

27. In finance, the _____ is the global financial market for short-term borrowing and lending. It provides short-term liquidity funding for the global financial system. The _____ is where short-term obligations such as Treasury bills, commercial paper and bankers' acceptances are bought and sold.

 a. Cramdown   b. Consumer debt
 c. Money market   d. Debt-for-equity swap

28. A _____ is a fungible, negotiable instrument representing financial value. They are broadly categorized into debt securities (such as banknotes, bonds and debentures), and equity securities; e.g., common stocks. The company or other entity issuing the _____ is called the issuer.

 a. Book entry   b. Securities lending
 c. Security   d. Tracking stock

Chapter 4. The Behavior of Interest Rates

29. _____ is concerned with the tasks of developing and applying quantitative or statistical methods to the study and elucidation of economic principles. _____ combines economic theory with statistics to analyze and test economic relationships. Theoretical _____ considers questions about the statistical properties of estimators and tests, while applied _____ is concerned with the application of econometric methods to assess economic theories.
    a. AAB
    b. ABN Amro
    c. A Random Walk Down Wall Street
    d. Econometrics

30. _____s are statistical models used in econometrics. An _____ specifies the statistical relationship that is believed to hold between the various economic quantities pertaining a particular economic phenomena under study. An _____ can be derived from a deterministic economic model by allowing for uncertainty or from an economic model which itself is stochastic.
    a. A Random Walk Down Wall Street
    b. ABN Amro
    c. AAB
    d. Econometric model

31. In the United States, _____ are overnight borrowings by banks to maintain their bank reserves at the Federal Reserve. Banks keep reserves at Federal Reserve Banks to meet their reserve requirements and to clear financial transactions. Transactions in the _____ market enable depository institutions with reserve balances in excess of reserve requirements to lend reserves to institutions with reserve deficiencies.
    a. 4-4-5 Calendar
    b. Federal funds rate
    c. Regulation T
    d. Federal funds

32. A _____ is something for which there is demand, but which is supplied without qualitative differentiation across a market. It is a product that is the same no matter who produces it, such as petroleum, notebook paper, or milk. In other words, copper is copper.
    a. 4-4-5 Calendar
    b. 7-Eleven
    c. Commodity
    d. 529 plan

33. In the original and simplified sense, _____ were things of value, of uniform quality, that were produced in large quantities by many different producers; the items from each different producer are considered equivalent. It is the contract and this underlying standard that define the commodity, not any quality inherent in the product.

_____ exchanges include:

- Chicago Board of Trade
- Kansas City Board of Trade
- Euronext.liffe
- Kuala Lumpur Futures Exchange
- Bhatinda Om ' Oil Exchange
- London Metal Exchange
- New York Mercantile Exchange
- Multi Commodity Exchange
- Dalian Commodity Exchange

Markets for trading _____ can be very efficient, particularly if the division into pools matches demand segments. These markets will quickly respond to changes in supply and demand to find an equilibrium price and quantity.

a. 529 plan
c. Commodities
b. 4-4-5 Calendar
d. 7-Eleven

Chapter 5. The Risk and Term Structure of Interest Rates

1. In finance, a _____ is a debt security, in which the authorized issuer owes the holders a debt and, depending on the terms of the _____, is obliged to pay interest (the coupon) and/or to repay the principal at a later date, termed maturity.

   Thus a _____ is a loan: the issuer is the borrower, the _____ holder is the lender, and the coupon is the interest. _____s provide the borrower with external funds to finance long-term investments, or, in the case of government _____s, to finance current expenditure.

   a. Puttable bond
   b. Catastrophe bonds
   c. Bond
   d. Convertible bond

2. In economic models, the _____ time frame assumes no fixed factors of production. Firms can enter or leave the marketplace, and the cost (and availability) of land, labor, raw materials, and capital goods can be assumed to vary. In contrast, in the short-run time frame, certain factors are assumed to be fixed, because there is not sufficient time for them to change.
   a. Short-run
   b. Long-run
   c. 529 plan
   d. 4-4-5 Calendar

3. In the United States, a _____ is a bond issued by a city or other local government, or their agencies. Potential issuers of these bonds include cities, counties, redevelopment agencies, school districts, publicly owned airports and seaports, and any other governmental entity (or group of governments) below the state level. They may be general obligations of the issuer or secured by specified revenues.
   a. Puttable bond
   b. Premium bond
   c. Senior debt
   d. Municipal bond

4. In finance, the yield curve is the relation between the interest rate (or cost of borrowing) and the time to maturity of the debt for a given borrower in a given currency. For example, the current U.S. dollar interest rates paid on U.S. Treasury securities for various maturities are closely watched by many traders, and are commonly plotted on a graph such as the one on the right which is informally called 'the yield curve.' More formal mathematical descriptions of this relation are often called the _____.

   The yield of a debt instrument is the annualized percentage increase in the value of the investment.

   a. 529 plan
   b. 7-Eleven
   c. Term structure of interest rates
   d. 4-4-5 Calendar

5. In finance, the term _____ describes the amount in cash that returns to the owners of a security. Normally it does not include the price variations, at the difference of the total return. _____ applies to various stated rates of return on stocks (common and preferred, and convertible), fixed income instruments (bonds, notes, bills, strips, zero coupon), and some other investment type insurance products (e.g. annuities.)
   a. Yield
   b. Yield to maturity
   c. 4-4-5 Calendar
   d. Macaulay duration

6. The _____ or redemption yield is the yield promised to the bondholder on the assumption that the bond or other fixed-interest security such as gilts will be held to maturity, that all coupon and principal payments will be made and coupon payments are reinvested at the bond's promised yield at the same rate as invested. It is a measure of the return of the bond. This technique in theory allows investors to calculate the fair value of different financial instruments.

a. Yield
b. Macaulay duration
c. 4-4-5 Calendar
d. Yield to maturity

7. _____ is a fee paid on borrowed assets. It is the price paid for the use of borrowed money, or, money earned by deposited funds. Assets that are sometimes lent with _____ include money, shares, consumer goods through hire purchase, major assets such as aircraft, and even entire factories in finance lease arrangements.
a. Interest
b. A Random Walk Down Wall Street
c. AAB
d. Insolvency

8. An _____ is the price a borrower pays for the use of money they do not own, and the return a lender receives for deferring the use of funds, by lending it to the borrower. _____s are normally expressed as a percentage rate over the period of one year.

_____s targets are also a vital tool of monetary policy and are used to control variables like investment, inflation, and unemployment.

a. A Random Walk Down Wall Street
b. AAB
c. Interest rate
d. ABN Amro

9. _____ is a life of security. It may also refer to the final payment date of a loan or other financial instrument, at which point all remaining interest and principal is due to be paid.

1, 3, 6 months _____ band can be calculated by using 30-day per month periods.

a. Primary market
b. Replacement cost
c. False billing
d. Maturity

10. In economics, the concept of the _____ refers to the decision-making time frame of a firm in which at least one factor of production is fixed. Costs which are fixed in the _____ have no impact on a firms decisions. For example a firm can raise output by increasing the amount of labour through overtime.
a. 4-4-5 Calendar
b. 529 plan
c. Short-run
d. Long-run

11. The institution most often referenced by the word '_____' is a public or publicly traded _____, the shares of which are traded on a public stock exchange (e.g., the New York Stock Exchange or Nasdaq in the United States) where shares of stock of _____s are bought and sold by and to the general public. Most of the largest businesses in the world are publicly traded _____s. However, the majority of _____s are said to be closely held, privately held or close _____s, meaning that no ready market exists for the trading of shares.
a. Protect
b. Depository Trust Company
c. Federal Home Loan Mortgage Corporation
d. Corporation

12. In finance, _____ occurs when a debtor has not met its legal obligations according to the debt contract, e.g. it has not made a scheduled payment, or has violated a loan covenant (condition) of the debt contract. _____ may occur if the debtor is either unwilling or unable to pay their debt. This can occur with all debt obligations including bonds, mortgages, loans, and promissory notes.

Chapter 5. The Risk and Term Structure of Interest Rates

a. Vendor finance
c. Credit crunch
b. Default
d. Debt validation

13. _____ is the risk of loss due to a debtor's non-payment of a loan or other line of credit (either the principal or interest (coupon) or both)

Most lenders employ their own models (credit scorecards) to rank potential and existing customers according to risk, and then apply appropriate strategies. With products such as unsecured personal loans or mortgages, lenders charge a higher price for higher risk customers and vice versa. With revolving products such as credit cards and overdrafts, risk is controlled through careful setting of credit limits.

a. Market risk
c. Transaction risk
b. Liquidity risk
d. Credit risk

14.

In finance, the _____ can be the expected rate of return above the risk-free interest rate. When measuring risk, a common sense approach is to compare the risk-free return on T-bills and the very risky return on other investments. The difference between these two returns can be interpreted as a measure of the excess return on the average risky asset. This excess return is known as the _____.

a. Risk aversion
c. Risk adjusted return on capital
b. Risk premium
d. Risk modeling

15. _____ are government bonds issued by the United States Department of the Treasury through the Bureau of the Public Debt. They are the debt financing instruments of the U.S. Federal government, and they are often referred to simply as Treasuries or Treasurys. There are four types of marketable _____: Treasury bills, Treasury notes, Treasury bonds, and Treasury Inflation Protected Securities (TIPS.)
a. 4-4-5 Calendar
c. Treasury Inflation-Protected Securities
b. Treasury securities
d. Treasury Inflation Protected Securities

16. A _____ is a fungible, negotiable instrument representing financial value. They are broadly categorized into debt securities (such as banknotes, bonds and debentures), and equity securities; e.g., common stocks. The company or other entity issuing the _____ is called the issuer.
a. Security
c. Tracking stock
b. Book entry
d. Securities lending

17. A _____ is a bond issued by a corporation. The term is usually applied to longer-term debt instruments, generally with a maturity date falling at least a year after their issue date. (The term 'commercial paper' is sometimes used for instruments with a shorter maturity.)
a. Corporate bond
c. Brady bonds
b. Government bond
d. Serial bond

18. _____ is an economic model based on price, utility and quantity in a market. It predicts that in a competitive market, price will function to equalize the quantity demanded by consumers, and the quantity supplied by producers, resulting in an economic equilibrium of price and quantity. Similarly, an increase in the number of workers tends to result in lower wages and vice-versa.
   a. Supply and demand
   b. Loan participation
   c. Rural credit cooperatives
   d. Price channel

19. In finance, a _____ (non-investment grade bond, speculative grade bond or junk bond) is a bond that is rated below investment grade at the time of purchase. These bonds have a higher risk of default or other adverse credit events, but typically pay higher yields than better quality bonds in order to make them attractive to investors.
   a. Volatility
   b. High yield bond
   c. Sharpe ratio
   d. Private equity

20. In finance, _____ refers to Monday, October 19, 1987, when stock markets around the world crashed, shedding a huge value in a very short time. The crash began in Hong Kong, spread west through international time zones to Europe, hitting the United States after other markets had already declined by a significant margin. The Dow Jones Industrial Average (DJIA) dropped by 508 points to 1738.74 (22.61%).
   a. 4-4-5 Calendar
   b. 529 plan
   c. 7-Eleven
   d. Black Monday

21. The _____ was a worldwide economic downturn starting in most places in 1929 and ending at different times in the 1930s or early 1940s for different countries. It was the largest and most important economic depression in the 20th century, and is used in the 21st century as an example of how far the world's economy can fall. The _____ originated in the United States; historians most often use as a starting date the stock market crash on October 29, 1929, known as Black Tuesday.
   a. 4-4-5 Calendar
   b. Great Depression
   c. 7-Eleven
   d. 529 plan

22. _____ are the means of implementing monetary policy by which a central bank controls its national money supply by buying and selling government securities, or other financial instruments. Monetary targets, such as interest rates or exchange rates, are used to guide this implementation.

Since most money is now in the form of electronic records, rather than paper records such as banknotes, _____ are conducted simply by electronically increasing or decreasing ('crediting' or 'debiting') the amount of money that a bank has, e.g., in its reserve account at the central bank, in exchange for a bank selling or buying a financial instrument.

   a. Open market operations
   b. AAB
   c. A Random Walk Down Wall Street
   d. ABN Amro

23. A _____ is a private or public market for the trading of company stock and derivatives of company stock at an agreed price; these are securities listed on a stock exchange as well as those only traded privately.

The size of the world _____ is estimated at about $36.6 trillion US at the beginning of October 2008 . The world derivatives market has been estimated at about $480 trillion face or nominal value, 12 times the size of the entire world economy.

Chapter 5. The Risk and Term Structure of Interest Rates

a. Anton Gelonkin
c. Adolph Coors
b. Stock market
d. Andrew Tobias

24. A _____ is a sudden dramatic decline of stock prices across a significant cross-section of a stock market. Crashes are driven by panic as much as by underlying economic factors. They often follow speculative stock market bubbles.
   a. 529 plan
   c. 4-4-5 Calendar
   b. 7-Eleven
   d. Stock market crash

25. In business and accounting, _____s are everything of value that is owned by a person or company. The balance sheet of a firm records the monetary value of the _____s owned by the firm. The two major _____ classes are tangible _____s and intangible _____s.
   a. Accounts payable
   c. Income
   b. EBITDA
   d. Asset

26. _____, refers to consumption opportunity gained by an entity within a specified time frame, which is generally expressed in monetary terms. However, for households and individuals, '_____ is the sum of all the wages, salaries, profits, interests payments, rents and other forms of earnings received... in a given period of time.' For firms, _____ generally refers to net-profit: what remains of revenue after expenses have been subtracted.
   a. Income
   c. Accrual
   b. OIBDA
   d. Annual report

27. An _____ is a tax levied on the financial income of people, corporations, or other legal entities. Various _____ systems exist, with varying degrees of tax incidence. Income taxation can be progressive, proportional, or regressive.
   a. A Random Walk Down Wall Street
   c. ABN Amro
   b. AAB
   d. Income tax

28. _____ is a measure of the ability of a debtor to pay their debts as and when they fall due. It is usually expressed as a ratio or a percentage of current liabilities.

For a corporation with a published balance sheet there are various ratios used to calculate a measure of liquidity.

   a. Operating leverage
   c. Accounting liquidity
   b. Operating profit margin
   d. Invested capital

29. _____ is a term used to explain a difference between two types of financial securities (e.g. stocks), that have all the same qualities except liquidity. For example:

_____ is a segment of a three-part theory that works to explain the behavior of yield curves for interest rates. The upwards-curving component of the interest yield can be explained by the _____.

   a. 4-4-5 Calendar
   c. 7-Eleven
   b. 529 plan
   d. Liquidity premium

30. _____ mature in one year or less. Like zero-coupon bonds, they do not pay interest prior to maturity; instead they are sold at a discount of the par value to create a positive yield to maturity. Many regard _____ as the least risky investment available to U.S. investors.
   a. Treasury securities
   b. 4-4-5 Calendar
   c. Treasury Inflation Protected Securities
   d. Treasury bills

31. A _____ is an exemption from all or certain taxes of a state or nation in which part of the taxes that would normally be collected from an individual or an organization are instead foregone.

Normally a _____ is provided to an individual or organization which falls within a class which the government wishes to promote economically, such as charitable organizations. _____s are usually meant to either reduce the tax burden on a particular segment of society in the interests of fairness or to promote some type of economic activity through reducing the tax burden on those organizations or individuals who are involved in that activity.

   a. Federal Open Market Committee
   b. Tax incidence
   c. Tax compliance solution
   d. Tax exemption

32. In finance, the _____ is the relation between the interest rate (or cost of borrowing) and the time to maturity of the debt for a given borrower in a given currency. For example, the current U.S. dollar interest rates paid on U.S. Treasury securities for various maturities are closely watched by many traders, and are commonly plotted on a graph such as the one on the right which is informally called 'the _____.' More formal mathematical descriptions of this relation are often called the term structure of interest rates.

The yield of a debt instrument is the annualized percentage increase in the value of the investment.

   a. 7-Eleven
   b. 529 plan
   c. 4-4-5 Calendar
   d. Yield curve

33. In finance, the _____ between two currencies specifies how much one currency is worth in terms of the other. For example an _____ of 102 Japanese yen to the United States dollar means that JPY 102 is worth the same as USD 1. The foreign exchange market is one of the largest markets in the world.
   a. ABN Amro
   b. A Random Walk Down Wall Street
   c. Exchange rate
   d. AAB

34. The _____ or forward rate is the agreed upon price of an asset in a forward contract. Using the rational pricing assumption, we can express the _____ in terms of the spot price and any dividends etc., so that there is no possibility for arbitrage.

The _____ is given by:

where

    F is the _____ to be paid at time T
    e^x is the exponential function
    r is the risk-free interest rate
    q is the cost-of-carry
    S_0 is the spot price of the asset (i.e. what it would sell for at time 0)
    D_i is a dividend which is guaranteed to be paid at time t_i where $0 < t_i < T$.

The two questions here are what price the short position (the seller of the asset) should offer to maximize his gain, and what price the long position (the buyer of the asset) should accept to maximize his gain?

At the very least we know that both do not want to lose any money in the deal.

a. Financial Gerontology	b. Security interest
c. Biweekly Mortgage	d. Forward price

35. The _____ of a commodity, a security or a currency is the price that is quoted for immediate (spot) settlement (payment and delivery.) Spot settlement is normally one or two business days from trade date. This is in contrast with the forward price established in a forward contract or futures contract, where contract terms (price) are set now, but delivery and payment will occur at a future date.

a. Spot rate	b. Market anomaly
c. Limits to arbitrage	d. Long position

Chapter 6. Structure of Central Banks and the Federal Reserve System

1. A _____, reserve bank, or monetary authority is the entity responsible for the monetary policy of a country or of a group of member states. It is a bank that can lend money to other banks in times of need. Its primary responsibility is to maintain the stability of the national currency and money supply, but more active duties include controlling subsidized-loan interest rates, and acting as a lender of last resort to the banking sector during times of financial crisis (private banks often being integral to the national financial system.)
   a. 7-Eleven
   b. 529 plan
   c. Central bank
   d. 4-4-5 Calendar

2. The _____, a component of the Federal Reserve System, is charged under United States law with overseeing the nation's open market operations. It is the Federal Reserve Committee that makes key decisions about interest rates and the growth jam of the United States money supply. It is the principal organ of United States national monetary policy.
   a. Tax exemption
   b. Tax incidence
   c. Fiscal policy
   d. Federal Open Market Committee

3. _____ is the process by which the government, or monetary authority of a country controls (i) the supply of money central bank (ii) availability of money, and (iii) cost of money or rate of interest, in order to attain a set of objectives oriented towards the growth and stability of the economy. Monetary theory provides insight into how to craft optimal _____.

   _____ is referred to as either being an expansionary policy where an expansionary policy increases the total supply of money in the economy, and a contractionary policy decreases the total money supply.

   a. Monetary policy
   b. Natural resources consumption tax
   c. Federal Open Market Committee
   d. Tax exemption

4. In financial accounting, the term _____ is most commonly used to describe any part of shareholders' equity, except for basic share capital. Sometimes, the term is used instead of the term provision; such a use, however, is inconsistent with the terminology suggested by International Accounting Standards Board. For more information about provisions, see provision (accounting.)
   a. Treasury stock
   b. Closing entries
   c. FIFO and LIFO accounting
   d. Reserve

5. The U.S. _____ is an independent agency of the United States government which holds primary responsibility for enforcing the federal securities laws and regulating the securities industry, the nation's stock and options exchanges, and other electronic securities markets. The SEC was created by section 4 of the SEC of 1934 (now codified as 15 U.S.C. § 78d and commonly referred to as the 1934 Act.)
   a. 4-4-5 Calendar
   b. 529 plan
   c. Securities and Exchange Commission
   d. 7-Eleven

6. _____ is the removal or simplification of government rules and regulations that constrain the operation of market forces. _____ does not mean elimination of laws against fraud, but eliminating or reducing government control of how business is done, thereby moving toward a more free market.

The stated rationale for '_____' is often that fewer and simpler regulations will lead to a raised level of competitiveness, therefore higher productivity, more efficiency and lower prices overall.

Chapter 6. Structure of Central Banks and the Federal Reserve System

a. Supply shock
c. Deregulation

b. Value added
d. Demand shock

7. In the United States, the Financial Industry Regulatory Authority (FINRA) is a self-regulatory organization (SRO) under the Securities Exchange Act of 1934, successor to the _____, Inc.

FINRA is responsible for regulatory oversight of all securities firms that do business with the public; professional training, testing and licensing of registered persons; arbitration and mediation; market regulation by contract for The NASDAQ Stock Market, Inc., the American Stock Exchange LLC, and the International Securities Exchange, LLC; and industry utilities, such as Trade Reporting Facilities and other over-the-counter operations.

a. 7-Eleven
c. National Association of Securities Dealers

b. 4-4-5 Calendar
d. 529 plan

8. _____ are the means of implementing monetary policy by which a central bank controls its national money supply by buying and selling government securities, or other financial instruments. Monetary targets, such as interest rates or exchange rates, are used to guide this implementation.

Since most money is now in the form of electronic records, rather than paper records such as banknotes, _____ are conducted simply by electronically increasing or decreasing ('crediting' or 'debiting') the amount of money that a bank has, e.g., in its reserve account at the central bank, in exchange for a bank selling or buying a financial instrument.

a. ABN Amro
c. AAB

b. A Random Walk Down Wall Street
d. Open market operations

9. The _____ is a bank regulation that sets the minimum reserves each bank must hold to customer deposits and notes. These reserves are designed to satisfy withdrawal demands, and would normally be in the form of fiat currency stored in a bank vault (vault cash), or with a central bank.

The reserve ratio is sometimes used as a tool in the monetary policy, influencing the country's economy, borrowing, and interest rates.

a. Variable rate mortgage
c. Reserve requirement

b. Wall Street Journal prime rate
d. Prime rate

10. A _____ is a fungible, negotiable instrument representing financial value. They are broadly categorized into debt securities (such as banknotes, bonds and debentures), and equity securities; e.g., common stocks. The company or other entity issuing the _____ is called the issuer.

a. Book entry
c. Securities lending

b. Tracking stock
d. Security

11. A _____ is a financial contract whose value is derived from the value of something else (known as the underlying.) The underlying on which a _____ is based can be an asset, weather conditions bonds or other forms of credit.

a. 7-Eleven
b. Derivative
c. 529 plan
d. 4-4-5 Calendar

12. _____ is the provision of resources (such as granting a loan) by one party to another party where that second party does not reimburse the first party immediately, thereby generating a debt, and instead arranges either to repay or return those resources (or material(s) of equal value) at a later date. The first party is called a creditor, also known as a lender, while the second party is called a debtor, also known as a borrower.

Movements of financial capital are normally dependent on either _____ or equity transfers.

a. Clearing house
b. Credit
c. Comparable
d. Warrant

13. A '_____' is a 'Charge' that is paid to obtain the right to delay a payment. Essentially, the payer purchases the right to make a given payment in the future instead of in the Present. The '_____', or 'Charge' that must be paid to delay the payment, is simply the difference between what the payment amount would be if it were paid in the present and what the payment amount would be paid if it were paid in the future.

a. Risk modeling
b. Value at risk
c. Risk aversion
d. Discount

14. The _____ is an interest rate a central bank charges depository institutions that borrow reserves from it.

The term _____ has two meanings:

- the same as interest rate; the term 'discount' does not refer to the meaning of the word, but to the purpose of using the quantity, such as computations of present value, e.g. net present value / discounted cash flow

- the annual effective _____, which is the annual interest divided by the capital including that interest; this rate is lower than the interest rate; it corresponds to using the value after a year as the nominal value, and seeing the initial value as the nominal value minus a discount; it is used for Treasury Bills and similar financial instruments

The annual effective _____ is the annual interest divided by the capital including that interest, which is the interest rate divided by 100% plus the interest rate. It is the annual discount factor to be applied to the future cash flow, to find the discount, subtracted from a future value to find the value one year earlier.

For example, suppose there is a government bond that sells for $95 and pays $100 in a year's time.

a. Black-Scholes
b. Stochastic volatility
c. Discount rate
d. Fisher equation

15. _____ is a United States government regulation that put a limit on the interest rates that banks could pay, including a rate of zero on demand deposits (checking accounts.) Section 11 of the Banking Act of 1933 (12 U.S.C. 371a) prohibits member banks from paying interest on demand deposits, which is implemented by _____.

Chapter 6. Structure of Central Banks and the Federal Reserve System

a. Fair Credit Billing Act
b. Regulation Q
c. Truth in Lending Act
d. Fair Credit Reporting Act

16. The _____ was a worldwide economic downturn starting in most places in 1929 and ending at different times in the 1930s or early 1940s for different countries. It was the largest and most important economic depression in the 20th century, and is used in the 21st century as an example of how far the world's economy can fall. The _____ originated in the United States; historians most often use as a starting date the stock market crash on October 29, 1929, known as Black Tuesday.
   a. Great Depression
   b. 7-Eleven
   c. 4-4-5 Calendar
   d. 529 plan

17. A _____ is a financial crisis that occurs when many banks suffer runs at the same time. A systemic banking crisis is one where all or almost all of the banking capital in a country is wiped out. The resulting chain of bankruptcies can cause a long economic recession. Much of the Great Depression's economic damage was caused directly by bank runs. The cost of cleaning up a systemic banking crisis can be huge, with fiscal costs averaging 13% of GDP and economic output losses averaging 20% of GDP for important crises from 1970 to 2007.
   a. Deposit insurance
   b. Banking panic
   c. Probability of default
   d. Credit bureau

18. The term _____ or economic cycle refers to the fluctuations of economic activity (business fluctuations) around a long-term growth trend. The cycle involves shifts over time between periods of relatively rapid growth of output (recovery and prosperity), and periods of relative stagnation or decline (contraction or recession.) These fluctuations are often measured using the real gross domestic product.
   a. Fixed exchange rate
   b. Behavioral finance
   c. Deflation
   d. Business cycle

19. In economics, _____ is a rise in the general level of prices of goods and services in an economy over a period of time. The term '_____' once referred to increases in the money supply (monetary _____); however, economic debates about the relationship between money supply and price levels have led to its primary use today in describing price _____. _____ can also be described as a decline in the real value of money--a loss of purchasing power in the medium of exchange which is also the monetary unit of account.
   a. A Random Walk Down Wall Street
   b. AAB
   c. ABN Amro
   d. Inflation

20. In business and accounting, _____s are everything of value that is owned by a person or company. The balance sheet of a firm records the monetary value of the _____s owned by the firm. The two major _____ classes are tangible _____s and intangible _____s.
   a. Income
   b. EBITDA
   c. Accounts payable
   d. Asset

21. The _____ is a stock exchange based in New York City, New York. It is the largest stock exchange in the world by dollar value of its listed companies securities. As of October 2008, the combined capitalization of all domestic _____ listed companies was $10.1 trillion.
   a. 7-Eleven
   b. 529 plan
   c. 4-4-5 Calendar
   d. New York Stock Exchange

22. A _____, securities exchange or (in Europe) bourse is a corporation or mutual organization which provides 'trading' facilities for stock brokers and traders, to trade stocks and other securities. _____s also provide facilities for the issue and redemption of securities as well as other financial instruments and capital events including the payment of income and dividends. The securities traded on a _____ include: shares issued by companies, unit trusts and other pooled investment products and bonds.
   a. 4-4-5 Calendar
   b. 529 plan
   c. 7-Eleven
   d. Stock Exchange

Chapter 7. Conduct of Monetary Policy: Tools, Goals, and Targets

1. In financial accounting, a _____ or statement of financial position is a summary of a person's or organization's balances. Assets, liabilities and ownership equity are listed as of a specific date, such as the end of its financial year. A _____ is often described as a snapshot of a company's financial condition.
    a. Statement of retained earnings
    b. Balance sheet
    c. Financial statements
    d. Statement on Auditing Standards No. 70: Service Organizations

2. _____ is the process by which the government, or monetary authority of a country controls (i) the supply of money central bank (ii) availability of money, and (iii) cost of money or rate of interest, in order to attain a set of objectives oriented towards the growth and stability of the economy. Monetary theory provides insight into how to craft optimal _____.

   _____ is referred to as either being an expansionary policy where an expansionary policy increases the total supply of money in the economy, and a contractionary policy decreases the total money supply.

    a. Tax exemption
    b. Federal Open Market Committee
    c. Natural resources consumption tax
    d. Monetary policy

3. In financial accounting, the term _____ is most commonly used to describe any part of shareholders' equity, except for basic share capital. Sometimes, the term is used instead of the term provision; such a use, however, is inconsistent with the terminology suggested by International Accounting Standards Board. For more information about provisions, see provision (accounting.)
    a. FIFO and LIFO accounting
    b. Closing entries
    c. Treasury stock
    d. Reserve

4. In business and accounting, _____s are everything of value that is owned by a person or company. The balance sheet of a firm records the monetary value of the _____s owned by the firm. The two major _____ classes are tangible _____s and intangible _____s.
    a. Income
    b. Accounts payable
    c. EBITDA
    d. Asset

5. The _____ is a bank regulation that sets the minimum reserves each bank must hold to customer deposits and notes. These reserves are designed to satisfy withdrawal demands, and would normally be in the form of fiat currency stored in a bank vault (vault cash), or with a central bank.

   The reserve ratio is sometimes used as a tool in the monetary policy, influencing the country's economy, borrowing, and interest rates.

    a. Variable rate mortgage
    b. Wall Street Journal prime rate
    c. Prime rate
    d. Reserve requirement

6. A '_____' is a 'Charge' that is paid to obtain the right to delay a payment. Essentially, the payer purchases the right to make a given payment in the future instead of in the Present. The '_____', or 'Charge' that must be paid to delay the payment, is simply the difference between what the payment amount would be if it were paid in the present and what the payment amount would be paid if it were paid in the future.
    a. Discount
    b. Risk aversion
    c. Value at risk
    d. Risk modeling

Chapter 7. Conduct of Monetary Policy: Tools, Goals, and Targets

7. The _____ is an interest rate a central bank charges depository institutions that borrow reserves from it.

The term _____ has two meanings:

- the same as interest rate; the term 'discount' does not refer to the meaning of the word, but to the purpose of using the quantity, such as computations of present value, e.g. net present value / discounted cash flow

- the annual effective _____, which is the annual interest divided by the capital including that interest; this rate is lower than the interest rate; it corresponds to using the value after a year as the nominal value, and seeing the initial value as the nominal value minus a discount; it is used for Treasury Bills and similar financial instruments

The annual effective _____ is the annual interest divided by the capital including that interest, which is the interest rate divided by 100% plus the interest rate. It is the annual discount factor to be applied to the future cash flow, to find the discount, subtracted from a future value to find the value one year earlier.

For example, suppose there is a government bond that sells for $95 and pays $100 in a year's time.

a. Stochastic volatility
c. Black-Scholes

b. Fisher equation
d. Discount rate

8. The _____ , a component of the Federal Reserve System, is charged under United States law with overseeing the nation's open market operations. It is the Federal Reserve Committee that makes key decisions about interest rates and the growth jam of the United States money supply. It is the principal organ of United States national monetary policy.

a. Tax incidence
c. Federal Open Market Committee

b. Fiscal policy
d. Tax exemption

9. _____ are the means of implementing monetary policy by which a central bank controls its national money supply by buying and selling government securities, or other financial instruments. Monetary targets, such as interest rates or exchange rates, are used to guide this implementation.

Since most money is now in the form of electronic records, rather than paper records such as banknotes, _____ are conducted simply by electronically increasing or decreasing ('crediting' or 'debiting') the amount of money that a bank has, e.g., in its reserve account at the central bank, in exchange for a bank selling or buying a financial instrument.

a. AAB
c. A Random Walk Down Wall Street

b. ABN Amro
d. Open market operations

10. In the United States, _____ are overnight borrowings by banks to maintain their bank reserves at the Federal Reserve. Banks keep reserves at Federal Reserve Banks to meet their reserve requirements and to clear financial transactions. Transactions in the _____ market enable depository institutions with reserve balances in excess of reserve requirements to lend reserves to institutions with reserve deficiencies.

Chapter 7. Conduct of Monetary Policy: Tools, Goals, and Targets   45

a. Regulation T
c. 4-4-5 Calendar
b. Federal funds rate
d. Federal funds

11. In the United States, the _____ is the interest rate at which private depository institutions (mostly banks) lend balances (federal funds) at the Federal Reserve to other depository institutions, usually overnight. Changing the target rate is one form of open market operations that the Chairman of the Federal Reserve uses to regulate the supply of money in the U.S. economy.

U.S. banks and thrift institutions are obligated by law to maintain certain levels of reserves, either as reserves with the Fed or as vault cash.

a. Taylor rule
c. 4-4-5 Calendar
b. Regulation T
d. Federal funds rate

12. A _____, reserve bank, or monetary authority is the entity responsible for the monetary policy of a country or of a group of member states. It is a bank that can lend money to other banks in times of need. Its primary responsibility is to maintain the stability of the national currency and money supply, but more active duties include controlling subsidized-loan interest rates, and acting as a lender of last resort to the banking sector during times of financial crisis (private banks often being integral to the national financial system.)

a. 4-4-5 Calendar
c. 7-Eleven
b. Central bank
d. 529 plan

13. _____ mature in one year or less. Like zero-coupon bonds, they do not pay interest prior to maturity; instead they are sold at a discount of the par value to create a positive yield to maturity. Many regard _____ as the least risky investment available to U.S. investors.

a. 4-4-5 Calendar
c. Treasury bills
b. Treasury Inflation Protected Securities
d. Treasury securities

14. _____ are government bonds issued by the United States Department of the Treasury through the Bureau of the Public Debt. They are the debt financing instruments of the U.S. Federal government, and they are often referred to simply as Treasuries or Treasurys. There are four types of marketable _____: Treasury bills, Treasury notes, Treasury bonds, and Treasury Inflation Protected Securities (TIPS.)

a. 4-4-5 Calendar
c. Treasury Inflation Protected Securities
b. Treasury Inflation-Protected Securities
d. Treasury securities

15. A _____ is a fungible, negotiable instrument representing financial value. They are broadly categorized into debt securities (such as banknotes, bonds and debentures), and equity securities; e.g., common stocks. The company or other entity issuing the _____ is called the issuer.

a. Tracking stock
c. Book entry
b. Securities lending
d. Security

16. A _____ is a bank or securities broker-dealer that may trade directly with the Federal Reserve System of the United States ('the Fed'.) Such firms are required to make bids or offers when the Fed conducts open market operations, provide information to the Fed's open market trading desk, and to participate actively in U.S. Treasury securities auctions. They consult with both the U.S. Treasury and the Fed about funding the budget deficit and implementing monetary policy.

a. 529 plan
c. 4-4-5 Calendar
b. 7-Eleven
d. Primary dealer

17. _____ means regulating, adapting or settling in a variety of contexts:

In commercial law, _____ means the settlement of a loss incurred on insured goods. The calculation of the amounts of compensation to be paid by or to the several interests is a complicated matter. It involves much detail and arithmetic, and requires a full and accurate knowledge of the principles of the subject.

a. Intelligent investor
c. Equity method
b. Asset recovery
d. Adjustment

18. A _____ allows a borrower to use a financial security as collateral for a cash loan at a fixed rate of interest. In a repo, the borrower agrees to immediately sell a security to a lender and also agrees to buy the same security from the lender at a fixed price at some later date. A repo is equivalent to a cash transaction combined with a forward contract.

a. Volatility arbitrage
c. Repurchase agreement
b. Contango
d. Total return swap

19. _____ is the provision of resources (such as granting a loan) by one party to another party where that second party does not reimburse the first party immediately, thereby generating a debt, and instead arranges either to repay or return those resources (or material(s) of equal value) at a later date. The first party is called a creditor, also known as a lender, while the second party is called a debtor, also known as a borrower.

Movements of financial capital are normally dependent on either _____ or equity transfers.

a. Warrant
c. Comparable
b. Clearing house
d. Credit

20. A _____ is a financial crisis that occurs when many banks suffer runs at the same time. A systemic banking crisis is one where all or almost all of the banking capital in a country is wiped out. The resulting chain of bankruptcies can cause a long economic recession. Much of the Great Depression's economic damage was caused directly by bank runs. The cost of cleaning up a systemic banking crisis can be huge, with fiscal costs averaging 13% of GDP and economic output losses averaging 20% of GDP for important crises from 1970 to 2007.

a. Probability of default
c. Credit bureau
b. Deposit insurance
d. Banking panic

21. The institution most often referenced by the word '_____' is a public or publicly traded _____, the shares of which are traded on a public stock exchange (e.g., the New York Stock Exchange or Nasdaq in the United States) where shares of stock of _____s are bought and sold by and to the general public. Most of the largest businesses in the world are publicly traded _____s. However, the majority of _____s are said to be closely held, privately held or close _____s, meaning that no ready market exists for the trading of shares.

a. Corporation
c. Federal Home Loan Mortgage Corporation
b. Protect
d. Depository Trust Company

Chapter 7. Conduct of Monetary Policy: Tools, Goals, and Targets 47

22. Explicit _____ is a measure implemented in many countries to protect bank depositors, in full or in part, from losses caused by a bank's inability to pay its debts when due. _____ systems are one component of a financial system safety net that promotes financial stability.
   a. Time deposit
   b. Reserve requirement
   c. Banking panic
   d. Deposit Insurance

23. The _____ is a United States government corporation created by the Glass-Steagall Act of 1933. It provides deposit insurance, which guarantees the safety of checking and savings deposits in member banks, currently up to $250,000 per depositor per bank. Insured deposits are backed by the full faith and credit of the United States.
   a. FASB
   b. Federal Deposit Insurance Corporation
   c. NYSE Group
   d. Ford Foundation

24. In business, _____ is the total assets minus total outside liabilities of an individual or a company. For a company, this is called shareholders' equity and may be referred to as book value. _____ is stated as at a particular point in time.
   a. Restructuring
   b. Moneylender
   c. Certified International Investment Analyst
   d. Net worth

25. In finance, _____ refers to Monday, October 19, 1987, when stock markets around the world crashed, shedding a huge value in a very short time. The crash began in Hong Kong, spread west through international time zones to Europe, hitting the United States after other markets had already declined by a significant margin. The Dow Jones Industrial Average (DJIA) dropped by 508 points to 1738.74 (22.61%).
   a. 4-4-5 Calendar
   b. 529 plan
   c. 7-Eleven
   d. Black Monday

26. _____ is the removal or simplification of government rules and regulations that constrain the operation of market forces. _____ does not mean elimination of laws against fraud, but eliminating or reducing government control of how business is done, thereby moving toward a more free market.

The stated rationale for '_____' is often that fewer and simpler regulations will lead to a raised level of competitiveness, therefore higher productivity, more efficiency and lower prices overall.

   a. Value added
   b. Deregulation
   c. Demand shock
   d. Supply shock

27. The _____ was a worldwide economic downturn starting in most places in 1929 and ending at different times in the 1930s or early 1940s for different countries. It was the largest and most important economic depression in the 20th century, and is used in the 21st century as an example of how far the world's economy can fall. The _____ originated in the United States; historians most often use as a starting date the stock market crash on October 29, 1929, known as Black Tuesday.
   a. Great Depression
   b. 4-4-5 Calendar
   c. 529 plan
   d. 7-Eleven

28. A _____ is a private or public market for the trading of company stock and derivatives of company stock at an agreed price; these are securities listed on a stock exchange as well as those only traded privately.

Chapter 7. Conduct of Monetary Policy: Tools, Goals, and Targets

The size of the world _____ is estimated at about $36.6 trillion US at the beginning of October 2008 . The world derivatives market has been estimated at about $480 trillion face or nominal value, 12 times the size of the entire world economy.

a. Stock market
c. Adolph Coors
b. Anton Gelonkin
d. Andrew Tobias

29. A _____ is a sudden dramatic decline of stock prices across a significant cross-section of a stock market. Crashes are driven by panic as much as by underlying economic factors. They often follow speculative stock market bubbles.
a. 529 plan
c. 7-Eleven
b. Stock market crash
d. 4-4-5 Calendar

30. _____ is the increase in the amount of the goods and services produced by an economy over time. It is conventionally measured as the percent rate of increase in real gross domestic product, or real GDP. Growth is usually calculated in real terms, i.e. inflation-adjusted terms, in order to net out the effect of inflation on the price of the goods and services produced.
a. A Random Walk Down Wall Street
c. Economic growth
b. ABN Amro
d. AAB

31. In finance, the _____ between two currencies specifies how much one currency is worth in terms of the other. For example an _____ of 102 Japanese yen to the United States dollar means that JPY 102 is worth the same as USD 1. The foreign exchange market is one of the largest markets in the world.
a. AAB
c. A Random Walk Down Wall Street
b. ABN Amro
d. Exchange rate

32. In economics, a _____ is a mechanism that allows people to easily buy and sell (trade) financial securities (such as stocks and bonds), commodities (such as precious metals or agricultural goods), and other fungible items of value at low transaction costs and at prices that reflect the efficient-market hypothesis.

_____s have evolved significantly over several hundred years and are undergoing constant innovation to improve liquidity.

Both general markets (where many commodities are traded) and specialized markets (where only one commodity is traded) exist.

a. Financial market
c. Cost of carry
b. Secondary market
d. Delta hedging

33. In economics, _____ is the total amount of money available in an economy at a particular point in time. There are several ways to define 'money', but each includes currency in circulation and demand deposits.

_____ data are recorded and published.

Chapter 7. Conduct of Monetary Policy: Tools, Goals, and Targets

a. 7-Eleven
c. 529 plan
b. Money supply
d. 4-4-5 Calendar

34. In economics, _____ is a rise in the general level of prices of goods and services in an economy over a period of time. The term '_____' once referred to increases in the money supply (monetary _____); however, economic debates about the relationship between money supply and price levels have led to its primary use today in describing price _____. _____ can also be described as a decline in the real value of money--a loss of purchasing power in the medium of exchange which is also the monetary unit of account.
a. Inflation
c. ABN Amro
b. A Random Walk Down Wall Street
d. AAB

35. In economics, a _____ is a general slowdown in economic activity in a country over a sustained period of time, or a business cycle contraction. During _____s, many macroeconomic indicators vary in a similar way. Production as measured by Gross Domestic Product (GDP), employment, investment spending, capacity utilization, household incomes and business profits all fall during _____s.
a. Fixed exchange rate
c. Mercantilism
b. Behavioral finance
d. Recession

36. In finance, the _____ is the global financial market for short-term borrowing and lending. It provides short-term liquidity funding for the global financial system. The _____ is where short-term obligations such as Treasury bills, commercial paper and bankers' acceptances are bought and sold.
a. Consumer debt
c. Debt-for-equity swap
b. Money market
d. Cramdown

37. _____ was an arrangement established in 1979 under the Jenkins European Commission where most nations of the European Economic Community (EEC) linked their currencies to prevent large fluctuations relative to one another.

After the collapse of the Bretton Woods system in 1971, most of the EEC countries agreed in 1972 to maintain stable exchange rates by preventing exchange fluctuations of more than 2.25% (the European 'currency snake'.) In March 1979, this system was replaced by the _____, and the European Currency Unit (ECU) was defined.

a. A Random Walk Down Wall Street
c. Euro Interbank Offered Rate
b. European Monetary System
d. Exchange Rate Mechanism

38. The _____ was signed by the then G6 on February 22, 1987 in Paris, France. Italy had been an invited member, but declined to finalize the agreement. The goal of the _____ was to stabilize the international currency markets and halt the continued decline of the US Dollar caused by the Plaza Accord .
a. 529 plan
c. Louvre Accord
b. 7-Eleven
d. 4-4-5 Calendar

39. A _____ secures the proper functioning of money by regulating economic agents, transaction types, and money supply.

They are traditionally formed by the policy decisions of individual governments and administrated as a domestic economic issue.

The current trend, however, is to use international trade and investment to alter the policy and legislation of individual governments.

- a. Pattern day trader
- b. Monetary System
- c. Bond credit rating
- d. Payback period

40. The _____ or Plaza Agreement was an agreement between the governments of France, West Germany, Japan, the United States and the United Kingdom, agreeing to depreciate the US dollar in relation to the Japanese yen and German Deutsche Mark by intervening in currency markets. The five governments signed the accord on September 22, 1985 at the Plaza Hotel in New York City.

The exchange rate value of the dollar versus the yen declined by 51% from 1985 to 1987.

- a. Plaza Accord
- b. 4-4-5 Calendar
- c. 7-Eleven
- d. 529 plan

41. A _____, sometimes called a pegged exchange rate, is a type of exchange rate regime wherein a currency's value is matched to the value of another single currency or to a basket of other currencies, or to another measure of value such as gold.

A _____ is usually used to stabilize the value of a currency, vis-a-vis the currency it is pegged to. This facilitates trade and investments between the two countries, and is especially useful for small economies where external trade forms a large part of their GDP.

- a. Human capital
- b. Fixed exchange rate
- c. Market structure
- d. Deflation

42. The _____ is where currency trading takes place. It is where banks and other official institutions facilitate the buying and selling of foreign currencies. FX transactions typically involve one party purchasing a quantity of one currency in exchange for paying a quantity of another.
- a. Floating exchange rate
- b. Foreign exchange option
- c. Spot market
- d. Foreign exchange market

43. _____ is an economic policy in which a central bank estimates and makes public a projected, or 'target,' inflation rate and then attempts to steer actual inflation towards the target through the use of interest rate changes and other monetary tools.

Chapter 7. Conduct of Monetary Policy: Tools, Goals, and Targets

Because interest rates and the inflation rate tend to be inversely related, the likely moves of the central bank to raise or lower interest rates become more transparent under the policy of _____. Examples:

- if inflation appears to be above the target, the bank is likely to raise interest rates. This usually (but not always) has the effect over time of cooling the economy and bringing down inflation.

- if inflation appears to be below the target, the bank is likely to lower interest rates. This usually (again, not always) has the effect over time of accelerating the economy and raising inflation.

a. A Random Walk Down Wall Street
b. AAB
c. Inflation targeting
d. Inflation accounting

44. The _____ is a stock exchange based in New York City, New York. It is the largest stock exchange in the world by dollar value of its listed companies securities. As of October 2008, the combined capitalization of all domestic _____ listed companies was $10.1 trillion.
   a. 7-Eleven
   b. 4-4-5 Calendar
   c. 529 plan
   d. New York Stock Exchange

45. A _____, securities exchange or (in Europe) bourse is a corporation or mutual organization which provides 'trading' facilities for stock brokers and traders, to trade stocks and other securities. _____s also provide facilities for the issue and redemption of securities as well as other financial instruments and capital events including the payment of income and dividends. The securities traded on a _____ include: shares issued by companies, unit trusts and other pooled investment products and bonds.
   a. 4-4-5 Calendar
   b. 7-Eleven
   c. 529 plan
   d. Stock Exchange

Chapter 8. The Money Markets

1. In finance, the _____ is the global financial market for short-term borrowing and lending. It provides short-term liquidity funding for the global financial system. The _____ is where short-term obligations such as Treasury bills, commercial paper and bankers' acceptances are bought and sold.
   a. Cramdown
   b. Money market
   c. Consumer debt
   d. Debt-for-equity swap

2. In economics, business, and accounting, a _____ is the value of money that has been used up to produce something, and hence is not available for use anymore. In business, the _____ may be one of acquisition, in which case the amount of money expended to acquire it is counted as _____. In this case, money is the input that is gone in order to acquire the thing.
   a. Sliding scale fees
   b. Fixed costs
   c. Marginal cost
   d. Cost

3. A _____ is a fungible, negotiable instrument representing financial value. They are broadly categorized into debt securities (such as banknotes, bonds and debentures), and equity securities; e.g., common stocks. The company or other entity issuing the _____ is called the issuer.
   a. Security
   b. Tracking stock
   c. Securities lending
   d. Book entry

4. The _____ is the financial market where previously issued securities and financial instruments such as stock, bonds, options, and futures are bought and sold. The term '_____' is also used refer to the market for any used goods or assets, or an alternative use for an existing product or asset where the customer base is the second market

   With primary issuances of securities or financial instruments, or the primary market, investors purchase these securities directly from issuers such as corporations issuing shares in an IPO or private placement, or directly from the federal government in the case of treasuries.

   a. Performance attribution
   b. Financial market
   c. Delta neutral
   d. Secondary market

5. A _____ is a financial contract whose value is derived from the value of something else (known as the underlying.) The underlying on which a _____ is based can be an asset, weather conditions bonds or other forms of credit.
   a. 4-4-5 Calendar
   b. 529 plan
   c. 7-Eleven
   d. Derivative

6. The _____ of 1933 established the Federal Deposit Insurance Corporation (FDIC) in the United States and included banking reforms, some of which were designed to control speculation. Some provisions such as Regulation Q, which allowed the Federal Reserve to regulate interest rates in savings accounts, were repealed by the Depository Institutions Deregulation and Monetary Control Act of 1980. Provisions that prohibit a bank holding company from owning other financial companies were repealed on November 12, 1999, by the Gramm-Leach-Bliley Act.
   a. 529 plan
   b. 7-Eleven
   c. 4-4-5 Calendar
   d. Glass-Steagall Act

7. The _____ was a worldwide economic downturn starting in most places in 1929 and ending at different times in the 1930s or early 1940s for different countries. It was the largest and most important economic depression in the 20th century, and is used in the 21st century as an example of how far the world's economy can fall. The _____ originated in the United States; historians most often use as a starting date the stock market crash on October 29, 1929, known as Black Tuesday.
   a. 4-4-5 Calendar
   b. 7-Eleven
   c. Great Depression
   d. 529 plan

8. _____ or economic opportunity loss is the value of the next best alternative foregone as the result of making a decision. _____ analysis is an important part of a company's decision-making processes but is not treated as an actual cost in any financial statement. The next best thing that a person can engage in is referred to as the _____ of doing the best thing and ignoring the next best thing to be done.
   a. ABN Amro
   b. AAB
   c. Opportunity cost
   d. A Random Walk Down Wall Street

9. In financial accounting, the term _____ is most commonly used to describe any part of shareholders' equity, except for basic share capital. Sometimes, the term is used instead of the term provision; such a use, however, is inconsistent with the terminology suggested by International Accounting Standards Board. For more information about provisions, see provision (accounting.)
   a. FIFO and LIFO accounting
   b. Treasury stock
   c. Closing entries
   d. Reserve

10. The _____ is a bank regulation that sets the minimum reserves each bank must hold to customer deposits and notes. These reserves are designed to satisfy withdrawal demands, and would normally be in the form of fiat currency stored in a bank vault (vault cash), or with a central bank.

The reserve ratio is sometimes used as a tool in the monetary policy, influencing the country's economy, borrowing, and interest rates.

   a. Prime rate
   b. Reserve requirement
   c. Wall Street Journal prime rate
   d. Variable rate mortgage

11. A _____ is an institution, firm or individual who mediates between two or more parties in a financial context. Typically the first party is a provider of a product or service and the second party is a consumer or customer.

In the U.S., a _____ is typically an institution that facilitates the channelling of funds between lenders and borrowers indirectly.

   a. Financial intermediary
   b. Net asset value
   c. Mutual fund
   d. Savings and loan association

12. The _____ , a component of the Federal Reserve System, is charged under United States law with overseeing the nation's open market operations. It is the Federal Reserve Committee that makes key decisions about interest rates and the growth jam of the United States money supply. It is the principal organ of United States national monetary policy.

a. Fiscal policy
b. Federal Open Market Committee
c. Tax incidence
d. Tax exemption

13. _____ mature in one year or less. Like zero-coupon bonds, they do not pay interest prior to maturity; instead they are sold at a discount of the par value to create a positive yield to maturity. Many regard _____ as the least risky investment available to U.S. investors.
   a. Treasury Inflation Protected Securities
   b. 4-4-5 Calendar
   c. Treasury securities
   d. Treasury bills

14. An _____ is a company whose main business is holding securities of other companies purely for investment purposes. The _____ invests money on behalf of its shareholders who in turn share in the profits and losses.
   a. AAB
   b. A Random Walk Down Wall Street
   c. Unit investment trust
   d. Investment company

15. A _____ or bank is a financial institution whose primary activity is to act as a payment agent for customers and to borrow and lend money.

The first modern bank was founded in Italy in Genoa in 1406, its name was Banco di San Giorgio (Bank of St. George.)

Many other financial activities were added over time.

   a. 4-4-5 Calendar
   b. Banker
   c. Black Sea Trade and Development Bank
   d. Bought deal

16. A _____ is a pool of assets forming an independent legal entity that are bought with the contributions to a pension plan for the exclusive purpose of financing pension plan benefits.

_____s are important shareholders of listed and private companies. They are especially important to the stock market where large institutional investors like the Ontario Teachers' Pension Plan dominate.

   a. Leveraged buyout
   b. Limited liability company
   c. Pension fund
   d. Leverage

17. The _____ is the market for securities, where companies and governments can raise longterm funds. The _____ includes the stock market and the bond market. Financial regulators, such as the U.S. Securities and Exchange Commission, oversee the _____s in their designated countries to ensure that investors are protected against fraud.
   a. Spot rate
   b. Forward market
   c. Delta neutral
   d. Capital market

18. A '_____' is a 'Charge' that is paid to obtain the right to delay a payment. Essentially, the payer purchases the right to make a given payment in the future instead of in the Present. The '_____', or 'Charge' that must be paid to delay the payment, is simply the difference between what the payment amount would be if it were paid in the present and what the payment amount would be paid if it were paid in the future.

Chapter 8. The Money Markets

a. Discount
b. Risk aversion
c. Risk modeling
d. Value at risk

19. _____ is a system of tracking ownership of securities where no certificate is given to investors. In the case of _____ only issues, while investors do not receive certificates, a custodian holds one or more global certificates. Dematerialized securities, in contrast are ones in which no certificates exist (instead, the security issuer or its agent keeps records, usually electronically, of who holds outstanding securities.)
a. Marketable
b. Securities lending
c. Tracking stock
d. Book entry

20. _____ is the acquisition of goods and/or services at the best possible total cost of ownership, in the right quantity and quality, at the right time, in the right place and from the right source for the direct benefit or use of corporations or individuals, generally via a contract. Simple _____ may involve nothing more than repeat purchasing. Complex _____ could involve finding long term partners - or even 'co-destiny' suppliers that might fundamentally commit one organization to another.
a. Procurement
b. Market capitalization
c. Pac-Man defense
d. Synthetic CDO

21. In finance, _____ occurs when a debtor has not met its legal obligations according to the debt contract, e.g. it has not made a scheduled payment, or has violated a loan covenant (condition) of the debt contract. _____ may occur if the debtor is either unwilling or unable to pay their debt. This can occur with all debt obligations including bonds, mortgages, loans, and promissory notes.
a. Vendor finance
b. Default
c. Credit crunch
d. Debt validation

22. _____ is the risk of loss due to a debtor's non-payment of a loan or other line of credit (either the principal or interest (coupon) or both)

Most lenders employ their own models (credit scorecards) to rank potential and existing customers according to risk, and then apply appropriate strategies. With products such as unsecured personal loans or mortgages, lenders charge a higher price for higher risk customers and vice versa. With revolving products such as credit cards and overdrafts, risk is controlled through careful setting of credit limits.

a. Liquidity risk
b. Transaction risk
c. Market risk
d. Credit risk

23. _____ are government bonds issued by the United States Department of the Treasury through the Bureau of the Public Debt. They are the debt financing instruments of the U.S. Federal government, and they are often referred to simply as Treasuries or Treasurys. There are four types of marketable _____: Treasury bills, Treasury notes, Treasury bonds, and Treasury Inflation Protected Securities (TIPS.)
a. 4-4-5 Calendar
b. Treasury Inflation-Protected Securities
c. Treasury securities
d. Treasury Inflation Protected Securities

24. _____ are the means of implementing monetary policy by which a central bank controls its national money supply by buying and selling government securities, or other financial instruments. Monetary targets, such as interest rates or exchange rates, are used to guide this implementation.

Since most money is now in the form of electronic records, rather than paper records such as banknotes, _____ are conducted simply by electronically increasing or decreasing ('crediting' or 'debiting') the amount of money that a bank has, e.g., in its reserve account at the central bank, in exchange for a bank selling or buying a financial instrument.

a. A Random Walk Down Wall Street
b. Open market operations
c. ABN Amro
d. AAB

25. _____s are deposits denominated in United States dollars at banks outside the United States, and thus are not under the jurisdiction of the Federal Reserve. Consequently, such deposits are subject to much less regulation than similar deposits within the United States, allowing for higher margins. There is nothing 'European' about _____ deposits; a US dollar-denominated deposit in Tokyo or Caracas would likewise be deemed _____ deposits.

a. Eurodollar
b. ABN Amro
c. AAB
d. A Random Walk Down Wall Street

26. In the United States, _____ are overnight borrowings by banks to maintain their bank reserves at the Federal Reserve. Banks keep reserves at Federal Reserve Banks to meet their reserve requirements and to clear financial transactions. Transactions in the _____ market enable depository institutions with reserve balances in excess of reserve requirements to lend reserves to institutions with reserve deficiencies.

a. Regulation T
b. Federal funds rate
c. 4-4-5 Calendar
d. Federal funds

27. The '_____' is approximately the nominal interest rate minus the inflation rate Since the inflation rate over the course of a loan is not known initially, volatility in inflation represents a risk to both the lender and the borrower.

In economics and finance, an individual who lends money for repayment at a later point in time expects to be compensated for the time value of money, or not having the use of that money while it is lent.

a. 4-4-5 Calendar
b. Real interest rate
c. 7-Eleven
d. 529 plan

28. In economics, _____ is a rise in the general level of prices of goods and services in an economy over a period of time. The term '_____' once referred to increases in the money supply (monetary _____); however, economic debates about the relationship between money supply and price levels have led to its primary use today in describing price _____.
_____ can also be described as a decline in the real value of money--a loss of purchasing power in the medium of exchange which is also the monetary unit of account.

a. A Random Walk Down Wall Street
b. AAB
c. ABN Amro
d. Inflation

29. _____ is a fee paid on borrowed assets. It is the price paid for the use of borrowed money , or, money earned by deposited funds . Assets that are sometimes lent with _____ include money, shares, consumer goods through hire purchase, major assets such as aircraft, and even entire factories in finance lease arrangements.

a. Insolvency
b. A Random Walk Down Wall Street
c. AAB
d. Interest

Chapter 8. The Money Markets

30. An _____ is the price a borrower pays for the use of money they do not own, and the return a lender receives for deferring the use of funds, by lending it to the borrower. _____s are normally expressed as a percentage rate over the period of one year.

_____s targets are also a vital tool of monetary policy and are used to control variables like investment, inflation, and unemployment.

   a. ABN Amro
   c. A Random Walk Down Wall Street
   b. Interest rate
   d. AAB

31. In the United States, the _____ is the interest rate at which private depository institutions (mostly banks) lend balances (federal funds) at the Federal Reserve to other depository institutions, usually overnight. Changing the target rate is one form of open market operations that the Chairman of the Federal Reserve uses to regulate the supply of money in the U.S. economy.

U.S. banks and thrift institutions are obligated by law to maintain certain levels of reserves, either as reserves with the Fed or as vault cash.

   a. Regulation T
   c. 4-4-5 Calendar
   b. Federal funds rate
   d. Taylor rule

32. A _____ allows a borrower to use a financial security as collateral for a cash loan at a fixed rate of interest. In a repo, the borrower agrees to immediately sell a security to a lender and also agrees to buy the same security from the lender at a fixed price at some later date. A repo is equivalent to a cash transaction combined with a forward contract.
   a. Contango
   c. Volatility arbitrage
   b. Total return swap
   d. Repurchase agreement

33. A _____ is a document that indicates that the bearer of the document has title to property, such as shares or bonds. They differ from normal registered instruments, in that no records are kept of who owns the underlying property, or of the transactions involving transfer of ownership. Whoever physically holds the bearer bond papers owns the property.
   a. Book entry
   c. Securities lending
   b. Marketable
   d. Bearer instrument

34. A _____ s a time deposit, a financial product commonly offered to consumers by banks, thrift institutions, and credit unions.

They are similar to savings accounts in that they are insured and thus virtually risk-free; they are 'money in the bank'. They are different from savings accounts in that they have a specific, fixed term (often three months, six months, or one to five years), and, usually, a fixed interest rate.

   a. Certificate of deposit
   c. Reserve requirement
   b. Variable rate mortgage
   d. Time deposit

35. _____ is a type of bank account where the money in the account is legally able to be withdrawn immediately upon demand (or 'at call'.) This type of bank account can also be referred to as a 'cheque' or 'checking' or transactional account.

Chapter 8. The Money Markets

This type of bank account, allowing immediate conversion of the account balance into cash or withdrawal to another account, can be contrasted with a time deposit (also known as a certificate of deposit or term deposit), where the funds are not legally available for immediate withdrawal by the depositor.

a. 4-4-5 Calendar
b. Synthetic lease
c. Demand deposit
d. 529 plan

36. _____ is a United States government regulation that put a limit on the interest rates that banks could pay, including a rate of zero on demand deposits (checking accounts.) Section 11 of the Banking Act of 1933 (12 U.S.C. 371a) prohibits member banks from paying interest on demand deposits, which is implemented by _____

a. Regulation Q
b. Fair Credit Reporting Act
c. Truth in Lending Act
d. Fair Credit Billing Act

37. In the global money market, _____ is an unsecured promissory note with a fixed maturity of one to 270 days. _____ is a money-market security issued (sold) by large banks and corporations to get money to meet short term debt obligations (for example, payroll), and is only backed by an issuing bank or corporation's promise to pay the face amount on the maturity date specified on the note. Since it is not backed by collateral, only firms with excellent credit ratings from a recognized rating agency will be able to sell their _____ at a reasonable price.

a. Book building
b. Trade-off theory
c. Financial distress
d. Commercial paper

38. _____ is the provision of resources (such as granting a loan) by one party to another party where that second party does not reimburse the first party immediately, thereby generating a debt, and instead arranges either to repay or return those resources (or material(s) of equal value) at a later date. The first party is called a creditor, also known as a lender, while the second party is called a debtor, also known as a borrower.

Movements of financial capital are normally dependent on either _____ or equity transfers.

a. Warrant
b. Credit
c. Comparable
d. Clearing house

39. The _____ (LIBID) is a bid rate; the rate bid by banks on Eurocurrency deposits (i.e., the rate at which a bank is willing to borrow from other banks.) It is 'the opposite' of the LIBOR (an offered, hence 'ask' rate.) Whilst the British Bankers' Association set LIBOR rates, there is no correspondent official LIBID fixing.

a. Cash accumulation equation
b. Shanghai Interbank Offered Rate
c. London interbank bid rate
d. Repo rate

40. _____ is a measure of the ability of a debtor to pay their debts as and when they fall due. It is usually expressed as a ratio or a percentage of current liabilities.

For a corporation with a published balance sheet there are various ratios used to calculate a measure of liquidity.

a. Invested capital
b. Operating leverage
c. Operating profit margin
d. Accounting liquidity

Chapter 8. The Money Markets

41. A _____ is a professionally managed type of collective investment scheme that pools money from many investors and invests it in stocks, bonds, short-term money market instruments, and/or other securities. The _____ will have a fund manager that trades the pooled money on a regular basis. Currently, the worldwide value of all _____s totals more than $26 trillion.

Since 1940, there have been three basic types of investment companies in the United States: open-end funds, also known in the US as _____s; unit investment trusts (UITs); and closed-end funds.

- a. Trust company
- b. Net asset value
- c. Financial intermediary
- d. Mutual fund

42. In business and accounting, _____s are everything of value that is owned by a person or company. The balance sheet of a firm records the monetary value of the _____s owned by the firm. The two major _____ classes are tangible _____s and intangible _____s.
- a. Asset
- b. Income
- c. Accounts payable
- d. EBITDA

43. _____ are sometimes the same as net worth, or shareholders' equity - assets minus liabilities. The term _____ is commonly used with charities or not for profit entities. Although these entities don't make money, it is important to maintain reasonable reserves to help future growth.
- a. Net assets
- b. Sharpe ratio
- c. Cash conversion cycle
- d. Sustainable growth rate

Chapter 9. The Capital Markets

1. The _____ is the market for securities, where companies and governments can raise longterm funds. The _____ includes the stock market and the bond market. Financial regulators, such as the U.S. Securities and Exchange Commission, oversee the _____s in their designated countries to ensure that investors are protected against fraud.
   - a. Delta neutral
   - b. Spot rate
   - c. Forward market
   - d. Capital market

2. A _____, reserve bank, or monetary authority is the entity responsible for the monetary policy of a country or of a group of member states. It is a bank that can lend money to other banks in times of need. Its primary responsibility is to maintain the stability of the national currency and money supply, but more active duties include controlling subsidized-loan interest rates, and acting as a lender of last resort to the banking sector during times of financial crisis (private banks often being integral to the national financial system.)
   - a. 529 plan
   - b. 7-Eleven
   - c. Central bank
   - d. 4-4-5 Calendar

3. In finance, a _____ is a debt security, in which the authorized issuer owes the holders a debt and, depending on the terms of the _____, is obliged to pay interest (the coupon) and/or to repay the principal at a later date, termed maturity.

   Thus a _____ is a loan: the issuer is the borrower, the _____ holder is the lender, and the coupon is the interest. _____s provide the borrower with external funds to finance long-term investments, or, in the case of government _____s, to finance current expenditure.

   - a. Puttable bond
   - b. Convertible bond
   - c. Bond
   - d. Catastrophe bonds

4. The institution most often referenced by the word '_____' is a public or publicly traded _____, the shares of which are traded on a public stock exchange (e.g., the New York Stock Exchange or Nasdaq in the United States) where shares of stock of _____s are bought and sold by and to the general public. Most of the largest businesses in the world are publicly traded _____s. However, the majority of _____s are said to be closely held, privately held or close _____s, meaning that no ready market exists for the trading of shares.
   - a. Depository Trust Company
   - b. Protect
   - c. Federal Home Loan Mortgage Corporation
   - d. Corporation

5. In economics, a _____ is a mechanism that allows people to easily buy and sell (trade) financial securities (such as stocks and bonds), commodities (such as precious metals or agricultural goods), and other fungible items of value at low transaction costs and at prices that reflect the efficient-market hypothesis.

   _____s have evolved significantly over several hundred years and are undergoing constant innovation to improve liquidity.

   Both general markets (where many commodities are traded) and specialized markets (where only one commodity is traded) exist.

   - a. Cost of carry
   - b. Delta hedging
   - c. Secondary market
   - d. Financial market

Chapter 9. The Capital Markets

6. A _____ is a bond issued by a national government denominated in the country's own currency. Bonds issued by national governments in foreign currencies are normally referred to as sovereign bonds. The first ever _____ was issued by the British government in 1693 to raise money to fund a war against France.
   a. Municipal bond
   b. Government bond
   c. Zero-coupon bond
   d. Collateralized debt obligations

7. _____, is when a company issues common stock or shares to the public for the first time. They are often issued by smaller, younger companies seeking capital to expand, but can also be done by large privately-owned companies looking to become publicly traded.

   In an _____ the issuer may obtain the assistance of an underwriting firm, which helps it determine what type of security to issue (common or preferred), best offering price and time to bring it to market.

   a. Interest
   b. Initial public offering
   c. Asian Financial Crisis
   d. Insolvency

8. The _____ is that part of the capital markets that deals with the issuance of new securities. Companies, governments or public sector institutions can obtain funding through the sale of a new stock or bond issue. This is typically done through a syndicate of securities dealers.
   a. Volatility clustering
   b. Sector rotation
   c. Primary market
   d. Peer group analysis

9. The _____ is the financial market where previously issued securities and financial instruments such as stock, bonds, options, and futures are bought and sold. The term '_____' is also used refer to the market for any used goods or assets, or an alternative use for an existing product or asset where the customer base is the second market

   With primary issuances of securities or financial instruments, or the primary market, investors purchase these securities directly from issuers such as corporations issuing shares in an IPO or private placement, or directly from the federal government in the case of treasuries.

   a. Performance attribution
   b. Financial market
   c. Delta neutral
   d. Secondary market

10. A _____ is a fungible, negotiable instrument representing financial value. They are broadly categorized into debt securities (such as banknotes, bonds and debentures), and equity securities; e.g., common stocks. The company or other entity issuing the _____ is called the issuer.
    a. Security
    b. Securities lending
    c. Book entry
    d. Tracking stock

11. The _____ is a stock exchange based in New York City, New York. It is the largest stock exchange in the world by dollar value of its listed companies securities. As of October 2008, the combined capitalization of all domestic _____ listed companies was $10.1 trillion.
    a. 529 plan
    b. New York Stock Exchange
    c. 4-4-5 Calendar
    d. 7-Eleven

12. A _____, securities exchange or (in Europe) bourse is a corporation or mutual organization which provides 'trading' facilities for stock brokers and traders, to trade stocks and other securities. _____s also provide facilities for the issue and redemption of securities as well as other financial instruments and capital events including the payment of income and dividends. The securities traded on a _____ include: shares issued by companies, unit trusts and other pooled investment products and bonds.

a. 529 plan
b. 7-Eleven
c. 4-4-5 Calendar
d. Stock Exchange

13. In the United States, the Financial Industry Regulatory Authority (FINRA) is a self-regulatory organization (SRO) under the Securities Exchange Act of 1934, successor to the _____, Inc.

FINRA is responsible for regulatory oversight of all securities firms that do business with the public; professional training, testing and licensing of registered persons; arbitration and mediation; market regulation by contract for The NASDAQ Stock Market, Inc., the American Stock Exchange LLC, and the International Securities Exchange, LLC; and industry utilities, such as Trade Reporting Facilities and other over-the-counter operations.

a. 7-Eleven
b. National Association of Securities Dealers
c. 4-4-5 Calendar
d. 529 plan

14. The coupon or _____ of a bond is the amount of interest paid per year expressed as a percentage of the face value of the bond.

For example if you hold $10,000 nominal of a bond described as a 4.5% loan stock, you will receive $450 in interest each year (probably in two installments of $225 each.)

Not all bonds have coupons.

a. Puttable bond
b. Revenue bonds
c. Coupon rate
d. Zero-coupon bond

15. A '_____' is a 'Charge' that is paid to obtain the right to delay a payment. Essentially, the payer purchases the right to make a given payment in the future instead of in the Present. The '_____', or 'Charge' that must be paid to delay the payment, is simply the difference between what the payment amount would be if it were paid in the present and what the payment amount would be paid if it were paid in the future.

a. Discount
b. Risk modeling
c. Risk aversion
d. Value at risk

16. A _____ is a bond bought at a price lower than its face value, with the face value repaid at the time of maturity. It does not make periodic interest payments, or so-called 'coupons,' hence the term zero-coupon bond. Investors earn return from the compounded interest all paid at maturity plus the difference between the discounted price of the bond and its par value.

a. Municipal bond
b. Bowie bonds
c. Callable bond
d. Zero coupon bond

Chapter 9. The Capital Markets

17. In economic models, the _____ time frame assumes no fixed factors of production. Firms can enter or leave the marketplace, and the cost (and availability) of land, labor, raw materials, and capital goods can be assumed to vary. In contrast, in the short-run time frame, certain factors are assumed to be fixed, because there is not sufficient time for them to change.
    a. 529 plan
    b. Short-run
    c. 4-4-5 Calendar
    d. Long-run

18. A _____ is a bond bought at a price lower than its face value, with the face value repaid at the time of maturity. It does not make periodic interest payments, or have so-called 'coupons,' hence the term _____. Investors earn return from the compounded interest all paid at maturity plus the difference between the discounted price of the bond and its par value.
    a. Clean price
    b. Zero-coupon bond
    c. Corporate bond
    d. Bond fund

19. _____ mature in one year or less. Like zero-coupon bonds, they do not pay interest prior to maturity; instead they are sold at a discount of the par value to create a positive yield to maturity. Many regard _____ as the least risky investment available to U.S. investors.
    a. Treasury securities
    b. Treasury Inflation Protected Securities
    c. 4-4-5 Calendar
    d. Treasury bills

20. _____ are government bonds issued by the United States Department of the Treasury through the Bureau of the Public Debt. They are the debt financing instruments of the U.S. Federal government, and they are often referred to simply as Treasuries or Treasurys. There are four types of marketable _____: Treasury bills, Treasury notes, Treasury bonds, and Treasury Inflation Protected Securities (TIPS.)
    a. Treasury Inflation Protected Securities
    b. Treasury Inflation-Protected Securities
    c. 4-4-5 Calendar
    d. Treasury securities

21. A _____ is a financial crisis that occurs when many banks suffer runs at the same time. A systemic banking crisis is one where all or almost all of the banking capital in a country is wiped out. The resulting chain of bankruptcies can cause a long economic recession. Much of the Great Depression's economic damage was caused directly by bank runs. The cost of cleaning up a systemic banking crisis can be huge, with fiscal costs averaging 13% of GDP and economic output losses averaging 20% of GDP for important crises from 1970 to 2007.
    a. Deposit insurance
    b. Credit bureau
    c. Probability of default
    d. Banking panic

22. _____ is a fee paid on borrowed assets. It is the price paid for the use of borrowed money, or, money earned by deposited funds. Assets that are sometimes lent with _____ include money, shares, consumer goods through hire purchase, major assets such as aircraft, and even entire factories in finance lease arrangements.
    a. AAB
    b. Insolvency
    c. Interest
    d. A Random Walk Down Wall Street

23. An _____ is the price a borrower pays for the use of money they do not own, and the return a lender receives for deferring the use of funds, by lending it to the borrower. _____s are normally expressed as a percentage rate over the period of one year.

Chapter 9. The Capital Markets

_____s targets are also a vital tool of monetary policy and are used to control variables like investment, inflation, and unemployment.

a. ABN Amro
c. Interest rate

b. AAB
d. A Random Walk Down Wall Street

24. _____ are the means of implementing monetary policy by which a central bank controls its national money supply by buying and selling government securities, or other financial instruments. Monetary targets, such as interest rates or exchange rates, are used to guide this implementation.

Since most money is now in the form of electronic records, rather than paper records such as banknotes, _____ are conducted simply by electronically increasing or decreasing ('crediting' or 'debiting') the amount of money that a bank has, e.g., in its reserve account at the central bank, in exchange for a bank selling or buying a financial instrument.

a. ABN Amro
c. Open market operations

b. A Random Walk Down Wall Street
d. AAB

25. _____ are bonds where the principal is indexed to inflation. They are thus designed to cut out the inflation risk of an investment. _____ pay a periodic coupon that is equal to the product of the inflation index and the nominal coupon rate. The relationship between coupon payments, breakeven inflation and real interest rates is given by the Fisher equation.

a. Inflation-indexed bonds
c. ABN Amro

b. AAB
d. A Random Walk Down Wall Street

26. The _____ (NYSE: FNM), commonly known as Fannie Mae, is a stockholder-owned corporation chartered by Congress in 1968 as a government sponsored enterprise (GSE), but founded in 1938 during the Great Depression. The corporation's purpose is to purchase and securitize mortgages in order to ensure that funds are consistently available to the institutions that lend money to home buyers.

On September 7, 2008, James Lockhart, director of the Federal Housing Finance Agency (FHFA), announced that Fannie Mae and Freddie Mac were being placed into conservatorship of the FHFA.

a. SPDR
c. General partnership

b. The Depository Trust ' Clearing Corporation
d. Federal National Mortgage Association

27. The _____ is a U.S. government-owned corporation within the Department of Housing and Urban Development

Ginnie Mae provides guarantees on mortgage-backed securities backed by federally insured or guaranteed loans, mainly loans issued by the Federal Housing Administration, Department of Veterans Affairs, Rural Housing Service, and Office of Public and Indian Housing. Ginnie Mae securities are the only MBS that are guaranteed by the United States government.

Chapter 9. The Capital Markets

a. GNMA
c. Cash budget
b. Certified Emission Reductions
d. Case-Shiller Home Price Indices

28. The _____ is a U.S. government-owned corporation within the Department of Housing and Urban Development

Ginnie Mae provides guarantees on mortgage-backed securities backed by federally insured or guaranteed loans, mainly loans issued by the Federal Housing Administration, Department of Veterans Affairs, Rural Housing Service, and Office of Public and Indian Housing. Ginnie Mae securities are the only MBS that are guaranteed by the United States government.

a. 4-4-5 Calendar
c. Graduated payment mortgage
b. Government National Mortgage Association
d. Jumbo mortgage

29. _____ or financing is to provide capital (funds), which means money for a project, a person, a business or any other private or public institutions.

Those funds can be allocated for either short term or long term purposes. The health fund is a new way of _____ private healthcare centers.

a. Proxy fight
c. Synthetic CDO
b. Product life cycle
d. Funding

30. The '_____' is approximately the nominal interest rate minus the inflation rate Since the inflation rate over the course of a loan is not known initially, volatility in inflation represents a risk to both the lender and the borrower.

In economics and finance, an individual who lends money for repayment at a later point in time expects to be compensated for the time value of money, or not having the use of that money while it is lent.

a. 7-Eleven
c. 529 plan
b. 4-4-5 Calendar
d. Real interest rate

31. A _____ is a legal pledge in United States municipal finance, in which an entity pledges its full faith and credit to repay its debt, typically a _____ bond.
a. Letter of credit
c. Financial Institutions Reform Recovery and Enforcement Act
b. Covenant
d. General obligation

32. In the United States, a _____ is a bond issued by a city or other local government, or their agencies. Potential issuers of these bonds include cities, counties, redevelopment agencies, school districts, publicly owned airports and seaports, and any other governmental entity (or group of governments) below the state level. They may be general obligations of the issuer or secured by specified revenues.
a. Puttable bond
c. Premium bond
b. Municipal bond
d. Senior debt

33. In business, _____ is income that a company receives from its normal business activities, usually from the sale of goods and services to customers. Some companies also receive _____ from interest, dividends or royalties paid to them by other companies. _____ may refer to business income in general, or it may refer to the amount, in a monetary unit, received during a period of time, as in 'Last year, Company X had _____ of $32 million.'

In many countries, including the UK, _____ is referred to as turnover.

   a. Furniture, Fixtures and Equipment   b. Revenue
   c. Matching principle   d. Bottom line

34. _____ are bonds issued by governments, authorities, or public benefit corporations that are guaranteed by the revenue flow of the issuing agency.

The Supreme Court decision of Pollock versus Farmer's Loan and Trust Company of 1895 initiated a wave or series of innovations for the financial services community in both tax-treatment and regulation from government. This specific case, according to a leading investment bank's research, resulted in the 'intergovernmental tax immunity doctrine,' ultimately leading to 'tax-free status.' Municipal bonds are generally exempt from federal tax on their interest payments (not capital gains.)

   a. Callable bond   b. Gilts
   c. Private activity bond   d. Revenue bonds

35. A _____ is an exemption from all or certain taxes of a state or nation in which part of the taxes that would normally be collected from an individual or an organization are instead foregone.

Normally a _____ is provided to an individual or organization which falls within a class which the government wishes to promote economically, such as charitable organizations. _____s are usually meant to either reduce the tax burden on a particular segment of society in the interests of fairness or to promote some type of economic activity through reducing the tax burden on those organizations or individuals who are involved in that activity.

   a. Tax exemption   b. Federal Open Market Committee
   c. Tax incidence   d. Tax compliance solution

36. _____ (also trust indenture or deed of trust) is a legal document issued to lenders and describes key terms such as the interest rate, maturity date, convertibility, pledge, promises, representations, covenants, and other terms of the bond offering. When the Offering Memorandum is prepared in advance of marketing a Bond, the indenture will typically be summarised in the 'Description of Notes' section.

   a. Fair Labor Standards Act   b. McFadden Act
   c. Court of Audit of Belgium   d. Bond indenture

37. A _____ is a bond issued by a corporation. The term is usually applied to longer-term debt instruments, generally with a maturity date falling at least a year after their issue date. (The term 'commercial paper' is sometimes used for instruments with a shorter maturity.)

a. Corporate bond	b. Government bond
c. Brady bonds	d. Serial bond

38. In finance, _____ occurs when a debtor has not met its legal obligations according to the debt contract, e.g. it has not made a scheduled payment, or has violated a loan covenant (condition) of the debt contract. _____ may occur if the debtor is either unwilling or unable to pay their debt. This can occur with all debt obligations including bonds, mortgages, loans, and promissory notes.

a. Credit crunch	b. Default
c. Vendor finance	d. Debt validation

39. _____ is the risk of loss due to a debtor's non-payment of a loan or other line of credit (either the principal or interest (coupon) or both)

Most lenders employ their own models (credit scorecards) to rank potential and existing customers according to risk, and then apply appropriate strategies. With products such as unsecured personal loans or mortgages, lenders charge a higher price for higher risk customers and vice versa. With revolving products such as credit cards and overdrafts, risk is controlled through careful setting of credit limits.

a. Transaction risk	b. Credit risk
c. Liquidity risk	d. Market risk

40. A _____ is a document that indicates that the bearer of the document has title to property, such as shares or bonds. They differ from normal registered instruments, in that no records are kept of who owns the underlying property, or of the transactions involving transfer of ownership. Whoever physically holds the bearer bond papers owns the property.

a. Bearer instrument	b. Book entry
c. Marketable	d. Securities lending

41. A _____ is different from normal stock in that it is unregistered - no records are kept of the owner, or the transactions involving ownership. Whoever physically holds the _____ papers owns the stock or corporation. This is useful for investors and corporate officers who wish to retain anonymity.

a. Clean price	b. Revenue bonds
c. Gilts	d. Bearer bond

42. _____ is that which is owed; usually referencing assets owed, but the term can cover other obligations. In the case of assets, _____ is a means of using future purchasing power in the present before a summation has been earned. Some companies and corporations use _____ as a part of their overall corporate finance strategy.

a. Partial Payment	b. Cross-collateralization
c. Credit cycle	d. Debt

43. A _____ is a fund established by a government agency or business for the purpose of reducing debt.

The _____ was first used in Great Britain in the 18th century to reduce national debt. While used by Robert Walpole in 1716 and effectively in the 1720s and early 1730s, it originated in the commercial tax syndicates of the Italian peninsula of the 14th century to retire redeemable public debt of those cities.

a. Sinking fund
b. Debtor
c. Security interest
d. Modern portfolio theory

44. A mutual shareholder or _____ is an individual or company (including a corporation) that legally owns one or more shares of stock in a joint stock company. A company's shareholders collectively own that company. Thus, the typical goal of such companies is to enhance shareholder value.
   a. Limit order
   b. Stock market bubble
   c. Stockholder
   d. Trading curb

45. A _____ is an exchange of promises between two or more parties to do an act which is enforceable in a court of law. It is where an unqualified offer meets a qualified acceptance and the parties reach Consensus ad Idem. The parties must have the necessary capacity to _____ and the _____ must not be either trifling, indeterminate, impossible or illegal.
   a. 4-4-5 Calendar
   b. 7-Eleven
   c. 529 plan
   d. Contract

46. A _____, in its most general sense, is a solemn promise to engage in or refrain from a specified action.

More specifically, a _____, in contrast to a contract, is a one-way agreement whereby the _____er is the only party bound by the promise. A _____ may have conditions and prerequisites that qualify the undertaking, including the actions of second or third parties, but there is no inherent agreement by such other parties to fulfill those requirements.

   a. Covenant
   b. Federal Trade Commission Act
   c. Partnership
   d. Clayton Antitrust Act

47. In financial accounting, _____s are precautions for which the amount or probability of occurrence are not known. Typical examples are _____s for warranty costs and _____ for taxes the term reserve is used instead of term _____; such a use, however, is inconsistent with the terminology suggested by International Accounting Standards Board.
   a. Momentum Accounting and Triple-Entry Bookkeeping
   b. Petty cash
   c. Money measurement concept
   d. Provision

48. In lending agreements, _____ is a borrower's pledge of specific property to a lender, to secure repayment of a loan. The _____ serves as protection for a lender against a borrower's risk of default - that is, a borrower failing to pay the principal and interest under the terms of a loan obligation. If a borrower does default on a loan (due to insolvency or other event), that borrower forfeits (gives up) the property pledged as _____ *ollateral* - and the lender then becomes the owner of the _____.
   a. Nominal value
   b. Futuro oriented
   c. Refinancing risk
   d. Collateral

49. In finance, a _____ is a type of bond that can be converted into shares of stock in the issuing company, usually at some pre-announced ratio. It is a hybrid security with debt- and equity-like features. Although it typically has a low coupon rate, the holder is compensated with the ability to convert the bond to common stock, usually at a substantial discount to the stock's market value.

Chapter 9. The Capital Markets

a. Convertible bond
b. Corporate bond
c. Bond fund
d. Gilts

50. A _____ is defined as a certificate of agreement of loans which is given under the company's stamp and carries an undertaking that the _____ holder will get a fixed return (fixed on the basis of interest rates) and the principal amount whenever the _____ matures.

In finance, a _____ is a long-term debt instrument used by governments and large companies to obtain funds. It is defined as 'a debt secured only by the debtor's earning power, not by a lien on any specific asset.' It is similar to a bond except the securitization conditions are different.

a. Collateral Management
b. Partial Payment
c. Collection agency
d. Debenture

51. An _____ is a financial security used in aircraft finance, most commonly to take advantage of tax benefits in North America.

In a typical _____ transaction, a 'trust certificate' is sold to investors in order to finance the purchase of an aircraft by a trust managed on the investors' behalf. The trust then leases the aircraft to an airline, and the trustee routes payments through the trust to the investors.

a. A Random Walk Down Wall Street
b. Equipment trust certificate
c. AAB
d. ABN Amro

52. In finance, a _____ (non-investment grade bond, speculative grade bond or junk bond) is a bond that is rated below investment grade at the time of purchase. These bonds have a higher risk of default or other adverse credit events, but typically pay higher yields than better quality bonds in order to make them attractive to investors.

a. Sharpe ratio
b. Volatility
c. High yield bond
d. Private equity

53. The _____ is a financial market where participants buy and sell debt securities, usually in the form of bonds. As of 2006, the size of the international _____ is an estimated $45 trillion, of which the size of the outstanding U.S. _____ debt was $25.2 trillion.

Nearly all of the $923 billion average daily trading volume in the U.S. _____ takes place between broker-dealers and large institutions in a decentralized, over-the-counter market.

a. Fixed income
b. 4-4-5 Calendar
c. 529 plan
d. Bond market

54. A _____ is the direction in which a financial market is moving. _____s can be classified as primary trends, secondary trends (short-term), and secular trends (long-term.) This principle incorporates the idea that market cycles occur with regularity and persistence.

a. 4-4-5 Calendar
b. Market trend
c. 7-Eleven
d. 529 plan

Chapter 9. The Capital Markets

55. _____ is a form of corporation equity ownership represented in the securities. It is dangerous in comparison to preferred shares and some other investment options, in that in the event of bankruptcy, _____ investors receive their funds after preferred stockholders, bondholders, creditors, etc. On the other hand, common shares on average perform better than preferred shares or bonds over time.
   a. Common stock
   b. Stock market bubble
   c. Stock split
   d. Stop-limit order

56. A _____ is a payment made by a corporation to its shareholder members. When a corporation earns a profit or surplus, that money can be put to two uses: it can either be re-invested in the business (called retained earnings), or it can be paid to the shareholders as a _____. Many corporations retain a portion of their earnings and pay the remainder as a _____.
   a. Dividend
   b. Special dividend
   c. Dividend yield
   d. Dividend puzzle

57. _____ is typically a higher ranking stock than voting shares, and its terms are negotiated between the corporation and the investor.

   _____ usually carry no voting rights, but may carry superior priority over common stock in the payment of dividends and upon liquidation. _____ may carry a dividend that is paid out prior to any dividends to common stock holders.

   a. Follow-on offering
   b. Second lien loan
   c. Preferred stock
   d. Trade-off theory

58. In business and finance, a _____ (also referred to as equity _____) of stock means a _____ of ownership in a corporation (company.) In the plural, stocks is often used as a synonym for _____s especially in the United States, but it is less commonly used that way outside of North America.

   In the United Kingdom, South Africa, and Australia, stock can also refer to completely different financial instruments such as government bonds or, less commonly, to all kinds of marketable securities.

   a. Margin
   b. Procter ' Gamble
   c. Bucket shop
   d. Share

59. A _____ is the price of a single share of a no. of saleable stocks of the company. Once the stock is purchased, the owner becomes a shareholder of the company that issued the share.
   a. Trading curb
   b. Whisper numbers
   c. Share price
   d. Stock split

60. The _____ is one of several stock market indices, created by nineteenth-century Wall Street Journal editor and Dow Jones ' Company co-founder Charles Dow. Dow compiled the index to gauge the performance of the industrial sector of the American stock market. It is the second-oldest U.S. market index, after the Dow Jones Transportation Average, which Dow also created.
   a. 4-4-5 Calendar
   b. 529 plan
   c. 7-Eleven
   d. Dow Jones Industrial Average

Chapter 9. The Capital Markets

61. A _____ is a private or public market for the trading of company stock and derivatives of company stock at an agreed price; these are securities listed on a stock exchange as well as those only traded privately.

The size of the world _____ is estimated at about $36.6 trillion US at the beginning of October 2008. The world derivatives market has been estimated at about $480 trillion face or nominal value, 12 times the size of the entire world economy.

a. Anton Gelonkin
b. Adolph Coors
c. Andrew Tobias
d. Stock market

62. A _____ is a method of measuring a section of the stock market. Many indices are cited by news or financial services firms and are used to benchmark the performance of portfolios such as mutual funds.

a. Stock market index
b. Stop order
c. Trading curb
d. Program trading

63. _____ in finance is a risk management technique, related to hedging, that mixes a wide variety of investments within a portfolio. Because the fluctuations of a single security have less impact on a diverse portfolio, _____ minimizes the risk from any one investment.

A simple example of _____ is the following: On a particular island the entire economy consists of two companies: one that sells umbrellas and another that sells sunscreen.

a. 7-Eleven
b. Diversification
c. 4-4-5 Calendar
d. 529 plan

64. An _____ represents the ownership in the shares of a foreign company trading on US financial markets. The stock of many non-US companies trades on US exchanges through the use of _____s. _____s enable US investors to buy shares in foreign companies without undertaking cross-border transactions.

a. AAB
b. ABN Amro
c. A Random Walk Down Wall Street
d. American depository receipt

Chapter 10. The Efficient Market Hypothesis

1. _____ is a form of corporation equity ownership represented in the securities. It is dangerous in comparison to preferred shares and some other investment options, in that in the event of bankruptcy, _____ investors receive their funds after preferred stockholders, bondholders, creditors, etc. On the other hand, common shares on average perform better than preferred shares or bonds over time.
   a. Stock split
   b. Stock market bubble
   c. Stop-limit order
   d. Common stock

2. A _____ is a private or public market for the trading of company stock and derivatives of company stock at an agreed price; these are securities listed on a stock exchange as well as those only traded privately.

   The size of the world _____ is estimated at about $36.6 trillion US at the beginning of October 2008 . The world derivatives market has been estimated at about $480 trillion face or nominal value, 12 times the size of the entire world economy.

   a. Adolph Coors
   b. Andrew Tobias
   c. Anton Gelonkin
   d. Stock market

3. A _____ is the price of a single share of a no. of saleable stocks of the company. Once the stock is purchased, the owner becomes a shareholder of the company that issued the share.
   a. Whisper numbers
   b. Stock split
   c. Trading curb
   d. Share price

4. _____ is an estimate of the fair value of corporations and their stocks, by using fundamental economic criteria. This theoretical valuation has to be perfected with market criteria, as the final purpose is to determine potential market prices.
   a. Growth stocks
   b. Security Analysis
   c. 4-4-5 Calendar
   d. Stock valuation

5. In finance, _____ is the process of estimating the potential market value of a financial asset or liability. they can be done on assets (for example, investments in marketable securities such as stocks, options, business enterprises, or intangible assets such as patents and trademarks) or on liabilities (e.g., Bonds issued by a company.) _____s are required in many contexts including investment analysis, capital budgeting, merger and acquisition transactions, financial reporting, taxable events to determine the proper tax liability, and in litigation.
   a. Share
   b. Valuation
   c. Margin
   d. Procter ' Gamble

6. _____ most frequently refers to the standard deviation of the continuously compounded returns of a financial instrument with a specific time horizon. It is often used to quantify the risk of the instrument over that time period. _____ is typically expressed in annualized terms, and it may either be an absolute number ($5) or a fraction of the mean (5%).
   a. Portfolio insurance
   b. Volatility
   c. Seasoned equity offering
   d. Currency swap

Chapter 10. The Efficient Market Hypothesis

7. _____ is the balance of the amounts of cash being received and paid by a business during a defined period of time, sometimes tied to a specific project. Measurement of _____ can be used

- to evaluate the state or performance of a business or project.
- to determine problems with liquidity. Being profitable does not necessarily mean being liquid. A company can fail because of a shortage of cash, even while profitable.
- to generate project rate of returns. The time of _____s into and out of projects are used as inputs to financial models such as internal rate of return, and net present value.
- to examine income or growth of a business when it is believed that accrual accounting concepts do not represent economic realities. Alternately, _____ can be used to 'validate' the net income generated by accrual accounting.

_____ as a generic term may be used differently depending on context, and certain _____ definitions may be adapted by analysts and users for their own uses. Common terms include operating _____ and free _____.

_____s can be classified into:

1. Operational _____s: Cash received or expended as a result of the company's core business activities.
2. Investment _____s: Cash received or expended through capital expenditure, investments or acquisitions.
3. Financing _____s: Cash received or expended as a result of financial activities, such as interests and dividends.

All three together - the net _____ - are necessary to reconcile the beginning cash balance to the ending cash balance. Loan draw downs or equity injections, that is just shifting of capital but no expenditure as such, are not considered in the net _____.

a. Real option
b. Shareholder value
c. Corporate finance
d. Cash flow

8. A _____ is a payment made by a corporation to its shareholder members. When a corporation earns a profit or surplus, that money can be put to two uses: it can either be re-invested in the business (called retained earnings), or it can be paid to the shareholders as a _____. Many corporations retain a portion of their earnings and pay the remainder as a _____.

a. Dividend yield
b. Dividend puzzle
c. Special dividend
d. Dividend

9. A mutual shareholder or _____ is an individual or company (including a corporation) that legally owns one or more shares of stock in a joint stock company. A company's shareholders collectively own that company. Thus, the typical goal of such companies is to enhance shareholder value.
a. Limit order
b. Stockholder
c. Trading curb
d. Stock market bubble

10. _____ is a variant of the Discounted cash flow model, a method for valuing a stock or business. Often used to provide difficult-to-resolve valuation issues for litigation, tax planning, and business transactions that are currently off market.

It assumes that the company issues a dividend that has a current value of D that grows at a constant rate g. It also assumes that the required rate of return for the stock remains constant at k which is equal to the cost of equity for that company. It involves summing the infinite series which gives the value of price current P.

    a. Securitization
    c. Special journals
    b. Stock or scrip dividends
    d. Gordon growth model

11. _____ is an economic concept with commonplace familiarity. It is the price that a good or service is offered at, or will fetch, in the marketplace. It is of interest mainly in the study of microeconomics.
    a. Delta hedging
    c. Central Securities Depository
    b. Convertible arbitrage
    d. Market price

12. In business and accounting, _____s are everything of value that is owned by a person or company. The balance sheet of a firm records the monetary value of the _____s owned by the firm. The two major _____ classes are tangible _____s and intangible _____s.
    a. Asset
    c. EBITDA
    b. Accounts payable
    d. Income

13. _____ is the difference between price and the costs of bringing to market whatever it is that is accounted as an enterprise (whether by harvest, extraction, manufacture, or purchase) in terms of the component costs of delivered goods and/or services and any operating or other expenses.

A key difficulty in measuring profit is in defining costs. Pure economic monetary profits can be zero or negative even in competitive equilibrium when accounted monetized costs exceed monetized price.

    a. AAB
    c. A Random Walk Down Wall Street
    b. Economic profit
    d. Accounting profit

14. A _____, securities analyst, research analyst, equity analyst, or investment analyst is a person who performs financial analysis for external or internal clients as a core part of the job.

An analyst studies companies and other entities to arrive at the estimate of their financial value. It is normally done by analyzing financial reports, aided by follow-up interviews with company representatives and industry experts.

    a. Purchasing manager
    c. Stockbroker
    b. Portfolio manager
    d. Financial analyst

15. In economics and contract theory, _____ deals with the study of decisions in transactions where one party has more or better information than the other. This creates an imbalance of power in transactions which can sometimes cause the transactions to go awry. Examples of this problem are adverse selection and moral hazard.
    a. AAB
    c. A Random Walk Down Wall Street
    b. ABN Amro
    d. Information asymmetry

Chapter 10. The Efficient Market Hypothesis

16. A _____ is a professionally managed type of collective investment scheme that pools money from many investors and invests it in stocks, bonds, short-term money market instruments, and/or other securities. The _____ will have a fund manager that trades the pooled money on a regular basis. Currently, the worldwide value of all _____ s totals more than $26 trillion.

Since 1940, there have been three basic types of investment companies in the United States: open-end funds, also known in the US as _____ s; unit investment trusts (UITs); and closed-end funds.

a. Mutual fund
c. Trust company
b. Net asset value
d. Financial intermediary

17. A _____, is a mathematical formalization of a trajectory that consists of taking successive random steps. The results of _____ analysis have been applied to computer science, physics, ecology, economics and a number of other fields as a fundamental model for random processes in time. For example, the path traced by a molecule as it travels in a liquid or a gas, the search path of a foraging animal, the price of a fluctuating stock and the financial status of a gambler can all be modeled as _____ s.

a. 7-Eleven
c. 4-4-5 Calendar
b. 529 plan
d. Random walk

18. In finance, the _____ between two currencies specifies how much one currency is worth in terms of the other. For example an _____ of 102 Japanese yen to the United States dollar means that JPY 102 is worth the same as USD 1. The foreign exchange market is one of the largest markets in the world.

a. AAB
c. A Random Walk Down Wall Street
b. ABN Amro
d. Exchange rate

19. _____ was an arrangement established in 1979 under the Jenkins European Commission where most nations of the European Economic Community (EEC) linked their currencies to prevent large fluctuations relative to one another.

After the collapse of the Bretton Woods system in 1971, most of the EEC countries agreed in 1972 to maintain stable exchange rates by preventing exchange fluctuations of more than 2.25% (the European 'currency snake'.) In March 1979, this system was replaced by the _____, and the European Currency Unit (ECU) was defined.

a. European Monetary System
c. Exchange Rate Mechanism
b. A Random Walk Down Wall Street
d. Euro Interbank Offered Rate

20. A _____ secures the proper functioning of money by regulating economic agents, transaction types, and money supply.

They are traditionally formed by the policy decisions of individual governments and administrated as a domestic economic issue.

The current trend, however, is to use international trade and investment to alter the policy and legislation of individual governments.

a. Payback period
b. Monetary System
c. Bond credit rating
d. Pattern day trader

21. _____ is a security analysis discipline for forecasting the future direction of prices through the study of past market data, primarily price and volume. In its purest form, _____ considers only the actual price and volume behavior of the market or instrument. Technical analysts may employ models and trading rules based on price and volume transformations, such as the relative strength index, moving averages, regressions, inter-market and intra-market price correlations, cycles or, classically, through recognition of chart patterns.
   a. Support and resistance
   b. Dow theory
   c. Technical analysis
   d. Point and figure

22. The _____ is the tendency of the stock market to rise between December 31 and the end of the first week in January. There are many theories for why this happens, the main one being that it occurs because many investors choose to sell some of their stock right before the end of the year in order to claim a capital loss for tax purposes. Once the tax calendar rolls over to a new year on January 1st these same investors quickly reinvest their money in the market, causing stock prices to rise.
   a. Sector rotation
   b. Death spiral financing
   c. Revaluation
   d. January effect

23. In statistics, _____ has two related meanings:

   - the arithmetic _____
   - the expected value of a random variable, which is also called the population _____.

It is sometimes stated that the '_____' is average. This is incorrect if '_____' is taken in the specific sense of 'arithmetic _____' as there are different types of averages: the _____, median, and mode. Other simple statistical analyses use measures of spread, such as range, interquartile range, or standard deviation. For a real-valued random variable X, the _____ is the expectation of X. Note that not every probability distribution has a defined _____; see the Cauchy distribution for an example.

   a. Harmonic mean
   b. Mean
   c. Probability distribution
   d. Sample size

24. In finance, a _____ is a debt security, in which the authorized issuer owes the holders a debt and, depending on the terms of the _____, is obliged to pay interest (the coupon) and/or to repay the principal at a later date, termed maturity.

Thus a _____ is a loan: the issuer is the borrower, the _____ holder is the lender, and the coupon is the interest. _____s provide the borrower with external funds to finance long-term investments, or, in the case of government _____s, to finance current expenditure.

   a. Catastrophe bonds
   b. Bond
   c. Convertible bond
   d. Puttable bond

Chapter 10. The Efficient Market Hypothesis

25. In finance, _____ refers to Monday, October 19, 1987, when stock markets around the world crashed, shedding a huge value in a very short time. The crash began in Hong Kong, spread west through international time zones to Europe, hitting the United States after other markets had already declined by a significant margin. The Dow Jones Industrial Average (DJIA) dropped by 508 points to 1738.74 (22.61%).
- a. 529 plan
- b. 7-Eleven
- c. Black Monday
- d. 4-4-5 Calendar

26. The _____ was a worldwide economic downturn starting in most places in 1929 and ending at different times in the 1930s or early 1940s for different countries. It was the largest and most important economic depression in the 20th century, and is used in the 21st century as an example of how far the world's economy can fall. The _____ originated in the United States; historians most often use as a starting date the stock market crash on October 29, 1929, known as Black Tuesday.
- a. 4-4-5 Calendar
- b. Great Depression
- c. 7-Eleven
- d. 529 plan

27. A _____ is a sudden dramatic decline of stock prices across a significant cross-section of a stock market. Crashes are driven by panic as much as by underlying economic factors. They often follow speculative stock market bubbles.
- a. 529 plan
- b. Stock market crash
- c. 7-Eleven
- d. 4-4-5 Calendar

28. In finance, _____, also known as return on investment is the ratio of money gained or lost on an investment relative to the amount of money invested. The amount of money gained or lost may be referred to as interest, profit/loss, gain/loss, or net income/loss. The money invested may be referred to as the asset, capital, principal, or the cost basis of the investment.
- a. Doctrine of the Proper Law
- b. Composiition of Creditors
- c. Stock or scrip dividends
- d. Rate of return

Chapter 11. The Mortgage Markets

1. The _____ is the market for securities, where companies and governments can raise longterm funds. The _____ includes the stock market and the bond market. Financial regulators, such as the U.S. Securities and Exchange Commission, oversee the _____s in their designated countries to ensure that investors are protected against fraud.
   a. Spot rate
   b. Forward market
   c. Delta neutral
   d. Capital market

2. _____ is the process of decreasing an amount over a period of time. The word comes from Middle English amortisen to kill, alienate in mortmain, from Anglo-French amorteser, alteration of amortir, from Vulgar Latin admortire to kill, from Latin ad- + mort-, mors death. Particular instances of the term include:

   - _____ (business), the allocation of a lump sum amount to different time periods, particularly for loans and other forms of finance, including related interest or other finance charges.
     - _____ schedule, a table detailing each periodic payment on a loan (typically a mortgage), as generated by an _____ calculator.
     - Negative _____, an _____ schedule where the loan amount actually increases through not paying the full interest
   - Amortized analysis, analyzing the execution cost of algorithms over a sequence of operations.
   - _____ of capital expenditures of certain assets under accounting rules, particularly intangible assets, in a manner analogous to depreciation.
   - _____ (tax law)

   _____ is also used in the context of zoning regulations and describes the time in which a property owner has to relocate when the property's use constitutes a preexisting nonconforming use under zoning regulations.

   - Depreciation

   a. Option
   b. Intrinsic value
   c. AT'T Inc.
   d. Amortization

3. In financial accounting, a _____ or statement of financial position is a summary of a person's or organization's balances. Assets, liabilities and ownership equity are listed as of a specific date, such as the end of its financial year. A _____ is often described as a snapshot of a company's financial condition.
   a. Statement on Auditing Standards No. 70: Service Organizations
   b. Balance sheet
   c. Financial statements
   d. Statement of retained earnings

4. The _____ is the financial market where previously issued securities and financial instruments such as stock, bonds, options, and futures are bought and sold. The term '_____' is also used refer to the market for any used goods or assets, or an alternative use for an existing product or asset where the customer base is the second market

With primary issuances of securities or financial instruments, or the primary market, investors purchase these securities directly from issuers such as corporations issuing shares in an IPO or private placement, or directly from the federal government in the case of treasuries.

Chapter 11. The Mortgage Markets

a. Delta neutral
b. Performance attribution
c. Financial market
d. Secondary market

5. _____ are government bonds issued by the United States Department of the Treasury through the Bureau of the Public Debt. They are the debt financing instruments of the U.S. Federal government, and they are often referred to simply as Treasuries or Treasurys. There are four types of marketable _____: Treasury bills, Treasury notes, Treasury bonds, and Treasury Inflation Protected Securities (TIPS.)

a. 4-4-5 Calendar
b. Treasury Inflation-Protected Securities
c. Treasury Inflation Protected Securities
d. Treasury securities

6. In finance, a _____ is a debt security, in which the authorized issuer owes the holders a debt and, depending on the terms of the _____, is obliged to pay interest (the coupon) and/or to repay the principal at a later date, termed maturity.

Thus a _____ is a loan: the issuer is the borrower, the _____ holder is the lender, and the coupon is the interest. _____s provide the borrower with external funds to finance long-term investments, or, in the case of government _____s, to finance current expenditure.

a. Puttable bond
b. Convertible bond
c. Catastrophe bonds
d. Bond

7. A _____ is an exchange of promises between two or more parties to do an act which is enforceable in a court of law. It is where an unqualified offer meets a qualified acceptance and the parties reach Consensus ad Idem. The parties must have the necessary capacity to _____ and the _____ must not be either trifling, indeterminate, impossible or illegal.

a. 7-Eleven
b. 529 plan
c. 4-4-5 Calendar
d. Contract

8. A _____ is an institution, firm or individual who mediates between two or more parties in a financial context. Typically the first party is a provider of a product or service and the second party is a consumer or customer.

In the U.S., a _____ is typically an institution that facilitates the channelling of funds between lenders and borrowers indirectly.

a. Savings and loan association
b. Mutual fund
c. Net asset value
d. Financial intermediary

9. _____ is a fee paid on borrowed assets. It is the price paid for the use of borrowed money, or, money earned by deposited funds. Assets that are sometimes lent with _____ include money, shares, consumer goods through hire purchase, major assets such as aircraft, and even entire factories in finance lease arrangements.

a. AAB
b. Insolvency
c. A Random Walk Down Wall Street
d. Interest

10. An _____ is the price a borrower pays for the use of money they do not own, and the return a lender receives for deferring the use of funds, by lending it to the borrower. _____s are normally expressed as a percentage rate over the period of one year.

_____s targets are also a vital tool of monetary policy and are used to control variables like investment, inflation, and unemployment.

a. A Random Walk Down Wall Street
b. ABN Amro
c. AAB
d. Interest rate

11. The _____ is the market for the sale of securities or bonds collateralized by the value of mortgage loans. The mortgage lender, commercial banks, or specialized firm will group together many loans and sell grouped loans as securities called collateralized mortgage obligations (CMOs.) The risk of the individual loans is reduced by that aggregation process.
a. 529 plan
b. Secondary Mortgage market
c. 7-Eleven
d. 4-4-5 Calendar

12. A '_____' is a 'Charge' that is paid to obtain the right to delay a payment. Essentially, the payer purchases the right to make a given payment in the future instead of in the Present. The '_____', or 'Charge' that must be paid to delay the payment, is simply the difference between what the payment amount would be if it were paid in the present and what the payment amount would be paid if it were paid in the future.
a. Value at risk
b. Risk aversion
c. Risk modeling
d. Discount

13. In lending agreements, _____ is a borrower's pledge of specific property to a lender, to secure repayment of a loan. The _____ serves as protection for a lender against a borrower's risk of default - that is, a borrower failing to pay the principal and interest under the terms of a loan obligation. If a borrower does default on a loan (due to insolvency or other event), that borrower forfeits (gives up) the property pledged as _____ _ollateral_ - and the lender then becomes the owner of the _____.
a. Collateral
b. Future-oriented
c. Refinancing risk
d. Nominal value

14. _____ is a term used in the context of the purchase of expensive items such as a car and a house, whereby the payment is the initial upfront portion of the total amount due and it is usually given in cash at the time of finalizing the transaction. A loan is then required to make the full payment.

The main purpose of a _____ is to ensure that the lending institution can recover the balance due on the loan in the event that the borrower defaults.

a. Financial Institutions Reform Recovery and Enforcement Act
b. Business valuation
c. Down payment
d. Royalties

15. In law, a _____ is a form of security interest granted over an item of property to secure the payment of a debt or performance of some other obligation. The owner of the property, who grants the _____, is referred to as the lienor and the person who has the benefit of the _____ is referred to as the _____ee.

The etymological root is: Anglo-French _____, loyen bond, restraint, from Latin ligamen, from ligare to bind.

Chapter 11. The Mortgage Markets

a. Family and Medical Leave Act
b. Joint venture
c. Sarbanes-Oxley Act
d. Lien

16. _____ is insurance payable to a lender or trustee for a pool of securities that may be required when taking out a mortgage loan. It is insurance to offset losses in the case where a mortgagor is not able to repay the loan and the lender is not able to recover its costs after foreclosure and sale of the mortgaged property. Typical rates are $55/mo. per $100,000 financed, or as high as $1,500/yr. for a typical $200,000 loan.

a. 4-4-5 Calendar
b. Lenders Mortgage Insurance
c. 529 plan
d. Property insurance

17. _____ is an insurance policy which compensates lenders or investors for losses due to the default of a mortgage loan. _____ can be either public or private depending upon the insurer. The policy is also known as a mortgage indemnity guarantee (Mortgage insuranceG), particularly in the UK.

a. Mortgage Insurance
b. Reverse mortgage
c. Mortgage-backed security
d. Subprime lending

18. In business, _____ is the total assets minus total outside liabilities of an individual or a company. For a company, this is called shareholders' equity and may be referred to as book value. _____ is stated as at a particular point in time.

a. Certified International Investment Analyst
b. Restructuring
c. Moneylender
d. Net worth

19. An _____ is a mortgage loan where the interest rate on the note is periodically adjusted based on a variety of indices. Among the most common indices are the rates on 1-year constant-maturity Treasury (CMT) securities, the Cost of Funds Index (COFI), and the London Interbank Offered Rate (LIBOR.) A few lenders use their own cost of funds as an index, rather than using other indices.

a. Adjustable rate mortgage
b. ABN Amro
c. AAB
d. A Random Walk Down Wall Street

20. A _____ is a professionally managed type of collective investment scheme that pools money from many investors and invests it in stocks, bonds, short-term money market instruments, and/or other securities. The _____ will have a fund manager that trades the pooled money on a regular basis. Currently, the worldwide value of all _____s totals more than $26 trillion.

Since 1940, there have been three basic types of investment companies in the United States: open-end funds, also known in the US as _____s; unit investment trusts (UITs); and closed-end funds.

a. Net asset value
b. Financial intermediary
c. Trust company
d. Mutual fund

21. In finance, a _____ is the party in a loan agreement which receives money or other instrument from a lender and promises to repay the lender in a specified time.

a. Line of credit
b. Borrower
c. Cash credit
d. Debt management plan

Chapter 11. The Mortgage Markets

22. In finance, 'participation' is an ownership interest in a mortgage or other loan. In particular, _____ is a cooperation of multiple lenders to issue a loan (known as participation loan) to one borrower. This is usually done in order to reduce individual risks of the lenders.

    a. Securitization
    b. Doctrine of the Proper Law
    c. Short positions
    d. Loan participation

23. _____ is the provision of resources (such as granting a loan) by one party to another party where that second party does not reimburse the first party immediately, thereby generating a debt, and instead arranges either to repay or return those resources (or material(s) of equal value) at a later date. The first party is called a creditor, also known as a lender, while the second party is called a debtor, also known as a borrower.

    Movements of financial capital are normally dependent on either _____ or equity transfers.

    a. Comparable
    b. Clearing house
    c. Warrant
    d. Credit

24. A _____ is a cooperative financial institution that is owned and controlled by its members, and operated for the purpose of promoting thrift, providing credit at reasonable rates, and providing other financial services to its members. Many _____s exist to further community development or sustainable international development on a local level. Worldwide, _____ systems vary significantly in terms of total system assets and average institution asset size since _____s exist in a wide range of sizes, ranging from volunteer operations with a handful of members to institutions with several billion dollars in assets and hundreds of thousands of members.

    a. Fi-linx
    b. Credit Union Service Organization
    c. Credit Union
    d. Corporate credit union

25. In business, _____ is income that a company receives from its normal business activities, usually from the sale of goods and services to customers. Some companies also receive _____ from interest, dividends or royalties paid to them by other companies. _____ may refer to business income in general, or it may refer to the amount, in a monetary unit, received during a period of time, as in 'Last year, Company X had _____ of $32 million.'

    In many countries, including the UK, _____ is referred to as turnover.

    a. Matching principle
    b. Furniture, Fixtures and Equipment
    c. Bottom line
    d. Revenue

26. _____ are bonds issued by governments, authorities, or public benefit corporations that are guaranteed by the revenue flow of the issuing agency.

    The Supreme Court decision of Pollock versus Farmer's Loan and Trust Company of 1895 initiated a wave or series of innovations for the financial services community in both tax-treatment and regulation from government. This specific case, according to a leading investment bank's research, resulted in the 'intergovernmental tax immunity doctrine,' ultimately leading to 'tax-free status.' Municipal bonds are generally exempt from federal tax on their interest payments (not capital gains.)

Chapter 11. The Mortgage Markets

a. Callable bond
c. Gilts
b. Private activity bond
d. Revenue bonds

27. An _____ can be defined as a contract which provides an income stream in return for an initial payment.

An immediate _____ is an _____ for which the time between the contract date and the date of the first payment is not longer than the time interval between payments. A common use for an immediate _____ is to provide a pension to a retired person or persons.

a. Amortization
c. Intrinsic value
b. Annuity
d. AT'T Inc.

28. In financial accounting, the term _____ is most commonly used to describe any part of shareholders' equity, except for basic share capital. Sometimes, the term is used instead of the term provision; such a use, however, is inconsistent with the terminology suggested by International Accounting Standards Board. For more information about provisions, see provision (accounting.)

a. Treasury stock
c. FIFO and LIFO accounting
b. Reserve
d. Closing entries

29. _____, in bookkeeping, refers to assets, liabilities, income, and expenses recorded on individual pages of the so called book of final entry or ledger. Changes in _____ value are made by chronologically posting debit (DR) and credit (CR) entries to its page. Examples of _____s are cash, _____s receivable, mortgages, loans, land and buildings, common stock, sales, services provided, wages, and payroll overhead.

a. Option
c. Alpha
b. Accretion
d. Account

30. In business and finance, a _____ (also referred to as equity _____) of stock means a _____ of ownership in a corporation (company.) In the plural, stocks is often used as a synonym for _____s especially in the United States, but it is less commonly used that way outside of North America.

In the United Kingdom, South Africa, and Australia, stock can also refer to completely different financial instruments such as government bonds or, less commonly, to all kinds of marketable securities.

a. Procter ' Gamble
c. Bucket shop
b. Share
d. Margin

31. The _____ (NYSE: FNM), commonly known as Fannie Mae, is a stockholder-owned corporation chartered by Congress in 1968 as a government sponsored enterprise (GSE), but founded in 1938 during the Great Depression. The corporation's purpose is to purchase and securitize mortgages in order to ensure that funds are consistently available to the institutions that lend money to home buyers.

On September 7, 2008, James Lockhart, director of the Federal Housing Finance Agency (FHFA), announced that Fannie Mae and Freddie Mac were being placed into conservatorship of the FHFA.

Chapter 11. The Mortgage Markets

a. General partnership
b. Federal National Mortgage Association
c. SPDR
d. The Depository Trust ' Clearing Corporation

32. A _____ is an asset-backed security whose cash flows are backed by the principal and interest payments of a set of mortgage loans. Payments are typically made monthly over the lifetime of the underlying loans.
a. Shared appreciation mortgage
b. Home equity line of credit
c. Conforming loan
d. Mortgage-backed security

33. _____ is a structured finance process that involves pooling and repackaging of cash-flow-producing financial assets into securities, which are then sold to investors. The term '_____' is derived from the fact that the form of financial instruments used to obtain funds from the investors are securities. As a portfolio risk backed by amortizing cash flows - and unlike general corporate debt - the credit quality of securitized debt is non-stationary due to changes in volatility that are time- and structure-dependent.
a. The Glass-Steagall Act of 1933
b. Special journals
c. Reputational risk
d. Securitization

34. A _____ is a financial contract whose value is derived from the value of something else (known as the underlying.) The underlying on which a _____ is based can be an asset, weather conditions bonds or other forms of credit.
a. 4-4-5 Calendar
b. 529 plan
c. 7-Eleven
d. Derivative

35. A _____ is a fungible, negotiable instrument representing financial value. They are broadly categorized into debt securities (such as banknotes, bonds and debentures), and equity securities; e.g., common stocks. The company or other entity issuing the _____ is called the issuer.
a. Securities lending
b. Tracking stock
c. Book entry
d. Security

36. The institution most often referenced by the word '_____' is a public or publicly traded _____, the shares of which are traded on a public stock exchange (e.g., the New York Stock Exchange or Nasdaq in the United States) where shares of stock of _____s are bought and sold by and to the general public. Most of the largest businesses in the world are publicly traded _____s. However, the majority of _____s are said to be closely held, privately held or close _____s, meaning that no ready market exists for the trading of shares.
a. Federal Home Loan Mortgage Corporation
b. Protect
c. Depository Trust Company
d. Corporation

37. The _____ (NYSE: FRE) is an insolvent government sponsored enterprise (GSE) of the United States federal government.

The _____ was created in 1970 to expand the secondary market for mortgages in the US. Along with other GSEs, Freddie Mac buys mortgages on the secondary market, pools them, and sells them as mortgage-backed securities to investors on the open market.

a. Federal Home Loan Mortgage Corporation
b. The Depository Trust ' Clearing Corporation
c. Governmental Accounting Standards Board
d. Public company

Chapter 11. The Mortgage Markets 85

38. The _____ is a U.S. government-owned corporation within the Department of Housing and Urban Development

Ginnie Mae provides guarantees on mortgage-backed securities backed by federally insured or guaranteed loans, mainly loans issued by the Federal Housing Administration, Department of Veterans Affairs, Rural Housing Service, and Office of Public and Indian Housing. Ginnie Mae securities are the only MBS that are guaranteed by the United States government.

a. Case-Shiller Home Price Indices
c. Cash budget
b. Certified Emission Reductions
d. GNMA

39. The _____ is a U.S. government-owned corporation within the Department of Housing and Urban Development

Ginnie Mae provides guarantees on mortgage-backed securities backed by federally insured or guaranteed loans, mainly loans issued by the Federal Housing Administration, Department of Veterans Affairs, Rural Housing Service, and Office of Public and Indian Housing. Ginnie Mae securities are the only MBS that are guaranteed by the United States government.

a. Jumbo mortgage
c. 4-4-5 Calendar
b. Graduated payment mortgage
d. Government National Mortgage Association

40. _____ is early repayment of a loan by a borrower.

In the case of a mortgage-backed security (MBS), _____ is perceived as a risk, because mortgage debts are often paid off early in order to incur lower total interest payments through cheaper refinancing. The new financing may be cheaper because the borrower's credit rating has improved or because interest rates are lower, but in either case, the payments that would have been made to the MBS investor would be above market rates.

a. Disposal tax effect
c. Bankruptcy remote
b. Retention ratio
d. Prepayment

41. A _____, reserve bank, or monetary authority is the entity responsible for the monetary policy of a country or of a group of member states. It is a bank that can lend money to other banks in times of need. Its primary responsibility is to maintain the stability of the national currency and money supply, but more active duties include controlling subsidized-loan interest rates, and acting as a lender of last resort to the banking sector during times of financial crisis (private banks often being integral to the national financial system.)

a. 7-Eleven
c. Central bank
b. 4-4-5 Calendar
d. 529 plan

42. _____ or financing is to provide capital (funds), which means money for a project, a person, a business or any other private or public institutions.

Those funds can be allocated for either short term or long term purposes. The health fund is a new way of _____ private healthcare centers.

Chapter 11. The Mortgage Markets

a. Synthetic CDO
b. Funding
c. Product life cycle
d. Proxy fight

43. A _____ is a financial debt vehicle that was first created in June 1983 by investment banks Salomon Brothers and First Boston for Freddie Mac. (The First Boston team was led by Dexter Senft.) Legally, a _____ is a special purpose entity that is wholly separate from the institution(s) that create it.
   a. Yield curve spread
   b. Collateralized mortgage obligation
   c. 4-4-5 Calendar
   d. Tranche

44. In banking and finance, _____ denotes all activities from the time a commitment is made for a transaction until it is settled. _____ is necessary because the speed of trades is much faster than the cycle time for completing the underlying transaction.

In its widest sense _____ involves the management of post-trading, pre-settlement credit exposures, to ensure that trades are settled in accordance with market rules, even if a buyer or seller should become insolvent prior to settlement.

   a. Clearing
   b. Procter ' Gamble
   c. Clearing house
   d. Share

45. In the United States, a _____ is a mortgage with a loan amount above the industry-standard definition of conventional conforming loan limits. This standard is set by the two largest secondary market lenders, Fannie Mae and Freddie Mac. Loans above the conforming limits may be offered by seller servicers of these wholesale institutions, as well as Wall Street conduits who provide warehouse financing for mortgage lenders.
   a. Government National Mortgage Association
   b. Graduated payment mortgage
   c. 4-4-5 Calendar
   d. Jumbo mortgage

46. A _____, securities exchange or (in Europe) bourse is a corporation or mutual organization which provides 'trading' facilities for stock brokers and traders, to trade stocks and other securities. _____s also provide facilities for the issue and redemption of securities as well as other financial instruments and capital events including the payment of income and dividends. The securities traded on a _____ include: shares issued by companies, unit trusts and other pooled investment products and bonds.
   a. 7-Eleven
   b. Stock Exchange
   c. 4-4-5 Calendar
   d. 529 plan

47. In finance, the _____ between two currencies specifies how much one currency is worth in terms of the other. For example an _____ of 102 Japanese yen to the United States dollar means that JPY 102 is worth the same as USD 1. The foreign exchange market is one of the largest markets in the world.
   a. AAB
   b. ABN Amro
   c. A Random Walk Down Wall Street
   d. Exchange rate

48. In finance, the _____ is the global financial market for short-term borrowing and lending. It provides short-term liquidity funding for the global financial system. The _____ is where short-term obligations such as Treasury bills, commercial paper and bankers' acceptances are bought and sold.

a. Cramdown
b. Debt-for-equity swap
c. Consumer debt
d. Money market

Chapter 12. The Foreign Exchange Market

1. _____ was an arrangement established in 1979 under the Jenkins European Commission where most nations of the European Economic Community (EEC) linked their currencies to prevent large fluctuations relative to one another.

After the collapse of the Bretton Woods system in 1971, most of the EEC countries agreed in 1972 to maintain stable exchange rates by preventing exchange fluctuations of more than 2.25% (the European 'currency snake'.) In March 1979, this system was replaced by the _____, and the European Currency Unit (ECU) was defined.

   a. Euro Interbank Offered Rate
   b. European Monetary System
   c. Exchange Rate Mechanism
   d. A Random Walk Down Wall Street

2. In finance, the _____ between two currencies specifies how much one currency is worth in terms of the other. For example an _____ of 102 Japanese yen to the United States dollar means that JPY 102 is worth the same as USD 1. The foreign exchange market is one of the largest markets in the world.
   a. AAB
   b. A Random Walk Down Wall Street
   c. ABN Amro
   d. Exchange rate

3. The _____ is where currency trading takes place. It is where banks and other official institutions facilitate the buying and selling of foreign currencies. FX transactions typically involve one party purchasing a quantity of one currency in exchange for paying a quantity of another.
   a. Foreign exchange option
   b. Spot market
   c. Foreign exchange market
   d. Floating exchange rate

4. A _____ secures the proper functioning of money by regulating economic agents, transaction types, and money supply.

They are traditionally formed by the policy decisions of individual governments and administrated as a domestic economic issue.

The current trend, however, is to use international trade and investment to alter the policy and legislation of individual governments.

   a. Monetary System
   b. Payback period
   c. Pattern day trader
   d. Bond credit rating

5. _____ is a term used in accounting relating to the increase in value of an asset. In this sense it is the reverse of depreciation, which measures the fall in value of assets over their normal life-time.

_____ is a rise of a currency in a floating exchange rate.

   a. Appreciation
   b. Operating cash flow
   c. Other Comprehensive Basis of Accounting
   d. A Random Walk Down Wall Street

6. _____ is a term used in accounting, economics and finance to spread the cost of an asset over the span of several years.

Chapter 12. The Foreign Exchange Market

In simple words we can say that _____ is the reduction in the value of an asset due to usage, passage of time, wear and tear, technological outdating or obsolescence, depletion or other such factors.

In accounting, _____ is a term used to describe any method of attributing the historical or purchase cost of an asset across its useful life, roughly corresponding to normal wear and tear.

a. Matching principle
b. Bottom line
c. Deferred financing costs
d. Depreciation

7. The _____ is an economic law stated as: 'In an efficient market all identical goods must have only one price.'

The intuition for this law is that all sellers will flock to the highest prevailing price, and all buyers to the lowest current market price. In an efficient market the convergence on one price is instant.

Commodities can be traded on financial markets, where there will be a single offer price, and bid price.

a. Law of one price
b. Personal property
c. Letter of credit
d. Liability

8. _____ refers to a business or organization attempting to acquire goods or services to accomplish the goals of the enterprise. Though there are several organizations that attempt to set standards in the _____ process, processes can vary greatly between organizations. Typically the word '_____' is not used interchangeably with the word 'procurement', since procurement typically includes Expediting, Supplier Quality, and Traffic and Logistics (T'L) in addition to _____.

a. 4-4-5 Calendar
b. 529 plan
c. 7-Eleven
d. Purchasing

9. _____ is the value of goods/services compared to the amount paid with a currency. Currency can be either a commodity money, like gold or silver, or fiat currency like US dollars which are the world reserve currency. As Adam Smith noted, having money gives one the ability to 'command' others' labor, so _____ to some extent is power over other people, to the extent that they are willing to trade their labor or goods for money or currency.

a. Purchasing power
b. 7-Eleven
c. 529 plan
d. 4-4-5 Calendar

10. The _____ theory uses the long-term equilibrium exchange rate of two currencies to equalize their purchasing power. Developed by Gustav Cassel in 1920, it is based on the law of one price: the theory states that, in ideally efficient markets, identical goods should have only one price.

This purchasing power SEM rate equalizes the purchasing power of different currencies in their home countries for a given basket of goods.

a. Purchasing power parity
b. TED spread
c. 4-4-5 Calendar
d. Gross national product

Chapter 12. The Foreign Exchange Market

11. In business and accounting, _____s are everything of value that is owned by a person or company. The balance sheet of a firm records the monetary value of the _____s owned by the firm. The two major _____ classes are tangible _____s and intangible _____s.
    a. EBITDA
    b. Income
    c. Accounts payable
    d. Asset

12. In economics, the concept of the _____ refers to the decision-making time frame of a firm in which at least one factor of production is fixed. Costs which are fixed in the _____ have no impact on a firms decisions. For example a firm can raise output by increasing the amount of labour through overtime.
    a. Long-run
    b. 4-4-5 Calendar
    c. Short-run
    d. 529 plan

13. _____ is a fee paid on borrowed assets. It is the price paid for the use of borrowed money, or, money earned by deposited funds. Assets that are sometimes lent with _____ include money, shares, consumer goods through hire purchase, major assets such as aircraft, and even entire factories in finance lease arrangements.
    a. Insolvency
    b. AAB
    c. A Random Walk Down Wall Street
    d. Interest

14. In economics, _____ is the total amount of money available in an economy at a particular point in time. There are several ways to define 'money', but each includes currency in circulation and demand deposits.

    _____ data are recorded and published.

    a. 7-Eleven
    b. Money supply
    c. 529 plan
    d. 4-4-5 Calendar

15. _____ most frequently refers to the standard deviation of the continuously compounded returns of a financial instrument with a specific time horizon. It is often used to quantify the risk of the instrument over that time period. _____ is typically expressed in annualized terms, and it may either be an absolute number ($5) or a fraction of the mean (5%).
    a. Seasoned equity offering
    b. Portfolio insurance
    c. Volatility
    d. Currency swap

16. The '_____' is approximately the nominal interest rate minus the inflation rate Since the inflation rate over the course of a loan is not known initially, volatility in inflation represents a risk to both the lender and the borrower.

    In economics and finance, an individual who lends money for repayment at a later point in time expects to be compensated for the time value of money, or not having the use of that money while it is lent.

    a. Real interest rate
    b. 4-4-5 Calendar
    c. 529 plan
    d. 7-Eleven

17. An _____ is the price a borrower pays for the use of money they do not own, and the return a lender receives for deferring the use of funds, by lending it to the borrower. _____s are normally expressed as a percentage rate over the period of one year.

_____s targets are also a vital tool of monetary policy and are used to control variables like investment, inflation, and unemployment.

a. ABN Amro
b. A Random Walk Down Wall Street
c. AAB
d. Interest rate

Chapter 13. The International Financial System

1. A _____, reserve bank, or monetary authority is the entity responsible for the monetary policy of a country or of a group of member states. It is a bank that can lend money to other banks in times of need. Its primary responsibility is to maintain the stability of the national currency and money supply, but more active duties include controlling subsidized-loan interest rates, and acting as a lender of last resort to the banking sector during times of financial crisis (private banks often being integral to the national financial system.)
   a. 4-4-5 Calendar
   b. 529 plan
   c. 7-Eleven
   d. Central bank

2. _____ was an arrangement established in 1979 under the Jenkins European Commission where most nations of the European Economic Community (EEC) linked their currencies to prevent large fluctuations relative to one another.

   After the collapse of the Bretton Woods system in 1971, most of the EEC countries agreed in 1972 to maintain stable exchange rates by preventing exchange fluctuations of more than 2.25% (the European 'currency snake'.) In March 1979, this system was replaced by the _____, and the European Currency Unit (ECU) was defined.

   a. A Random Walk Down Wall Street
   b. Euro Interbank Offered Rate
   c. European Monetary System
   d. Exchange Rate Mechanism

3. In finance, the _____ between two currencies specifies how much one currency is worth in terms of the other. For example an _____ of 102 Japanese yen to the United States dollar means that JPY 102 is worth the same as USD 1. The foreign exchange market is one of the largest markets in the world.
   a. ABN Amro
   b. Exchange rate
   c. A Random Walk Down Wall Street
   d. AAB

4. A _____ is a bond issued by a national government denominated in the country's own currency. Bonds issued by national governments in foreign currencies are normally referred to as sovereign bonds. The first ever _____ was issued by the British government in 1693 to raise money to fund a war against France.
   a. Government bond
   b. Municipal bond
   c. Collateralized debt obligations
   d. Zero-coupon bond

5. A _____ secures the proper functioning of money by regulating economic agents, transaction types, and money supply.

   They are traditionally formed by the policy decisions of individual governments and administrated as a domestic economic issue.

   The current trend, however, is to use international trade and investment to alter the policy and legislation of individual governments.

   a. Payback period
   b. Pattern day trader
   c. Monetary System
   d. Bond credit rating

6. _____ is the process by which the government, or monetary authority of a country controls (i) the supply of money central bank (ii) availability of money, and (iii) cost of money or rate of interest, in order to attain a set of objectives oriented towards the growth and stability of the economy. Monetary theory provides insight into how to craft optimal _____.

Chapter 13. The International Financial System

_____ is referred to as either being an expansionary policy where an expansionary policy increases the total supply of money in the economy, and a contractionary policy decreases the total money supply.

a. Monetary policy
b. Tax exemption
c. Federal Open Market Committee
d. Natural resources consumption tax

7. In economics, _____ is the total amount of money available in an economy at a particular point in time. There are several ways to define 'money', but each includes currency in circulation and demand deposits.

_____ data are recorded and published.

a. Money supply
b. 4-4-5 Calendar
c. 529 plan
d. 7-Eleven

8. In financial accounting, the term _____ is most commonly used to describe any part of shareholders' equity, except for basic share capital. Sometimes, the term is used instead of the term provision; such a use, however, is inconsistent with the terminology suggested by International Accounting Standards Board. For more information about provisions, see provision (accounting.)

a. FIFO and LIFO accounting
b. Closing entries
c. Treasury stock
d. Reserve

9. In finance, a _____ is a debt security, in which the authorized issuer owes the holders a debt and, depending on the terms of the _____, is obliged to pay interest (the coupon) and/or to repay the principal at a later date, termed maturity.

Thus a _____ is a loan: the issuer is the borrower, the _____ holder is the lender, and the coupon is the interest. _____s provide the borrower with external funds to finance long-term investments, or, in the case of government _____s, to finance current expenditure.

a. Catastrophe bonds
b. Bond
c. Convertible bond
d. Puttable bond

10. In finance, the _____ is the system that allows the transfer of money between savers and borrowers.

Put another way: the _____ is a set of complex and closely interconnected financial institutions, markets, instruments, services, practices, and transactions.

a. Financial system
b. Horizontal merger
c. 4-4-5 Calendar
d. Passive income

11. The free _____ of a public company is an estimate of the proportion of shares that are not held by large owners and that are not stock with sales restrictions (restricted stock that cannot be sold until they become unrestricted stock.)

The free _____ or a public _____ is usually defined as being all shares held by investors other than:

- shares held by owners owning more than 5% of all shares (those could be institutional investors, 'strategic shareholders,' founders, executives, and other insiders' holdings)
- restricted stocks (granted to executives that can be, but don't have to be, registered insiders)
- insider holdings (it is assumed that insiders hold stock for the very long term)

The free _____ is an important criterion in quoting a share on the stock market.

To _____ a company means to list its shares on a public stock exchange through an initial public offering (or 'flotation'.)

- Open market
- Outstanding shares
- Market capitalization
- Public _____ loat
- Reverse takeover

a. Synthetic CDO
c. Trade finance
b. Golden parachute
d. Float

12. The _____ is where currency trading takes place. It is where banks and other official institutions facilitate the buying and selling of foreign currencies. FX transactions typically involve one party purchasing a quantity of one currency in exchange for paying a quantity of another.
a. Foreign exchange option
c. Foreign exchange market
b. Floating exchange rate
d. Spot market

13. In economic models, the _____ time frame assumes no fixed factors of production. Firms can enter or leave the marketplace, and the cost (and availability) of land, labor, raw materials, and capital goods can be assumed to vary. In contrast, in the short-run time frame, certain factors are assumed to be fixed, because there is not sufficient time for them to change.
a. Short-run
c. 4-4-5 Calendar
b. 529 plan
d. Long-run

14. In economics, the _____, measures the payments that flow between any individual country and all other countries. It is used to summarize all international economic transactions for that country during a specific time period, usually a year. The _____ is determined by the country's exports and imports of goods, services, and financial capital, as well as financial transfers.
a. Gross national product
c. 4-4-5 Calendar
b. Purchasing power parity
d. Balance of payments

15. In economics, the _____ is one of the two primary components of the balance of payments, the other being the capital account. It is the sum of the balance of trade (exports minus imports of goods and services), net factor income (such as interest and dividends) and net transfer payments (such as foreign aid.)

The _____ balance is one of two major metrics of the nature of a country's foreign trade (the other being the net capital outflow).

   a. Consols
   b. Cash budget
   c. Rights issue
   d. Current account

16. _____, in bookkeeping, refers to assets, liabilities, income, and expenses recorded on individual pages of the so called book of final entry or ledger. Changes in _____ value are made by chronologically posting debit (DR) and credit (CR) entries to its page. Examples of _____s are cash, _____s receivable, mortgages, loans, land and buildings, common stock, sales, services provided, wages, and payroll overhead.
   a. Option
   b. Alpha
   c. Accretion
   d. Account

17. In financial accounting, the _____ is one of the accounts in shareholders' equity. Sole proprietorships have a single _____ in the owner's equity. Partnerships maintain a _____ for each of the partners.
   a. Bed Bath ' Beyond Inc.
   b. Market maker
   c. Duty of loyalty
   d. Capital account

18. The _____, an agency of the United States Department of the Treasury, is the primary regulator of federal savings associations (sometimes referred to as federal thrifts.) Federal savings associations include both federal savings banks and federal savings and loans. The OTS is also responsible for supervising savings and loan holding companies (SLHCs) and some state-chartered institutions.
   a. AAB
   b. Office of Thrift Supervision
   c. ABN Amro
   d. A Random Walk Down Wall Street

19. The _____ is a monetary system in which a region's common medium of exchange are paper notes that are normally freely convertible into pre-set, fixed quantities of gold. The _____ is not currently used by any government, having been replaced completely by fiat currency.
   a. 529 plan
   b. 7-Eleven
   c. 4-4-5 Calendar
   d. Gold standard

20. _____ or financing is to provide capital (funds), which means money for a project, a person, a business or any other private or public institutions.

Those funds can be allocated for either short term or long term purposes. The health fund is a new way of _____ private healthcare centers.

a. Proxy fight
c. Product life cycle
b. Synthetic CDO
d. Funding

21. The _____ of monetary management established the rules for commercial and financial relations among the world's major industrial states in the mid 20th Century. The _____ was the first example of a fully negotiated monetary order intended to govern monetary relations among independent nation-states.

Preparing to rebuild the international economic system as World War II was still raging, 730 delegates from all 44 Allied nations gathered at the Mount Washington Hotel in Bretton Woods, New Hampshire, United States, for the United Nations Monetary and Financial Conference.

a. The Hong Kong Securities Institute
c. Cash budget
b. Bretton Woods system
d. Fixed Asset Register

22. A _____, sometimes called a pegged exchange rate, is a type of exchange rate regime wherein a currency's value is matched to the value of another single currency or to a basket of other currencies, or to another measure of value such as gold.

A _____ is usually used to stabilize the value of a currency, vis-a-vis the currency it is pegged to. This facilitates trade and investments between the two countries, and is especially useful for small economies where external trade forms a large part of their GDP.

a. Deflation
c. Fixed exchange rate
b. Market structure
d. Human capital

23. A _____ is a currency which is held in significant quantities by many governments and institutions as part of their foreign exchange reserves. It also tends to be the international pricing currency for products traded on a global market, such as oil, gold, etc.

This permits the issuing country to purchase the commodities at a marginally cheaper rate than other nations, which must exchange their currency with each purchase and pay a transaction cost.

a. Devaluation
c. Hard currency
b. Functional currency
d. Reserve currency

24. The _____ is a bank that provides financial and technical assistance to developing countries for development programs (e.g. bridges, roads, schools, etc.) with the stated goal of reducing poverty

The _____ differs from the _____ Group, in that the _____ comprises only two institutions:

- International Bank for Reconstruction and Development (IBRD)
- International Development Association (IDA)

Chapter 13. The International Financial System

Whereas the latter incorporates these two in addition to three more:

- International Finance Corporation (IFC)
- Multilateral Investment Guarantee Agency (MIGA)
- International Centre for Settlement of Investment Disputes (ICSID)

John Maynard Keynes (right) represented the UK at the conference, and Harry Dexter White represented the US.

The _____ was created following the ratification of the United Nations Monetary and Financial Conference | Bretton Woods agreement. The concept was originally conceived in July 1944 at the United Nations Monetary and Financial Conference.

a. 7-Eleven
b. 4-4-5 Calendar
c. World Bank
d. 529 plan

25. _____ is a reduction in the value of a currency with respect to other monetary units. In common modern usage, it specifically implies an official lowering of the value of a country's currency within a fixed exchange rate system, by which the monetary authority formally sets a new fixed rate with respect to a foreign reference currency. In contrast, (currency) depreciation is used for the unofficial decrease in the exchange rate in a floating exchange rate system.
a. Petrodollar recycling
b. Devaluation
c. Reserve currency
d. Currency board

26. _____ means a rise of a price of goods or products. This term is specially used as _____ of a currency, where it means a rise of currency to the relation with a foreign currency in a fixed exchange rate. In floating exchange rate correct term would be appreciation.
a. Holding period return
b. Common pool problem
c. Correlation trading
d. Revaluation

27. A _____ is a monetary authority which is required to maintain a fixed exchange rate with a foreign currency. This policy objective requires the conventional objectives of a central bank to be subordinated to the exchange rate target.
a. Hard currency
b. Devaluation
c. Functional currency
d. Currency board

28. The _____, a component of the Federal Reserve System, is charged under United States law with overseeing the nation's open market operations. It is the Federal Reserve Committee that makes key decisions about interest rates and the growth jam of the United States money supply. It is the principal organ of United States national monetary policy.
a. Tax exemption
b. Federal Open Market Committee
c. Tax incidence
d. Fiscal policy

29. In economics, _____ is a rise in the general level of prices of goods and services in an economy over a period of time. The term '_____' once referred to increases in the money supply (monetary _____); however, economic debates about the relationship between money supply and price levels have led to its primary use today in describing price _____. _____ can also be described as a decline in the real value of money--a loss of purchasing power in the medium of exchange which is also the monetary unit of account.

a. A Random Walk Down Wall Street
b. AAB
c. ABN Amro
d. Inflation

30. In business and accounting, _____s are everything of value that is owned by a person or company. The balance sheet of a firm records the monetary value of the _____s owned by the firm. The two major _____ classes are tangible _____s and intangible _____s.
   a. Asset
   b. Accounts payable
   c. Income
   d. EBITDA

31. In business, _____ is income that a company receives from its normal business activities, usually from the sale of goods and services to customers. Some companies also receive _____ from interest, dividends or royalties paid to them by other companies. _____ may refer to business income in general, or it may refer to the amount, in a monetary unit, received during a period of time, as in 'Last year, Company X had _____ of $32 million.'

In many countries, including the UK, _____ is referred to as turnover.

   a. Furniture, Fixtures and Equipment
   b. Matching principle
   c. Bottom line
   d. Revenue

32. The _____ was a worldwide economic downturn starting in most places in 1929 and ending at different times in the 1930s or early 1940s for different countries. It was the largest and most important economic depression in the 20th century, and is used in the 21st century as an example of how far the world's economy can fall. The _____ originated in the United States; historians most often use as a starting date the stock market crash on October 29, 1929, known as Black Tuesday.
   a. 7-Eleven
   b. 4-4-5 Calendar
   c. 529 plan
   d. Great Depression

33. _____ is the provision of resources (such as granting a loan) by one party to another party where that second party does not reimburse the first party immediately, thereby generating a debt, and instead arranges either to repay or return those resources (or material(s) of equal value) at a later date. The first party is called a creditor, also known as a lender, while the second party is called a debtor, also known as a borrower.

Movements of financial capital are normally dependent on either _____ or equity transfers.

   a. Warrant
   b. Clearing house
   c. Comparable
   d. Credit

34. A _____ is the maximum amount of credit that a financial institution or other lender will extend to a debtor for a particular line of credit. For example, the maximum that a credit card company will allow a card holder to borrow at any given point on a specific card.

This limit is based on a variety of factors ranging from an individual's ability to make interest payments, an organization's cashflow and/or ability to repay the principal, to the credit standards employed by the lender.

a. 529 plan	b. 7-Eleven
c. 4-4-5 Calendar	d. Credit limit

35. In economics, _____ is the monetary policy device that a country's government (i.e., sovereign power) uses to regulate the flows into and out of a country's capital account, i.e., the flows of investment-oriented money into and out of a country or currency. _____ has become more prominent in the years since the Clinton administration blessed the efforts of the world community to create the World Trade Organization (WTO), primarily because globalization has increased the acceleration of currency domain strength, in other words, giving some currencies utility far beyond their physical geographic boundaries.

a. Capital control	b. Monte Carlo methods
c. Debtor-in-possession financing	d. Tail risk

36. In business, _____ is the total assets minus total outside liabilities of an individual or a company. For a company, this is called shareholders' equity and may be referred to as book value. _____ is stated as at a particular point in time.

a. Certified International Investment Analyst	b. Moneylender
c. Restructuring	d. Net worth

37. In finance, _____ refers to Monday, October 19, 1987, when stock markets around the world crashed, shedding a huge value in a very short time. The crash began in Hong Kong, spread west through international time zones to Europe, hitting the United States after other markets had already declined by a significant margin. The Dow Jones Industrial Average (DJIA) dropped by 508 points to 1738.74 (22.61%).

a. 529 plan	b. 4-4-5 Calendar
c. 7-Eleven	d. Black Monday

38. A _____ is a private or public market for the trading of company stock and derivatives of company stock at an agreed price; these are securities listed on a stock exchange as well as those only traded privately.

The size of the world _____ is estimated at about $36.6 trillion US at the beginning of October 2008 . The world derivatives market has been estimated at about $480 trillion face or nominal value, 12 times the size of the entire world economy.

a. Anton Gelonkin	b. Adolph Coors
c. Andrew Tobias	d. Stock market

39. A _____ is a sudden dramatic decline of stock prices across a significant cross-section of a stock market. Crashes are driven by panic as much as by underlying economic factors. They often follow speculative stock market bubbles.

a. 7-Eleven	b. 529 plan
c. 4-4-5 Calendar	d. Stock market crash

40. The _____ or Plaza Agreement was an agreement between the governments of France, West Germany, Japan, the United States and the United Kingdom, agreeing to depreciate the US dollar in relation to the Japanese yen and German Deutsche Mark by intervening in currency markets. The five governments signed the accord on September 22, 1985 at the Plaza Hotel in New York City.

The exchange rate value of the dollar versus the yen declined by 51% from 1985 to 1987.

a. 4-4-5 Calendar
b. Plaza Accord
c. 7-Eleven
d. 529 plan

Chapter 14. Theory of Financial Structure

1. In economics, a _____ is a mechanism that allows people to easily buy and sell (trade) financial securities (such as stocks and bonds), commodities (such as precious metals or agricultural goods), and other fungible items of value at low transaction costs and at prices that reflect the efficient-market hypothesis.

_____s have evolved significantly over several hundred years and are undergoing constant innovation to improve liquidity.

Both general markets (where many commodities are traded) and specialized markets (where only one commodity is traded) exist.

   a. Cost of carry
   b. Delta hedging
   c. Secondary market
   d. Financial market

2. _____ or financing is to provide capital (funds), which means money for a project, a person, a business or any other private or public institutions.

Those funds can be allocated for either short term or long term purposes. The health fund is a new way of _____ private healthcare centers.

   a. Proxy fight
   b. Synthetic CDO
   c. Product life cycle
   d. Funding

3. In finance, the _____ is the global financial market for short-term borrowing and lending. It provides short-term liquidity funding for the global financial system. The _____ is where short-term obligations such as Treasury bills, commercial paper and bankers' acceptances are bought and sold.
   a. Consumer debt
   b. Money market
   c. Cramdown
   d. Debt-for-equity swap

4. In lending agreements, _____ is a borrower's pledge of specific property to a lender, to secure repayment of a loan. The _____ serves as protection for a lender against a borrower's risk of default - that is, a borrower failing to pay the principal and interest under the terms of a loan obligation. If a borrower does default on a loan (due to insolvency or other event), that borrower forfeits (gives up) the property pledged as _____ *ollateral* - and the lender then becomes the owner of the _____.
   a. Nominal value
   b. Refinancing risk
   c. Future-oriented
   d. Collateral

5. _____ is that which is owed; usually referencing assets owed, but the term can cover other obligations. In the case of assets, _____ is a means of using future purchasing power in the present before a summation has been earned. Some companies and corporations use _____ as a part of their overall corporate finance strategy.
   a. Debt
   b. Credit cycle
   c. Cross-collateralization
   d. Partial Payment

6. A secured loan is a loan in which the borrower pledges some asset (e.g. a car or property) as collateral for the loan, which then becomes a _____ owed to the creditor who gives the loan. The debt is thus secured against the collateral -- in the event that the borrower defaults, the creditor takes possession of the asset used as collateral and may sell it to satisfy the debt by regaining the amount originally lent to the borrower. From the creditor's perspective this is a category of debt in which a lender has been granted a portion of the bundle of rights to specified property.

Chapter 14. Theory of Financial Structure

a. Market value added
b. Secured debt
c. Barcampbank
d. CFA Institute

7. In finance, _____ refers to any type of debt or general obligation that is not collateralized by a lien on specific assets of the borrower in the case of a bankruptcy or liquidation.

In the event of the bankruptcy of the borrower, the unsecured creditors will have a general claim on the assets of the borrower after the specific pledged assets have been assigned to the secured creditors, although the unsecured creditors will usually realize a smaller proportion of their claims than the secured creditors.

In some legal systems, unsecured creditors who are also indebted to the insolvent debtor are able (and in some jurisdictions, required) to set-off the debts, which actually puts the unsecured creditor with a matured liability to the debtor in a pre-preferential position.

a. A Random Walk Down Wall Street
b. ABN Amro
c. Unsecured debt
d. AAB

8. A _____ is an exchange of promises between two or more parties to do an act which is enforceable in a court of law. It is where an unqualified offer meets a qualified acceptance and the parties reach Consensus ad Idem. The parties must have the necessary capacity to _____ and the _____ must not be either trifling, indeterminate, impossible or illegal.

a. 7-Eleven
b. 529 plan
c. 4-4-5 Calendar
d. Contract

9. A _____, in its most general sense, is a solemn promise to engage in or refrain from a specified action.

More specifically, a _____, in contrast to a contract, is a one-way agreement whereby the _____er is the only party bound by the promise. A _____ may have conditions and prerequisites that qualify the undertaking, including the actions of second or third parties, but there is no inherent agreement by such other parties to fulfill those requirements.

a. Federal Trade Commission Act
b. Partnership
c. Covenant
d. Clayton Antitrust Act

10. _____, in microeconomics, are the cost advantages that a business obtains due to expansion. _____ may be utilized by any size firm expanding its scale of operation.

a. Economies of scale
b. Employee Retirement Income Security Act
c. Uniform Commercial Code
d. Articles of incorporation

11. A _____ is an institution, firm or individual who mediates between two or more parties in a financial context. Typically the first party is a provider of a product or service and the second party is a consumer or customer.

In the U.S., a _____ is typically an institution that facilitates the channelling of funds between lenders and borrowers indirectly.

Chapter 14. Theory of Financial Structure

a. Net asset value
b. Mutual fund
c. Savings and loan association
d. Financial intermediary

12. In economics and related disciplines, a _____ is a cost incurred in making an economic exchange. For example, most people, when buying or selling a stock, must pay a commission to their broker; that commission is a _____ of doing the stock deal. Or consider buying a banana from a store; to purchase the banana, your costs will be not only the price of the banana itself, but also the energy and effort it requires to find out which of the various banana products you prefer, where to get them and at what price, the cost of traveling from your house to the store and back, the time waiting in line, and the effort of the paying itself; the costs above and beyond the cost of the banana are the _____s.
   a. Fixed costs
   b. Variable costs
   c. Marginal cost
   d. Transaction cost

13. In economics, business, and accounting, a _____ is the value of money that has been used up to produce something, and hence is not available for use anymore. In business, the _____ may be one of acquisition, in which case the amount of money expended to acquire it is counted as _____. In this case, money is the input that is gone in order to acquire the thing.
   a. Marginal cost
   b. Cost
   c. Sliding scale fees
   d. Fixed costs

14. _____ is an area of finance dealing with the financial decisions corporations make and the tools and analysis used to make these decisions. The primary goal of _____ is to maximize corporate value while managing the firm's financial risks. Although it is in principle different from managerial finance which studies the financial decisions of all firms, rather than corporations alone, the main concepts in the study of _____ are applicable to the financial problems of all kinds of firms.
   a. Gross profit
   b. Cash flow
   c. Special purpose entity
   d. Corporate finance

15. In economics and contract theory, _____ deals with the study of decisions in transactions where one party has more or better information than the other. This creates an imbalance of power in transactions which can sometimes cause the transactions to go awry. Examples of this problem are adverse selection and moral hazard.
   a. ABN Amro
   b. Information asymmetry
   c. A Random Walk Down Wall Street
   d. AAB

16. _____ is a measure of the ability of a debtor to pay their debts as and when they fall due. It is usually expressed as a ratio or a percentage of current liabilities.

For a corporation with a published balance sheet there are various ratios used to calculate a measure of liquidity.

   a. Operating leverage
   b. Operating profit margin
   c. Invested capital
   d. Accounting liquidity

17. A _____ is a professionally managed type of collective investment scheme that pools money from many investors and invests it in stocks, bonds, short-term money market instruments, and/or other securities. The _____ will have a fund manager that trades the pooled money on a regular basis. Currently, the worldwide value of all _____s totals more than $26 trillion.

Chapter 14. Theory of Financial Structure

Since 1940, there have been three basic types of investment companies in the United States: open-end funds, also known in the US as _____s; unit investment trusts (UITs); and closed-end funds.

a. Trust company
c. Mutual fund
b. Net asset value
d. Financial intermediary

18. '_____' is a 1970 paper by the economist George Akerlof. It discusses information asymmetry, which occurs when the seller knows more about a product than the buyer. Akerlof, Michael Spence, and Joseph Stiglitz jointly received the Nobel Memorial Prize in Economic Sciences in 2001 for their research related to asymmetric information.

a. 529 plan
c. 7-Eleven
b. 4-4-5 Calendar
d. The Market for Lemons: Quality Uncertainty and the Market Mechanism

19. In finance, a _____ is a debt security, in which the authorized issuer owes the holders a debt and, depending on the terms of the _____, is obliged to pay interest (the coupon) and/or to repay the principal at a later date, termed maturity.

Thus a _____ is a loan: the issuer is the borrower, the _____ holder is the lender, and the coupon is the interest. _____s provide the borrower with external funds to finance long-term investments, or, in the case of government _____s, to finance current expenditure.

a. Catastrophe bonds
c. Puttable bond
b. Convertible bond
d. Bond

20. The _____ is a financial market where participants buy and sell debt securities, usually in the form of bonds. As of 2006, the size of the international _____ is an estimated $45 trillion, of which the size of the outstanding U.S. _____ debt was $25.2 trillion.

Nearly all of the $923 billion average daily trading volume in the U.S. _____ takes place between broker-dealers and large institutions in a decentralized, over-the-counter market.

a. 529 plan
c. 4-4-5 Calendar
b. Bond market
d. Fixed income

21. In business and accounting, _____s are everything of value that is owned by a person or company. The balance sheet of a firm records the monetary value of the _____s owned by the firm. The two major _____ classes are tangible _____s and intangible _____s.

a. Asset
c. Income
b. EBITDA
d. Accounts payable

22. In finance, _____ is the process of estimating the potential market value of a financial asset or liability. they can be done on assets (for example, investments in marketable securities such as stocks, options, business enterprises, or intangible assets such as patents and trademarks) or on liabilities (e.g., Bonds issued by a company.) _____s are required in many contexts including investment analysis, capital budgeting, merger and acquisition transactions, financial reporting, taxable events to determine the proper tax liability, and in litigation.

Chapter 14. Theory of Financial Structure

a. Valuation
c. Share
b. Procter ' Gamble
d. Margin

23. A _____ is a financial crisis that occurs when many banks suffer runs at the same time. A systemic banking crisis is one where all or almost all of the banking capital in a country is wiped out. The resulting chain of bankruptcies can cause a long economic recession. Much of the Great Depression's economic damage was caused directly by bank runs. The cost of cleaning up a systemic banking crisis can be huge, with fiscal costs averaging 13% of GDP and economic output losses averaging 20% of GDP for important crises from 1970 to 2007.
   a. Credit bureau
   c. Banking panic
   b. Deposit insurance
   d. Probability of default

24. The institution most often referenced by the word '_____' is a public or publicly traded _____, the shares of which are traded on a public stock exchange (e.g., the New York Stock Exchange or Nasdaq in the United States) where shares of stock of _____s are bought and sold by and to the general public. Most of the largest businesses in the world are publicly traded _____s. However, the majority of _____s are said to be closely held, privately held or close _____s, meaning that no ready market exists for the trading of shares.
   a. Federal Home Loan Mortgage Corporation
   c. Corporation
   b. Depository Trust Company
   d. Protect

25. In economics, collective bargaining, psychology and political science, 'free riders' are those who consume more than their fair share of a resource, or shoulder less than a fair share of the costs of its production. Free riding is usually considered to be an economic 'problem' only when it leads to the non-production or under-production of a public good (and thus to Pareto inefficiency), or when it leads to the excessive use of a common property resource. The _____ is the question of how to prevent free riding from taking place (or at least limit its negative effects) in these situations.
   a. Free rider problem
   c. 7-Eleven
   b. 4-4-5 Calendar
   d. 529 plan

26. A _____ is a fungible, negotiable instrument representing financial value. They are broadly categorized into debt securities (such as banknotes, bonds and debentures), and equity securities; e.g., common stocks. The company or other entity issuing the _____ is called the issuer.
   a. Book entry
   c. Tracking stock
   b. Securities lending
   d. Security

27. The U.S. _____ is an independent agency of the United States government which holds primary responsibility for enforcing the federal securities laws and regulating the securities industry, the nation's stock and options exchanges, and other electronic securities markets. The SEC was created by section 4 of the SEC of 1934 (now codified as 15 U.S.C. Â§ 78d and commonly referred to as the 1934 Act.)
   a. 529 plan
   c. 4-4-5 Calendar
   b. 7-Eleven
   d. Securities and Exchange Commission

28. A _____ is a financial contract whose value is derived from the value of something else (known as the underlying.) The underlying on which a _____ is based can be an asset, weather conditions bonds or other forms of credit.
   a. 7-Eleven
   c. 4-4-5 Calendar
   b. 529 plan
   d. Derivative

Chapter 14. Theory of Financial Structure

29. In business, _____ is the total assets minus total outside liabilities of an individual or a company. For a company, this is called shareholders' equity and may be referred to as book value. _____ is stated as at a particular point in time.
   a. Certified International Investment Analyst
   b. Net worth
   c. Restructuring
   d. Moneylender

30. In political science and economics, the _____ or agency dilemma treats the difficulties that arise under conditions of incomplete and asymmetric information when a principal hires an agent. Various mechanisms may be used to try to align the interests of the agent with those of the principal, such as piece rates/commissions, profit sharing, efficiency wages, performance measurement (including financial statements), the agent posting a bond, or fear of firing. The _____ is found in most employer/employee relationships, for example, when stockholders hire top executives of corporations.
   a. 529 plan
   b. 7-Eleven
   c. Principal-agent problem
   d. 4-4-5 Calendar

31. A mutual shareholder or _____ is an individual or company (including a corporation) that legally owns one or more shares of stock in a joint stock company. A company's shareholders collectively own that company. Thus, the typical goal of such companies is to enhance shareholder value.
   a. Trading curb
   b. Stockholder
   c. Limit order
   d. Stock market bubble

32. _____ is the provision of resources (such as granting a loan) by one party to another party where that second party does not reimburse the first party immediately, thereby generating a debt, and instead arranges either to repay or return those resources (or material(s) of equal value) at a later date. The first party is called a creditor, also known as a lender, while the second party is called a debtor, also known as a borrower.

   Movements of financial capital are normally dependent on either _____ or equity transfers.

   a. Warrant
   b. Clearing house
   c. Credit
   d. Comparable

33. _____ is the risk of loss due to a debtor's non-payment of a loan or other line of credit (either the principal or interest (coupon) or both)

   Most lenders employ their own models (credit scorecards) to rank potential and existing customers according to risk, and then apply appropriate strategies. With products such as unsecured personal loans or mortgages, lenders charge a higher price for higher risk customers and vice versa. With revolving products such as credit cards and overdrafts, risk is controlled through careful setting of credit limits.

   a. Credit risk
   b. Transaction risk
   c. Market risk
   d. Liquidity risk

34. _____ is the discipline of identifying, monitoring and limiting risks. In some cases the acceptable risk may be near zero. Risks can come from accidents, natural causes and disasters as well as deliberate attacks from an adversary.
   a. Risk management
   b. Penny stock
   c. 4-4-5 Calendar
   d. FIFO

Chapter 14. Theory of Financial Structure

35. _____ is a type of private equity capital typically provided to early-stage, high-potential, growth companies in the interest of generating a return through an eventual realization event such as an IPO or trade sale of the company. _____ investments are generally made as cash in exchange for shares in the invested company. It is typical for _____ investors to identify and back companies in high technology industries such as biotechnology and ICT.
    a. Probability distribution
    b. Tail risk
    c. Treasury Inflation-Protected Securities
    d. Venture capital

36. _____ is the increase in the amount of the goods and services produced by an economy over time. It is conventionally measured as the percent rate of increase in real gross domestic product, or real GDP. Growth is usually calculated in real terms, i.e. inflation-adjusted terms, in order to net out the effect of inflation on the price of the goods and services produced.
    a. A Random Walk Down Wall Street
    b. Economic growth
    c. ABN Amro
    d. AAB

37. In finance, the _____ is the system that allows the transfer of money between savers and borrowers.

    Put another way: the _____ is a set of complex and closely interconnected financial institutions, markets, instruments, services, practices, and transactions.

    a. 4-4-5 Calendar
    b. Horizontal merger
    c. Passive income
    d. Financial system

38. _____ is a legally declared inability or impairment of ability of an individual or organization to pay their creditors. Creditors may file a _____ petition against a debtor ('involuntary _____') in an effort to recoup a portion of what they are owed or initiate a restructuring. In the majority of cases, however, _____ is initiated by the debtor (a 'voluntary _____' that is filed by the bankrupt individual or organization.)
    a. Bankruptcy
    b. 529 plan
    c. 4-4-5 Calendar
    d. Debt settlement

39. A _____ is a party (e.g. person, organization, company, or government) that has a claim to the services of a second party. The first party, in general, has provided some property or service to the second party under the assumption (usually enforced by contract) that the second party will return an equivalent property or service. The second party is frequently called a debtor or borrower.
    a. NOPLAT
    b. Redemption value
    c. False billing
    d. Creditor

40. In financial accounting, a _____ or statement of financial position is a summary of a person's or organization's balances. Assets, liabilities and ownership equity are listed as of a specific date, such as the end of its financial year. A _____ is often described as a snapshot of a company's financial condition.
    a. Financial statements
    b. Statement of retained earnings
    c. Statement on Auditing Standards No. 70: Service Organizations
    d. Balance sheet

41. The _____ is the market for securities, where companies and governments can raise longterm funds. The _____ includes the stock market and the bond market. Financial regulators, such as the U.S. Securities and Exchange Commission, oversee the _____s in their designated countries to ensure that investors are protected against fraud.

Chapter 14. Theory of Financial Structure

a. Capital market
c. Delta neutral
b. Forward market
d. Spot rate

42. _____ is the balance of the amounts of cash being received and paid by a business during a defined period of time, sometimes tied to a specific project. Measurement of _____ can be used

- to evaluate the state or performance of a business or project.
- to determine problems with liquidity. Being profitable does not necessarily mean being liquid. A company can fail because of a shortage of cash, even while profitable.
- to generate project rate of returns. The time of _____s into and out of projects are used as inputs to financial models such as internal rate of return, and net present value.
- to examine income or growth of a business when it is believed that accrual accounting concepts do not represent economic realities. Alternately, _____ can be used to 'validate' the net income generated by accrual accounting.

_____ as a generic term may be used differently depending on context, and certain _____ definitions may be adapted by analysts and users for their own uses. Common terms include operating _____ and free _____.

_____s can be classified into:

1. Operational _____s: Cash received or expended as a result of the company's core business activities.
2. Investment _____s: Cash received or expended through capital expenditure, investments or acquisitions.
3. Financing _____s: Cash received or expended as a result of financial activities, such as interests and dividends.

All three together - the net _____ - are necessary to reconcile the beginning cash balance to the ending cash balance. Loan draw downs or equity injections, that is just shifting of capital but no expenditure as such, are not considered in the net _____.

a. Real option
c. Shareholder value
b. Corporate finance
d. Cash flow

43. In finance, the _____ between two currencies specifies how much one currency is worth in terms of the other. For example an _____ of 102 Japanese yen to the United States dollar means that JPY 102 is worth the same as USD 1. The foreign exchange market is one of the largest markets in the world.
a. AAB
c. A Random Walk Down Wall Street
b. ABN Amro
d. Exchange rate

44. _____ is a fee paid on borrowed assets. It is the price paid for the use of borrowed money, or, money earned by deposited funds. Assets that are sometimes lent with _____ include money, shares, consumer goods through hire purchase, major assets such as aircraft, and even entire factories in finance lease arrangements.
a. A Random Walk Down Wall Street
c. AAB
b. Insolvency
d. Interest

Chapter 14. Theory of Financial Structure

45. An _____ is the price a borrower pays for the use of money they do not own, and the return a lender receives for deferring the use of funds, by lending it to the borrower. _____s are normally expressed as a percentage rate over the period of one year.

_____s targets are also a vital tool of monetary policy and are used to control variables like investment, inflation, and unemployment.

a. A Random Walk Down Wall Street
b. AAB
c. ABN Amro
d. Interest rate

46. In financial accounting, the term _____ is most commonly used to describe any part of shareholders' equity, except for basic share capital. Sometimes, the term is used instead of the term provision; such a use, however, is inconsistent with the terminology suggested by International Accounting Standards Board. For more information about provisions, see provision (accounting.)

a. Closing entries
b. FIFO and LIFO accounting
c. Reserve
d. Treasury stock

47. The _____ was a worldwide economic downturn starting in most places in 1929 and ending at different times in the 1930s or early 1940s for different countries. It was the largest and most important economic depression in the 20th century, and is used in the 21st century as an example of how far the world's economy can fall. The _____ originated in the United States; historians most often use as a starting date the stock market crash on October 29, 1929, known as Black Tuesday.

a. 4-4-5 Calendar
b. 7-Eleven
c. 529 plan
d. Great Depression

48. _____ means the inability to pay one's debts as they fall due. Usually used in Business terms, _____ refers to the inability for a 'limited liability' company to pay off debts.

This is defined in two different ways:

Cash flow _____ -
    Unable to pay debts as they fall due.
Balance sheet _____ -
    Having negative net assets: liabilities exceed assets; or net liabilities.

a. A Random Walk Down Wall Street
b. AAB
c. Interest
d. Insolvency

49. A _____ is a private or public market for the trading of company stock and derivatives of company stock at an agreed price; these are securities listed on a stock exchange as well as those only traded privately.

The size of the world _____ is estimated at about $36.6 trillion US at the beginning of October 2008 . The world derivatives market has been estimated at about $480 trillion face or nominal value, 12 times the size of the entire world economy.

a. Adolph Coors
c. Anton Gelonkin
b. Andrew Tobias
d. Stock market

50. A _____ is a sudden dramatic decline of stock prices across a significant cross-section of a stock market. Crashes are driven by panic as much as by underlying economic factors. They often follow speculative stock market bubbles.

a. 7-Eleven
c. 4-4-5 Calendar
b. 529 plan
d. Stock market crash

51. The _____ was the most devastating stock market crash in the history of the United States, taking into consideration the full extent and duration of its fallout.

Three phrases--Black Thursday, Black Monday, and Black Tuesday--are commonly used to describe this collapse of stock values. All three are appropriate, for the crash was not a one-day affair. The initial crash occurred on Thursday, October 24, 1929, but the catastrophic downturn of Monday, October 28 and Tuesday, October 29 precipitated widespread alarm and the onset of an unprecedented and long-lasting economic depression for the United States and the world. This stock market collapse continued for a month.

a. Securitization
c. Board of Audit
b. Wall Street Crash of 1929
d. Legal and regulatory risk

52. _____ in economics is a persistent decrease in the general price level of goods and services - a negative inflation rate. When the inflation rate slows down (decreases, but remains positive), this is known as disinflation.

Inflation destroys real value in money.

a. Fixed exchange rate
c. Mercantilism
b. Recession
d. Deflation

53. A _____ is the maximum amount of credit that a financial institution or other lender will extend to a debtor for a particular line of credit. For example, the maximum that a credit card company will allow a card holder to borrow at any given point on a specific card.

This limit is based on a variety of factors ranging from an individual's ability to make interest payments, an organization's cashflow and/or ability to repay the principal, to the credit standards employed by the lender.

a. 529 plan
c. 7-Eleven
b. 4-4-5 Calendar
d. Credit limit

Chapter 15. The Banking Firm and Bank Management

1. In financial accounting, a _____ or statement of financial position is a summary of a person's or organization's balances. Assets, liabilities and ownership equity are listed as of a specific date, such as the end of its financial year. A _____ is often described as a snapshot of a company's financial condition.
   a. Financial statements
   b. Balance sheet
   c. Statement on Auditing Standards No. 70: Service Organizations
   d. Statement of retained earnings

2. A _____ s a time deposit, a financial product commonly offered to consumers by banks, thrift institutions, and credit unions.

   They are similar to savings accounts in that they are insured and thus virtually risk-free; they are 'money in the bank'. They are different from savings accounts in that they have a specific, fixed term (often three months, six months, or one to five years), and, usually, a fixed interest rate.

   a. Reserve requirement
   b. Variable rate mortgage
   c. Time deposit
   d. Certificate of deposit

3. A '_____' is a 'Charge' that is paid to obtain the right to delay a payment. Essentially, the payer purchases the right to make a given payment in the future instead of in the Present. The '_____', or 'Charge' that must be paid to delay the payment, is simply the difference between what the payment amount would be if it were paid in the present and what the payment amount would be paid if it were paid in the future.
   a. Value at risk
   b. Risk aversion
   c. Risk modeling
   d. Discount

4. _____s are deposits denominated in United States dollars at banks outside the United States, and thus are not under the jurisdiction of the Federal Reserve. Consequently, such deposits are subject to much less regulation than similar deposits within the United States, allowing for higher margins. There is nothing 'European' about _____ deposits; a US dollar-denominated deposit in Tokyo or Caracas would likewise be deemed _____ deposits.
   a. ABN Amro
   b. A Random Walk Down Wall Street
   c. AAB
   d. Eurodollar

5. _____ is a fee paid on borrowed assets. It is the price paid for the use of borrowed money , or, money earned by deposited funds . Assets that are sometimes lent with _____ include money, shares, consumer goods through hire purchase, major assets such as aircraft, and even entire factories in finance lease arrangements.
   a. AAB
   b. Insolvency
   c. Interest
   d. A Random Walk Down Wall Street

6. A _____ is a money deposit at a banking institution that cannot be withdrawn for a certain 'term' or period of time. When the term is over it can be withdrawn or it can be held for another term. Generally speaking, the longer the term the better the yield on the money.
   a. Basel Accord
   b. Private money
   c. Time deposit
   d. Certificate of deposit

7. _____, in bookkeeping, refers to assets, liabilities, income, and expenses recorded on individual pages of the so called book of final entry or ledger. Changes in _____ value are made by chronologically posting debit (DR) and credit (CR) entries to its page. Examples of _____s are cash, _____s receivable, mortgages, loans, land and buildings, common stock, sales, services provided, wages, and payroll overhead.

a. Alpha
b. Account
c. Accretion
d. Option

8. In business and accounting, _____s are everything of value that is owned by a person or company. The balance sheet of a firm records the monetary value of the _____s owned by the firm. The two major _____ classes are tangible _____s and intangible _____s.

a. EBITDA
b. Accounts payable
c. Income
d. Asset

9. The _____ is a bank regulation that sets the minimum reserves each bank must hold to customer deposits and notes. These reserves are designed to satisfy withdrawal demands, and would normally be in the form of fiat currency stored in a bank vault (vault cash), or with a central bank.

The reserve ratio is sometimes used as a tool in the monetary policy, influencing the country's economy, borrowing, and interest rates.

a. Variable rate mortgage
b. Prime rate
c. Wall Street Journal prime rate
d. Reserve requirement

10. In financial accounting, the term _____ is most commonly used to describe any part of shareholders' equity, except for basic share capital. Sometimes, the term is used instead of the term provision; such a use, however, is inconsistent with the terminology suggested by International Accounting Standards Board. For more information about provisions, see provision (accounting.)

a. Closing entries
b. FIFO and LIFO accounting
c. Treasury stock
d. Reserve

11. In finance, the _____ between two currencies specifies how much one currency is worth in terms of the other. For example an _____ of 102 Japanese yen to the United States dollar means that JPY 102 is worth the same as USD 1. The foreign exchange market is one of the largest markets in the world.

a. A Random Walk Down Wall Street
b. Exchange rate
c. AAB
d. ABN Amro

12. In finance, a _____ is a debt security, in which the authorized issuer owes the holders a debt and, depending on the terms of the _____, is obliged to pay interest (the coupon) and/or to repay the principal at a later date, termed maturity.

Thus a _____ is a loan: the issuer is the borrower, the _____ holder is the lender, and the coupon is the interest. _____s provide the borrower with external funds to finance long-term investments, or, in the case of government _____s, to finance current expenditure.

a. Bond
b. Convertible bond
c. Catastrophe bonds
d. Puttable bond

Chapter 15. The Banking Firm and Bank Management 113

13. The term _____ is often used to refer to the investment management of collective investments, (not necessarily) whilst the more generic fund management may refer to all forms of institutional investment as well as investment management for private investors. Investment managers who specialize in advisory or discretionary management on behalf of (normally wealthy) private investors may often refer to their services as wealth management or portfolio management often within the context of so-called 'private banking'.

The provision of 'investment management services' includes elements of financial analysis, asset selection, stock selection, plan implementation and ongoing monitoring of investments.

a. ABN Amro
c. AAB
b. Asset management
d. A Random Walk Down Wall Street

14. _____ is the provision of resources (such as granting a loan) by one party to another party where that second party does not reimburse the first party immediately, thereby generating a debt, and instead arranges either to repay or return those resources (or material(s) of equal value) at a later date. The first party is called a creditor, also known as a lender, while the second party is called a debtor, also known as a borrower.

Movements of financial capital are normally dependent on either _____ or equity transfers.

a. Comparable
c. Warrant
b. Credit
d. Clearing house

15. _____ is the risk of loss due to a debtor's non-payment of a loan or other line of credit (either the principal or interest (coupon) or both)

Most lenders employ their own models (credit scorecards) to rank potential and existing customers according to risk, and then apply appropriate strategies. With products such as unsecured personal loans or mortgages, lenders charge a higher price for higher risk customers and vice versa. With revolving products such as credit cards and overdrafts, risk is controlled through careful setting of credit limits.

a. Liquidity risk
c. Market risk
b. Transaction risk
d. Credit risk

16. In the most general sense, a _____ is anything that is a hindrance, or puts individuals at a disadvantage.

Before we discuss the financial terms, we should note that a _____ can also have a much more important slang meaning.

This is best described in an example.

a. Covenant
c. McFadden Act
b. Limited liability
d. Liability

17. _____ is a measure of the ability of a debtor to pay their debts as and when they fall due. It is usually expressed as a ratio or a percentage of current liabilities.

For a corporation with a published balance sheet there are various ratios used to calculate a measure of liquidity.

   a. Accounting liquidity
   b. Invested capital
   c. Operating profit margin
   d. Operating leverage

18. A _____ is a financial contract whose value is derived from the value of something else (known as the underlying.) The underlying on which a _____ is based can be an asset, weather conditions bonds or other forms of credit.
   a. 7-Eleven
   b. Derivative
   c. 4-4-5 Calendar
   d. 529 plan

19. _____ is a business, economics or investment term that refers to an asset's ability to be easily converted through an act of buying or selling without causing a significant movement in the price and with minimum loss of value. Money, or cash on hand, is the most liquid asset. An act of exchange of a less liquid asset with a more liquid asset is called liquidation.
   a. 529 plan
   b. 4-4-5 Calendar
   c. 7-Eleven
   d. Market liquidity

20. The _____ is an interest rate a central bank charges depository institutions that borrow reserves from it.

The term _____ has two meanings:

- the same as interest rate; the term 'discount' does not refer to the meaning of the word, but to the purpose of using the quantity, such as computations of present value, e.g. net present value / discounted cash flow

- the annual effective _____, which is the annual interest divided by the capital including that interest; this rate is lower than the interest rate; it corresponds to using the value after a year as the nominal value, and seeing the initial value as the nominal value minus a discount; it is used for Treasury Bills and similar financial instruments

The annual effective _____ is the annual interest divided by the capital including that interest, which is the interest rate divided by 100% plus the interest rate. It is the annual discount factor to be applied to the future cash flow, to find the discount, subtracted from a future value to find the value one year earlier.

For example, suppose there is a government bond that sells for $95 and pays $100 in a year's time.

   a. Fisher equation
   b. Stochastic volatility
   c. Black-Scholes
   d. Discount rate

21. _____ measures the rate of return on the ownership interest (shareholders' equity) of the common stock owners. _____ is viewed as one of the most important financial ratios. It measures a firm's efficiency at generating profits from every dollar of shareholders' equity (also known as net assets or assets minus liabilities.)
   a. Return on sales
   b. Diluted Earnings Per Share
   c. Return of capital
   d. Return on equity

Chapter 15. The Banking Firm and Bank Management

22. The _____ percentage shows how profitable a company's assets are in generating revenue.

_____ can be computed as:

$$\text{ROA} = \frac{\text{Net Income}}{\text{Total Assets}}$$

This number tells you 'what the company can do with what it's got', i.e. how many dollars of earnings they derive from each dollar of assets they control. It's a useful number for comparing competing companies in the same industry.

a. Receivables turnover ratio
c. P/E ratio
b. Return on sales
d. Return on assets

23. A _____ is a sudden reduction in the general availability of loans, or a sudden increase in the cost of obtaining loans from banks.

There are a number of reasons why banks may suddenly increase the costs of borrowing or make borrowing more difficult. It may be due to an anticipated decline in value of the collateral used by the banks when issuing loans, or even an increased perception of risk regarding the solvency of other banks within the banking system.

a. Credit cycle
c. Credit crunch
b. Credit report monitoring
d. Capital note

24. In economics, a _____ is a general slowdown in economic activity in a country over a sustained period of time, or a business cycle contraction. During _____s, many macroeconomic indicators vary in a similar way. Production as measured by Gross Domestic Product (GDP), employment, investment spending, capacity utilization, household incomes and business profits all fall during _____s.

a. Recession
c. Fixed exchange rate
b. Behavioral finance
d. Mercantilism

25. In finance, 'participation' is an ownership interest in a mortgage or other loan. In particular, _____ is a cooperation of multiple lenders to issue a loan (known as participation loan) to one borrower. This is usually done in order to reduce individual risks of the lenders.

a. Loan participation
c. Securitization
b. Short positions
d. Doctrine of the Proper Law

26. A _____ is an international bond that is denominated in a currency not native to the country where it is issued. It can be categorised according to the currency in which it is issued. London is one of the centers of the _____ market, but _____s may be traded throughout the world - for example in Singapore or Tokyo.

a. Eurobond
c. Interest rate option
b. Education production function
d. Economic entity

Chapter 15. The Banking Firm and Bank Management

27. In political science and economics, the _____ or agency dilemma treats the difficulties that arise under conditions of incomplete and asymmetric information when a principal hires an agent. Various mechanisms may be used to try to align the interests of the agent with those of the principal, such as piece rates/commissions, profit sharing, efficiency wages, performance measurement (including financial statements), the agent posting a bond, or fear of firing. The _____ is found in most employer/employee relationships, for example, when stockholders hire top executives of corporations.

   a. Principal-agent problem   b. 529 plan
   c. 4-4-5 Calendar   d. 7-Eleven

28. A _____ is a general term that describes any government policy or regulation that restricts international trade. The barriers can take many forms, including the following terms that include many restrictions in international trade within multiple countries that import and export any items of trade.

- Import duty
- Import licenses
- Export licenses
- Import quotas
- Tariffs
- Subsidies
- Non-tariff barriers to trade
- Voluntary Export Restraints
- Local Content Requirements
- Embargo

   a. Foreign exchange reserves   b. World Trade Organization
   c. Median   d. Trade barrier

29. In financial mathematics and financial risk management, _____ is a widely used measure of the risk of loss on a specific portfolio of financial assets. For a given portfolio, probability and time horizon, VaR is defined as a threshold value such that the probability that the mark-to-market loss on the portfolio over the given time horizon exceeds this value (assuming normal markets and no trading) is the given probability level.

For example, if a portfolio of stocks has a one-day 5% VaR of $1 million, there is a 5% probability that the portfolio will fall in value by more than $1 million over a one day period, assuming markets are normal and there is no trading.

   a. Risk aversion   b. Risk modeling
   c. Value at risk   d. Discount factor

30. The institution most often referenced by the word '_____' is a public or publicly traded _____, the shares of which are traded on a public stock exchange (e.g., the New York Stock Exchange or Nasdaq in the United States) where shares of stock of _____s are bought and sold by and to the general public. Most of the largest businesses in the world are publicly traded _____s. However, the majority of _____s are said to be closely held, privately held or close _____s, meaning that no ready market exists for the trading of shares.

Chapter 15. The Banking Firm and Bank Management 117

a. Protect
b. Depository Trust Company
c. Federal Home Loan Mortgage Corporation
d. Corporation

31. In business, _____ is the total assets minus total outside liabilities of an individual or a company. For a company, this is called shareholders' equity and may be referred to as book value. _____ is stated as at a particular point in time.
a. Certified International Investment Analyst
b. Moneylender
c. Net worth
d. Restructuring

32. A _____, securities exchange or (in Europe) bourse is a corporation or mutual organization which provides 'trading' facilities for stock brokers and traders, to trade stocks and other securities. _____s also provide facilities for the issue and redemption of securities as well as other financial instruments and capital events including the payment of income and dividends. The securities traded on a _____ include: shares issued by companies, unit trusts and other pooled investment products and bonds.
a. 4-4-5 Calendar
b. 529 plan
c. 7-Eleven
d. Stock exchange

33. _____, refers to consumption opportunity gained by an entity within a specified time frame, which is generally expressed in monetary terms. However, for households and individuals, '_____ is the sum of all the wages, salaries, profits, interests payments, rents and other forms of earnings received... in a given period of time.' For firms, _____ generally refers to net-profit: what remains of revenue after expenses have been subtracted.
a. Income
b. Accrual
c. OIBDA
d. Annual report

34. An _____ is a financial statement for companies that indicates how Revenue is transformed into net income The purpose of the _____ is to show managers and investors whether the company made or lost money during the period being reported.

The important thing to remember about an _____ is that it represents a period of time.

a. AAB
b. A Random Walk Down Wall Street
c. ABN Amro
d. Income statement

35. _____ is the difference between operating revenues and operating expenses, but it is also sometimes used as a synonym for EBIT and operating profit. This is true if the firm has no non-_____.

A professional investor contemplating a change to the capital structure of a firm (e.g., through a leveraged buyout) first evaluates a firm's fundamental earnings potential (reflected by Earnings Before Interest, Taxes, Depreciation and Amortization EBITDA and EBIT), and then determines the optimal use of debt vs. equity.

a. ABN Amro
b. A Random Walk Down Wall Street
c. AAB
d. Operating income

36. An _____, operating expenditure, operational expense, operational expenditure or OPEX is an on-going cost for running a product, business, or system. Its counterpart, a capital expenditure (CAPEX), is the cost of developing or providing non-consumable parts for the product or system. For example, the purchase of a photocopier is the CAPEX, and the annual paper and toner cost is the OPEX.

a. ABN Amro
b. AAB
c. Operating expense
d. A Random Walk Down Wall Street

37. In finance, a _____ is collateral that the holder of a position in securities, options, or futures contracts has to deposit to cover the credit risk of his counterparty (most often his broker.) This risk can arise if the holder has done any of the following:

- borrowed cash from the counterparty to buy securities or options,
- sold securities or options short, or
- entered into a futures contract.

The collateral can be in the form of cash or securities, and it is deposited in a _____ account. On U.S. futures exchanges, '_____' was formally called performance bond.

_____ buying is buying securities with cash borrowed from a broker, using other securities as collateral.

a. Procter ' Gamble
b. Credit
c. Margin
d. Share

38. An _____ is a mortgage loan where the interest rate on the note is periodically adjusted based on a variety of indices. Among the most common indices are the rates on 1-year constant-maturity Treasury (CMT) securities, the Cost of Funds Index (COFI), and the London Interbank Offered Rate (LIBOR.) A few lenders use their own cost of funds as an index, rather than using other indices.

a. A Random Walk Down Wall Street
b. AAB
c. ABN Amro
d. Adjustable rate mortgage

39. _____ is an economic model based on price, utility and quantity in a market. It predicts that in a competitive market, price will function to equalize the quantity demanded by consumers, and the quantity supplied by producers, resulting in an economic equilibrium of price and quantity. Similarly, an increase in the number of workers tends to result in lower wages and vice-versa.

a. Rural credit cooperatives
b. Supply and demand
c. Price channel
d. Loan participation

40. _____ or amalgamation is the act of merging many things into one. In business, it often refers to the mergers or acquisitions of many smaller companies into much larger ones. The financial accounting term of _____ refers to the aggregated financial statements of a group company as consolidated account.

a. Write-off
b. Retained earnings
c. Consolidation
d. Cost of goods sold

41. A _____ is a fungible, negotiable instrument representing financial value. They are broadly categorized into debt securities (such as banknotes, bonds and debentures), and equity securities; e.g., common stocks. The company or other entity issuing the _____ is called the issuer.

a. Securities lending
b. Book entry
c. Tracking stock
d. Security

Chapter 15. The Banking Firm and Bank Management

42. A _____ is a financial crisis that occurs when many banks suffer runs at the same time. A systemic banking crisis is one where all or almost all of the banking capital in a country is wiped out. The resulting chain of bankruptcies can cause a long economic recession. Much of the Great Depression's economic damage was caused directly by bank runs. The cost of cleaning up a systemic banking crisis can be huge, with fiscal costs averaging 13% of GDP and economic output losses averaging 20% of GDP for important crises from 1970 to 2007.
   a. Deposit insurance
   b. Credit bureau
   c. Banking panic
   d. Probability of default

43. A _____, reserve bank, or monetary authority is the entity responsible for the monetary policy of a country or of a group of member states. It is a bank that can lend money to other banks in times of need. Its primary responsibility is to maintain the stability of the national currency and money supply, but more active duties include controlling subsidized-loan interest rates, and acting as a lender of last resort to the banking sector during times of financial crisis (private banks often being integral to the national financial system.)
   a. 7-Eleven
   b. Central bank
   c. 529 plan
   d. 4-4-5 Calendar

44. In the global money market, _____ is an unsecured promissory note with a fixed maturity of one to 270 days. _____ is a money-market security issued (sold) by large banks and corporations to get money to meet short term debt obligations (for example, payroll), and is only backed by an issuing bank or corporation's promise to pay the face amount on the maturity date specified on the note. Since it is not backed by collateral, only firms with excellent credit ratings from a recognized rating agency will be able to sell their _____ at a reasonable price.
   a. Trade-off theory
   b. Financial distress
   c. Book building
   d. Commercial paper

45. In economics, _____ is the removal of intermediaries in a supply chain: 'cutting out the middleman'. Instead of going through traditional distribution channels, which had some type of intermediate (such as a distributor, wholesaler, broker, or agent), companies may now deal with every customer directly, for example via the Internet. One important factor is a drop in the cost of servicing customers directly.
   a. 4-4-5 Calendar
   b. 7-Eleven
   c. 529 plan
   d. Disintermediation

46. The _____ , a component of the Federal Reserve System, is charged under United States law with overseeing the nation's open market operations. It is the Federal Reserve Committee that makes key decisions about interest rates and the growth jam of the United States money supply. It is the principal organ of United States national monetary policy.
   a. Federal Open Market Committee
   b. Tax incidence
   c. Fiscal policy
   d. Tax exemption

47. _____ is a United States government regulation that put a limit on the interest rates that banks could pay, including a rate of zero on demand deposits (checking accounts.) Section 11 of the Banking Act of 1933 (12 U.S.C. 371a) prohibits member banks from paying interest on demand deposits, which is implemented by _____
   a. Truth in Lending Act
   b. Fair Credit Reporting Act
   c. Regulation Q
   d. Fair Credit Billing Act

48. A _____ allows a borrower to use a financial security as collateral for a cash loan at a fixed rate of interest. In a repo, the borrower agrees to immediately sell a security to a lender and also agrees to buy the same security from the lender at a fixed price at some later date. A repo is equivalent to a cash transaction combined with a forward contract.

Chapter 15. The Banking Firm and Bank Management

a. Total return swap
b. Volatility arbitrage
c. Contango
d. Repurchase agreement

49. In business and finance, a _____ (also referred to as equity _____) of stock means a _____ of ownership in a corporation (company.) In the plural, stocks is often used as a synonym for _____s especially in the United States, but it is less commonly used that way outside of North America.

In the United Kingdom, South Africa, and Australia, stock can also refer to completely different financial instruments such as government bonds or, less commonly, to all kinds of marketable securities.

a. Procter ' Gamble
b. Margin
c. Share
d. Bucket shop

50. A _____ can require immediate payment by the second party to the third upon presentation of the _____. This is called a sight _____. A Cheques is a sight _____. An importer might write a _____ promising payment to an exporter for delivery of goods with payment to occur 60 days after the goods are delivered. Such a _____ is called a time _____.

a. Gross profit margin
b. Second lien loan
c. Cashflow matching
d. Draft

51. A _____ is a bond bought at a price lower than its face value, with the face value repaid at the time of maturity. It does not make periodic interest payments, or so-called 'coupons,' hence the term zero-coupon bond. Investors earn return from the compounded interest all paid at maturity plus the difference between the discounted price of the bond and its par value.

a. Bowie bonds
b. Municipal bond
c. Callable bond
d. Zero coupon bond

52. _____ is one of the main genres of financial risk. The term describes the risk that a particular investment might be canceled or stopped somehow, that one may have to find a new place to invest that money with the risk being there might not be a similarly attractive investment available. This primarily occurs if bonds (which are portions of loans to entities) are paid back earlier then expected.

a. Standard of deferred payment
b. Biweekly Mortgage
c. Debt cash flow
d. Reinvestment risk

53. _____ are government bonds issued by the United States Department of the Treasury through the Bureau of the Public Debt. They are the debt financing instruments of the U.S. Federal government, and they are often referred to simply as Treasuries or Treasurys. There are four types of marketable _____: Treasury bills, Treasury notes, Treasury bonds, and Treasury Inflation Protected Securities (TIPS.)

a. 4-4-5 Calendar
b. Treasury Inflation-Protected Securities
c. Treasury Inflation Protected Securities
d. Treasury securities

54. A _____ is a bond bought at a price lower than its face value, with the face value repaid at the time of maturity. It does not make periodic interest payments, or have so-called 'coupons,' hence the term _____. Investors earn return from the compounded interest all paid at maturity plus the difference between the discounted price of the bond and its par value.

a. Clean price	b. Zero-coupon bond
c. Bond fund	d. Corporate bond

55. _____ are the means of implementing monetary policy by which a central bank controls its national money supply by buying and selling government securities, or other financial instruments. Monetary targets, such as interest rates or exchange rates, are used to guide this implementation.

Since most money is now in the form of electronic records, rather than paper records such as banknotes, _____ are conducted simply by electronically increasing or decreasing ('crediting' or 'debiting') the amount of money that a bank has, e.g., in its reserve account at the central bank, in exchange for a bank selling or buying a financial instrument.

a. ABN Amro	b. A Random Walk Down Wall Street
c. AAB	d. Open market operations

Chapter 16. Commercial Banking Industry: Structure and Competition

1. The U.S. _____ is an independent agency of the United States government which holds primary responsibility for enforcing the federal securities laws and regulating the securities industry, the nation's stock and options exchanges, and other electronic securities markets. The SEC was created by section 4 of the SEC of 1934 (now codified as 15 U.S.C. § 78d and commonly referred to as the 1934 Act.)
   - a. 4-4-5 Calendar
   - b. 7-Eleven
   - c. Securities and Exchange Commission
   - d. 529 plan

2. The institution most often referenced by the word '_____' is a public or publicly traded _____, the shares of which are traded on a public stock exchange (e.g., the New York Stock Exchange or Nasdaq in the United States) where shares of stock of _____s are bought and sold by and to the general public. Most of the largest businesses in the world are publicly traded _____s. However, the majority of _____s are said to be closely held, privately held or close _____s, meaning that no ready market exists for the trading of shares.
   - a. Corporation
   - b. Depository Trust Company
   - c. Federal Home Loan Mortgage Corporation
   - d. Protect

3. Explicit _____ is a measure implemented in many countries to protect bank depositors, in full or in part, from losses caused by a bank's inability to pay its debts when due. _____ systems are one component of a financial system safety net that promotes financial stability.
   - a. Time deposit
   - b. Reserve requirement
   - c. Deposit Insurance
   - d. Banking panic

4. The _____ is a United States government corporation created by the Glass-Steagall Act of 1933. It provides deposit insurance, which guarantees the safety of checking and savings deposits in member banks, currently up to $250,000 per depositor per bank. Insured deposits are backed by the full faith and credit of the United States.
   - a. NYSE Group
   - b. Ford Foundation
   - c. Federal Deposit Insurance Corporation
   - d. FASB

5. The _____ of 1933 established the Federal Deposit Insurance Corporation (FDIC) in the United States and included banking reforms, some of which were designed to control speculation. Some provisions such as Regulation Q, which allowed the Federal Reserve to regulate interest rates in savings accounts, were repealed by the Depository Institutions Deregulation and Monetary Control Act of 1980. Provisions that prohibit a bank holding company from owning other financial companies were repealed on November 12, 1999, by the Gramm-Leach-Bliley Act.
   - a. 529 plan
   - b. 7-Eleven
   - c. 4-4-5 Calendar
   - d. Glass-Steagall Act

6. The _____ was a worldwide economic downturn starting in most places in 1929 and ending at different times in the 1930s or early 1940s for different countries. It was the largest and most important economic depression in the 20th century, and is used in the 21st century as an example of how far the world's economy can fall. The _____ originated in the United States; historians most often use as a starting date the stock market crash on October 29, 1929, known as Black Tuesday.
   - a. Great Depression
   - b. 529 plan
   - c. 7-Eleven
   - d. 4-4-5 Calendar

7. In the United States, the Financial Industry Regulatory Authority (FINRA) is a self-regulatory organization (SRO) under the Securities Exchange Act of 1934, successor to the _____, Inc.

Chapter 16. Commercial Banking Industry: Structure and Competition

FINRA is responsible for regulatory oversight of all securities firms that do business with the public; professional training, testing and licensing of registered persons; arbitration and mediation; market regulation by contract for The NASDAQ Stock Market, Inc., the American Stock Exchange LLC, and the International Securities Exchange, LLC; and industry utilities, such as Trade Reporting Facilities and other over-the-counter operations.

a. 529 plan
b. 4-4-5 Calendar
c. National Association of Securities Dealers
d. 7-Eleven

8. In financial accounting, the term _____ is most commonly used to describe any part of shareholders' equity, except for basic share capital. Sometimes, the term is used instead of the term provision; such a use, however, is inconsistent with the terminology suggested by International Accounting Standards Board. For more information about provisions, see provision (accounting.)

a. Reserve
b. Closing entries
c. Treasury stock
d. FIFO and LIFO accounting

9. A _____ is a fungible, negotiable instrument representing financial value. They are broadly categorized into debt securities (such as banknotes, bonds and debentures), and equity securities; e.g., common stocks. The company or other entity issuing the _____ is called the issuer.

a. Book entry
b. Security
c. Securities lending
d. Tracking stock

10. In finance, a _____ is a debt security, in which the authorized issuer owes the holders a debt and, depending on the terms of the _____, is obliged to pay interest (the coupon) and/or to repay the principal at a later date, termed maturity.

Thus a _____ is a loan: the issuer is the borrower, the _____ holder is the lender, and the coupon is the interest. _____s provide the borrower with external funds to finance long-term investments, or, in the case of government _____s, to finance current expenditure.

a. Bond
b. Catastrophe bonds
c. Puttable bond
d. Convertible bond

11. A _____ is a financial contract whose value is derived from the value of something else (known as the underlying.) The underlying on which a _____ is based can be an asset, weather conditions bonds or other forms of credit.

a. 7-Eleven
b. Derivative
c. 4-4-5 Calendar
d. 529 plan

12. A _____ is a bond issued by a national government denominated in the country's own currency. Bonds issued by national governments in foreign currencies are normally referred to as sovereign bonds. The first ever _____ was issued by the British government in 1693 to raise money to fund a war against France.

a. Government bond
b. Municipal bond
c. Zero-coupon bond
d. Collateralized debt obligations

Chapter 16. Commercial Banking Industry: Structure and Competition

13. A _____, reserve bank, or monetary authority is the entity responsible for the monetary policy of a country or of a group of member states. It is a bank that can lend money to other banks in times of need. Its primary responsibility is to maintain the stability of the national currency and money supply, but more active duties include controlling subsidized-loan interest rates, and acting as a lender of last resort to the banking sector during times of financial crisis (private banks often being integral to the national financial system.)

   a. 529 plan
   c. Central bank
   b. 4-4-5 Calendar
   d. 7-Eleven

14.

A _____ is a type of financial intermediary and a type of bank. Commercial banking is also known as business banking. It is a bank that provides checking accounts, savings accounts, and money market accounts and that accepts time deposits.

   a. 7-Eleven
   c. Commercial bank
   b. 529 plan
   d. 4-4-5 Calendar

15. A _____ is a company that owns other companies' outstanding stock. It usually refers to a company which does not produce goods or services itself, rather its only purpose is owning shares of other companies. They allow the reduction of risk for the owners and can allow the ownership and control of a number of different companies.

   a. Privately held company
   c. Holding company
   b. Federal National Mortgage Association
   d. MRU Holdings

16. The _____ is a United States federal law enacted in 1927 from recommendations made by the comptroller of the currency Henry May Dawes.

The Act sought to give national banks competitive equality with state-chartered banks by letting national banks branch to the extent permitted by state law. The _____ specifically prohibited interstate branching by allowing each national bank to branch only within the state in which it is situated.

   a. McFadden Act
   c. Duty of loyalty
   b. Covenant
   d. Business valuation

17. The _____ of 1956 (12 U.S.C. § 1841, et seq.) is a United States Act of Congress that regulates the actions of bank holding companies.

The original law (subsequently amended), specified that the Federal Reserve Board of Governors must approve the establishment of a bank holding company, and prohibited bank holding companies headquartered in one state from acquiring a bank in another state. The law was implemented in part to regulate and control banks that had formed bank holding companies in order to own both banking and non-banking businesses.

   a. Fair Credit Billing Act
   c. Truth in Lending Act
   b. Fair Credit Reporting Act
   d. Bank Holding Company Act

Chapter 16. Commercial Banking Industry: Structure and Competition

18. A _____ is a financial crisis that occurs when many banks suffer runs at the same time. A systemic banking crisis is one where all or almost all of the banking capital in a country is wiped out. The resulting chain of bankruptcies can cause a long economic recession. Much of the Great Depression's economic damage was caused directly by bank runs. The cost of cleaning up a systemic banking crisis can be huge, with fiscal costs averaging 13% of GDP and economic output losses averaging 20% of GDP for important crises from 1970 to 2007.
 a. Probability of default
 b. Banking panic
 c. Credit bureau
 d. Deposit insurance

19. _____ or amalgamation is the act of merging many things into one. In business, it often refers to the mergers or acquisitions of many smaller companies into much larger ones. The financial accounting term of _____ refers to the aggregated financial statements of a group company as consolidated account.
 a. Consolidation
 b. Retained earnings
 c. Cost of goods sold
 d. Write-off

20. The phrase _____ refers to the aspect of corporate strategy, corporate finance and management dealing with the buying, selling and combining of different companies that can aid, finance, or help a growing company in a given industry grow rapidly without having to create another business entity.

An acquisition, also known as a takeover, is the buying of one company (the 'target') by another. An acquisition may be friendly or hostile.

 a. 4-4-5 Calendar
 b. 529 plan
 c. 7-Eleven
 d. Mergers and acquisitions

21. _____ is the provision of resources (such as granting a loan) by one party to another party where that second party does not reimburse the first party immediately, thereby generating a debt, and instead arranges either to repay or return those resources (or material(s) of equal value) at a later date. The first party is called a creditor, also known as a lender, while the second party is called a debtor, also known as a borrower.

Movements of financial capital are normally dependent on either _____ or equity transfers.

 a. Comparable
 b. Credit
 c. Warrant
 d. Clearing house

22. _____ refer to services provided by the finance industry.

The finance industry encompasses a broad range of organizations that deal with the management of money. Among these organizations are banks, credit card companies, insurance companies, consumer finance companies, stock brokerages, investment funds and some government sponsored enterprises.

 a. Cost of carry
 b. Financial instruments
 c. Delta hedging
 d. Financial Services

Chapter 16. Commercial Banking Industry: Structure and Competition

23. The _____ Act is an Act of the 106th United States Congress which repealed part of the Glass-Steagall Act of 1933, opening up competition among banks, securities companies and insurance companies. The Glass-Steagall Act prohibited any one institution from acting as both an investment bank and a commercial bank, or as both a bank and an insurer.

The _____ Act (GLBA) allowed commercial and investment banks to consolidate.

   a. 7-Eleven
   b. Gramm-Leach-Bliley
   c. 4-4-5 Calendar
   d. 529 plan

24. A _____, securities exchange or (in Europe) bourse is a corporation or mutual organization which provides 'trading' facilities for stock brokers and traders, to trade stocks and other securities. _____s also provide facilities for the issue and redemption of securities as well as other financial instruments and capital events including the payment of income and dividends. The securities traded on a _____ include: shares issued by companies, unit trusts and other pooled investment products and bonds.
   a. 4-4-5 Calendar
   b. Stock Exchange
   c. 529 plan
   d. 7-Eleven

25. In finance, the _____ between two currencies specifies how much one currency is worth in terms of the other. For example an _____ of 102 Japanese yen to the United States dollar means that JPY 102 is worth the same as USD 1. The foreign exchange market is one of the largest markets in the world.
   a. ABN Amro
   b. AAB
   c. A Random Walk Down Wall Street
   d. Exchange rate

26. _____s are deposits denominated in United States dollars at banks outside the United States, and thus are not under the jurisdiction of the Federal Reserve. Consequently, such deposits are subject to much less regulation than similar deposits within the United States, allowing for higher margins. There is nothing 'European' about _____ deposits; a US dollar-denominated deposit in Tokyo or Caracas would likewise be deemed _____ deposits.
   a. A Random Walk Down Wall Street
   b. ABN Amro
   c. AAB
   d. Eurodollar

27. In finance, the _____ is the global financial market for short-term borrowing and lending. It provides short-term liquidity funding for the global financial system. The _____ is where short-term obligations such as Treasury bills, commercial paper and bankers' acceptances are bought and sold.
   a. Consumer debt
   b. Money market
   c. Cramdown
   d. Debt-for-equity swap

28. A _____ is a professionally managed type of collective investment scheme that pools money from many investors and invests it in stocks, bonds, short-term money market instruments, and/or other securities. The _____ will have a fund manager that trades the pooled money on a regular basis. Currently, the worldwide value of all _____s totals more than $26 trillion.

Since 1940, there have been three basic types of investment companies in the United States: open-end funds, also known in the US as _____s; unit investment trusts (UITs); and closed-end funds.

Chapter 16. Commercial Banking Industry: Structure and Competition

a. Financial intermediary
c. Trust company
b. Mutual fund
d. Net asset value

29. The value of speculative bonds is affected to a higher degree than investment grade bonds by the possibility of default. For example, in a recession interest rates may drop, and the drop in interest rates tends to increase the value of investment grade bonds; however, a recession tends to increase the possibility of default in speculative-grade bonds.

The original speculative grade bonds were bonds that once had been investment grade at time of issue, but where the credit rating of the issuer had slipped and the possibility of default increased significantly. These bonds are called '_____'.

a. Sharpe ratio
c. Seed round
b. Return on capital employed
d. Fallen angels

30. In finance, a _____ (non-investment grade bond, speculative grade bond or junk bond) is a bond that is rated below investment grade at the time of purchase. These bonds have a higher risk of default or other adverse credit events, but typically pay higher yields than better quality bonds in order to make them attractive to investors.

a. High yield bond
c. Sharpe ratio
b. Volatility
d. Private equity

31. In the global money market, _____ is an unsecured promissory note with a fixed maturity of one to 270 days. _____ is a money-market security issued (sold) by large banks and corporations to get money to meet short term debt obligations (for example, payroll), and is only backed by an issuing bank or corporation's promise to pay the face amount on the maturity date specified on the note. Since it is not backed by collateral, only firms with excellent credit ratings from a recognized rating agency will be able to sell their _____ at a reasonable price.

a. Commercial paper
c. Trade-off theory
b. Financial distress
d. Book building

32. _____ is a structured finance process that involves pooling and repackaging of cash-flow-producing financial assets into securities, which are then sold to investors. The term '_____' is derived from the fact that the form of financial instruments used to obtain funds from the investors are securities. As a portfolio risk backed by amortizing cash flows - and unlike general corporate debt - the credit quality of securitized debt is non-stationary due to changes in volatility that are time- and structure-dependent.

a. Reputational risk
c. Securitization
b. The Glass-Steagall Act of 1933
d. Special journals

33. Accrual, in accounting, describes the accounting method known as _____, whereby revenues and expenses are recognized when they are accrued, i.e. accumulated (earned or incurred), regardless when the actual cash is received or paid out.

E.g. a company delivers a product to a customer who will pay for it 30 days later in the next fiscal year starting a week after the delivery. The company recognizes the proceeds as a revenue in its current income statement still for the fiscal year of the delivery, even though it will get paid in cash during the following accounting period.

a. Accrual basis
b. AAB
c. A Random Walk Down Wall Street
d. ABN Amro

34. A _____ is a financial debt vehicle that was first created in June 1983 by investment banks Salomon Brothers and First Boston for Freddie Mac. (The First Boston team was led by Dexter Senft.) Legally, a _____ is a special purpose entity that is wholly separate from the institution(s) that create it.
   a. 4-4-5 Calendar
   b. Collateralized mortgage obligation
   c. Yield curve spread
   d. Tranche

35. In structured finance, a _____ is one of a number of related securities offered as part of the same transaction. The word _____ is French for slice, section, series, or portion. In the financial sense of the word, each bond is a different slice of the deal's risk.
   a. Credit enhancement
   b. Tranche
   c. 4-4-5 Calendar
   d. Yield curve spread

36. In business and finance, a _____ (also referred to as equity _____) of stock means a _____ of ownership in a corporation (company.) In the plural, stocks is often used as a synonym for _____s especially in the United States, but it is less commonly used that way outside of North America.

In the United Kingdom, South Africa, and Australia, stock can also refer to completely different financial instruments such as government bonds or, less commonly, to all kinds of marketable securities.

   a. Margin
   b. Share
   c. Bucket shop
   d. Procter ' Gamble

Chapter 17. Savings Associations and Credit Unions

1. A _____ is a financial contract whose value is derived from the value of something else (known as the underlying.) The underlying on which a _____ is based can be an asset, weather conditions bonds or other forms of credit.
   a. 529 plan
   b. 4-4-5 Calendar
   c. Derivative
   d. 7-Eleven

2. The institution most often referenced by the word '_____' is a public or publicly traded _____, the shares of which are traded on a public stock exchange (e.g., the New York Stock Exchange or Nasdaq in the United States) where shares of stock of _____s are bought and sold by and to the general public. Most of the largest businesses in the world are publicly traded _____s. However, the majority of _____s are said to be closely held, privately held or close _____s, meaning that no ready market exists for the trading of shares.
   a. Protect
   b. Federal Home Loan Mortgage Corporation
   c. Depository Trust Company
   d. Corporation

3. The _____ (FSLIC) was an institution that administered deposit insurance for savings and loan institutions in the United States. It was abolished in 1989 by the Financial Institutions Reform, Recovery and Enforcement Act, which passed responsibility for savings and loan deposit insurance to the Federal Deposit Insurance Corporation (FDIC.)

   The FSLIC was created as part of the National Housing Act of 1934 in order to insure deposits in savings and loans, a year after the FDIC was created to insure deposits in commercial banks.

   a. Federal Savings and Loan Insurance Corporation
   b. SIPC
   c. Prudent man rule
   d. Securities Investor Protection Corporation

4. The _____ provide stable, on-demand, low-cost funding to American financial institutions for home mortgage loans, small business, rural, agricultural, and economic development lending. With their members, the _____ank System represents the largest collective source of home mortgage and community credit in the United States. The banks do not provide loans directly to individuals, only to other banks.
   a. 7-Eleven
   b. 529 plan
   c. 4-4-5 Calendar
   d. Federal Home Loan Banks

5. A _____ is a financial institution that specializes in accepting savings deposits and making mortgage and other loans. The S'L or thrift term is mainly used in the United States; similar institutions in the United Kingdom, Ireland and some Commonwealth countries include building societies and trustee savings banks.

   They are often mutually held, meaning that the depositors and borrowers are members with voting rights, and have the ability to direct the financial and managerial goals of the organization, not unlike the poliyholders of a mutual insurance company.

   a. Savings and loan association
   b. Net asset value
   c. Person-to-person lending
   d. Mutual fund

6. In finance, the _____ is the global financial market for short-term borrowing and lending. It provides short-term liquidity funding for the global financial system. The _____ is where short-term obligations such as Treasury bills, commercial paper and bankers' acceptances are bought and sold.
   a. Cramdown
   b. Debt-for-equity swap
   c. Consumer debt
   d. Money market

Chapter 17. Savings Associations and Credit Unions

7. A _____ is a fungible, negotiable instrument representing financial value. They are broadly categorized into debt securities (such as banknotes, bonds and debentures), and equity securities; e.g., common stocks. The company or other entity issuing the _____ is called the issuer.
   a. Tracking stock
   b. Book entry
   c. Securities lending
   d. Security

8. In political science and economics, the _____ or agency dilemma treats the difficulties that arise under conditions of incomplete and asymmetric information when a principal hires an agent. Various mechanisms may be used to try to align the interests of the agent with those of the principal, such as piece rates/commissions, profit sharing, efficiency wages, performance measurement (including financial statements), the agent posting a bond, or fear of firing. The _____ is found in most employer/employee relationships, for example, when stockholders hire top executives of corporations.
   a. 4-4-5 Calendar
   b. 529 plan
   c. 7-Eleven
   d. Principal-agent problem

9. In financial accounting, the term _____ is most commonly used to describe any part of shareholders' equity, except for basic share capital. Sometimes, the term is used instead of the term provision; such a use, however, is inconsistent with the terminology suggested by International Accounting Standards Board. For more information about provisions, see provision (accounting.)
   a. Reserve
   b. Treasury stock
   c. FIFO and LIFO accounting
   d. Closing entries

10. The _____ of the 1980s and 1990s (commonly referred to as the S'L crisis) was the failure of 745 savings and loan associations (S'Ls aka thrifts.) An S'L association is a financial institution in the United States that accepts savings deposits and makes mortgage loans. The ultimate cost of the crisis is estimated to have totaled around $160.1 billion, about $124.6 billion of which was directly paid for by the U.S. government--that is, the U.S. taxpayer, either directly or through charges on their savings and loan accounts--which contributed to the large budget deficits of the early 1990s.
    a. 529 plan
    b. 7-Eleven
    c. Savings and loan crisis
    d. 4-4-5 Calendar

11. In economics, business, and accounting, a _____ is the value of money that has been used up to produce something, and hence is not available for use anymore. In business, the _____ may be one of acquisition, in which case the amount of money expended to acquire it is counted as _____. In this case, money is the input that is gone in order to acquire the thing.
    a. Sliding scale fees
    b. Cost
    c. Marginal cost
    d. Fixed costs

12. _____, in bookkeeping, refers to assets, liabilities, income, and expenses recorded on individual pages of the so called book of final entry or ledger. Changes in _____ value are made by chronologically posting debit (DR) and credit (CR) entries to its page. Examples of _____s are cash, _____s receivable, mortgages, loans, land and buildings, common stock, sales, services provided, wages, and payroll overhead.
    a. Option
    b. Accretion
    c. Alpha
    d. Account

Chapter 17. Savings Associations and Credit Unions

13. _____ is an accounting term used to reflect the portion of the book value of a business entity not directly attributable to its assets and liabilities; it normally arises only in case of an acquisition. It reflects the ability of the entity to make a higher profit than would be derived from selling the tangible assets. _____ is also known as an intangible asset.
    a. Cost of goods sold
    b. Net profit
    c. Goodwill
    d. Consolidation

14. _____ measures the rate of return on the ownership interest (shareholders' equity) of the common stock owners. _____ is viewed as one of the most important financial ratios. It measures a firm's efficiency at generating profits from every dollar of shareholders' equity (also known as net assets or assets minus liabilities.)
    a. Return on equity
    b. Return of capital
    c. Return on sales
    d. Diluted Earnings Per Share

15. In business and accounting, _____s are everything of value that is owned by a person or company. The balance sheet of a firm records the monetary value of the _____s owned by the firm. The two major _____ classes are tangible _____s and intangible _____s.
    a. Accounts payable
    b. EBITDA
    c. Income
    d. Asset

16. In finance, the _____ between two currencies specifies how much one currency is worth in terms of the other. For example an _____ of 102 Japanese yen to the United States dollar means that JPY 102 is worth the same as USD 1. The foreign exchange market is one of the largest markets in the world.
    a. ABN Amro
    b. AAB
    c. A Random Walk Down Wall Street
    d. Exchange rate

17. _____ is the provision of resources (such as granting a loan) by one party to another party where that second party does not reimburse the first party immediately, thereby generating a debt, and instead arranges either to repay or return those resources (or material(s) of equal value) at a later date. The first party is called a creditor, also known as a lender, while the second party is called a debtor, also known as a borrower.

    Movements of financial capital are normally dependent on either _____ or equity transfers.

    a. Comparable
    b. Clearing house
    c. Warrant
    d. Credit

18. A _____ is a cooperative financial institution that is owned and controlled by its members, and operated for the purpose of promoting thrift, providing credit at reasonable rates, and providing other financial services to its members. Many _____s exist to further community development or sustainable international development on a local level. Worldwide, _____ systems vary significantly in terms of total system assets and average institution asset size since _____s exist in a wide range of sizes, ranging from volunteer operations with a handful of members to institutions with several billion dollars in assets and hundreds of thousands of members.
    a. Credit Union Service Organization
    b. Credit union
    c. Fi-linx
    d. Corporate credit union

19. In finance, a _____ is a debt security, in which the authorized issuer owes the holders a debt and, depending on the terms of the _____, is obliged to pay interest (the coupon) and/or to repay the principal at a later date, termed maturity.

Thus a _____ is a loan: the issuer is the borrower, the _____ holder is the lender, and the coupon is the interest. _____s provide the borrower with external funds to finance long-term investments, or, in the case of government _____s, to finance current expenditure.

a. Catastrophe bonds
b. Convertible bond
c. Puttable bond
d. Bond

20. _____ is a measure of the ability of a debtor to pay their debts as and when they fall due. It is usually expressed as a ratio or a percentage of current liabilities.

For a corporation with a published balance sheet there are various ratios used to calculate a measure of liquidity.

a. Operating leverage
b. Invested capital
c. Operating profit margin
d. Accounting liquidity

21. In business and finance, a _____ (also referred to as equity _____) of stock means a _____ of ownership in a corporation (company.) In the plural, stocks is often used as a synonym for _____s especially in the United States, but it is less commonly used that way outside of North America.

In the United Kingdom, South Africa, and Australia, stock can also refer to completely different financial instruments such as government bonds or, less commonly, to all kinds of marketable securities.

a. Procter ' Gamble
b. Margin
c. Bucket shop
d. Share

Chapter 18. Banking Regulation

1. The _____ was a worldwide economic downturn starting in most places in 1929 and ending at different times in the 1930s or early 1940s for different countries. It was the largest and most important economic depression in the 20th century, and is used in the 21st century as an example of how far the world's economy can fall. The _____ originated in the United States; historians most often use as a starting date the stock market crash on October 29, 1929, known as Black Tuesday.
   a. 7-Eleven
   b. 4-4-5 Calendar
   c. Great Depression
   d. 529 plan

2. In economics and contract theory, _____ deals with the study of decisions in transactions where one party has more or better information than the other. This creates an imbalance of power in transactions which can sometimes cause the transactions to go awry. Examples of this problem are adverse selection and moral hazard.
   a. ABN Amro
   b. A Random Walk Down Wall Street
   c. AAB
   d. Information asymmetry

3. A _____ is a financial crisis that occurs when many banks suffer runs at the same time. A systemic banking crisis is one where all or almost all of the banking capital in a country is wiped out. The resulting chain of bankruptcies can cause a long economic recession. Much of the Great Depression's economic damage was caused directly by bank runs. The cost of cleaning up a systemic banking crisis can be huge, with fiscal costs averaging 13% of GDP and economic output losses averaging 20% of GDP for important crises from 1970 to 2007.
   a. Deposit insurance
   b. Credit bureau
   c. Probability of default
   d. Banking panic

4. The institution most often referenced by the word '_____' is a public or publicly traded _____, the shares of which are traded on a public stock exchange (e.g., the New York Stock Exchange or Nasdaq in the United States) where shares of stock of _____s are bought and sold by and to the general public. Most of the largest businesses in the world are publicly traded _____s. However, the majority of _____s are said to be closely held, privately held or close _____s, meaning that no ready market exists for the trading of shares.
   a. Protect
   b. Corporation
   c. Depository Trust Company
   d. Federal Home Loan Mortgage Corporation

5. Explicit _____ is a measure implemented in many countries to protect bank depositors, in full or in part, from losses caused by a bank's inability to pay its debts when due. _____ systems are one component of a financial system safety net that promotes financial stability.
   a. Deposit Insurance
   b. Banking panic
   c. Time deposit
   d. Reserve requirement

6. The _____ is a United States government corporation created by the Glass-Steagall Act of 1933. It provides deposit insurance, which guarantees the safety of checking and savings deposits in member banks, currently up to $250,000 per depositor per bank. Insured deposits are backed by the full faith and credit of the United States.
   a. Federal Deposit Insurance Corporation
   b. Ford Foundation
   c. NYSE Group
   d. FASB

7. A _____, reserve bank, or monetary authority is the entity responsible for the monetary policy of a country or of a group of member states. It is a bank that can lend money to other banks in times of need. Its primary responsibility is to maintain the stability of the national currency and money supply, but more active duties include controlling subsidized-loan interest rates, and acting as a lender of last resort to the banking sector during times of financial crisis (private banks often being integral to the national financial system.)

Chapter 18. Banking Regulation

a. 4-4-5 Calendar
b. 529 plan
c. 7-Eleven
d. Central bank

8. In business, _____ is the total assets minus total outside liabilities of an individual or a company. For a company, this is called shareholders' equity and may be referred to as book value. _____ is stated as at a particular point in time.
   a. Restructuring
   b. Certified International Investment Analyst
   c. Moneylender
   d. Net worth

9. _____ refer to services provided by the finance industry.

The finance industry encompasses a broad range of organizations that deal with the management of money. Among these organizations are banks, credit card companies, insurance companies, consumer finance companies, stock brokerages, investment funds and some government sponsored enterprises.

   a. Financial instruments
   b. Cost of carry
   c. Delta hedging
   d. Financial Services

10. The _____ Act is an Act of the 106th United States Congress which repealed part of the Glass-Steagall Act of 1933, opening up competition among banks, securities companies and insurance companies. The Glass-Steagall Act prohibited any one institution from acting as both an investment bank and a commercial bank, or as both a bank and an insurer.

The _____ Act (GLBA) allowed commercial and investment banks to consolidate.

   a. Gramm-Leach-Bliley
   b. 529 plan
   c. 7-Eleven
   d. 4-4-5 Calendar

11. In business and accounting, _____s are everything of value that is owned by a person or company. The balance sheet of a firm records the monetary value of the _____s owned by the firm. The two major _____ classes are tangible _____s and intangible _____s.
   a. EBITDA
   b. Income
   c. Accounts payable
   d. Asset

12. _____ or amalgamation is the act of merging many things into one. In business, it often refers to the mergers or acquisitions of many smaller companies into much larger ones. The financial accounting term of _____ refers to the aggregated financial statements of a group company as consolidated account.
   a. Write-off
   b. Cost of goods sold
   c. Consolidation
   d. Retained earnings

13. In finance, the _____ between two currencies specifies how much one currency is worth in terms of the other. For example an _____ of 102 Japanese yen to the United States dollar means that JPY 102 is worth the same as USD 1. The foreign exchange market is one of the largest markets in the world.
   a. ABN Amro
   b. A Random Walk Down Wall Street
   c. Exchange rate
   d. AAB

Chapter 18. Banking Regulation

14. The _____ refers to the banking supervision Accords (recommendations on banking laws and regulations), Basel I and Basel II issued by the Basel Committee on Banking Supervision (BCBS.) They are called the _____s as the BCBS maintains its secretariat at the Bank of International Settlements in Basel, Switzerland and the committee normally meets there.

The Basel Committee consists of representatives from central banks and regulatory authorities of the Group of Ten (economic) countries, plus others (specifically Luxembourg and Spain).

a. Private money
b. Basel Accord
c. Banking panic
d. Variable rate mortgage

15. In finance, _____ (or gearing) is borrowing money to supplement existing funds for investment in such a way that the potential positive or negative outcome is magnified and/or enhanced. It generally refers to using borrowed funds, or debt, so as to attempt to increase the returns to equity. Deleveraging is the action of reducing borrowings.

a. Pension fund
b. Financial endowment
c. Limited partnership
d. Leverage

16. In economics and finance, _____ is the practice of taking advantage of a price differential between two or more markets: striking a combination of matching deals that capitalize upon the imbalance, the profit being the difference between the market prices. When used by academics, an _____ is a transaction that involves no negative cash flow at any probabilistic or temporal state and a positive cash flow in at least one state; in simple terms, a risk-free profit.

a. Arbitrage
b. Initial margin
c. Issuer
d. Efficient-market hypothesis

17. A _____ is a financial contract whose value is derived from the value of something else (known as the underlying.) The underlying on which a _____ is based can be an asset, weather conditions bonds or other forms of credit.

a. 529 plan
b. 7-Eleven
c. Derivative
d. 4-4-5 Calendar

18. _____ is the discipline of identifying, monitoring and limiting risks. In some cases the acceptable risk may be near zero. Risks can come from accidents, natural causes and disasters as well as deliberate attacks from an adversary.

a. Penny stock
b. FIFO
c. 4-4-5 Calendar
d. Risk management

19. _____ is the provision of resources (such as granting a loan) by one party to another party where that second party does not reimburse the first party immediately, thereby generating a debt, and instead arranges either to repay or return those resources (or material(s) of equal value) at a later date. The first party is called a creditor, also known as a lender, while the second party is called a debtor, also known as a borrower.

Movements of financial capital are normally dependent on either _____ or equity transfers.

a. Comparable
b. Credit
c. Warrant
d. Clearing house

Chapter 18. Banking Regulation

20. The _____, a component of the Federal Reserve System, is charged under United States law with overseeing the nation's open market operations. It is the Federal Reserve Committee that makes key decisions about interest rates and the growth jam of the United States money supply. It is the principal organ of United States national monetary policy.
    a. Tax incidence
    b. Fiscal policy
    c. Federal Open Market Committee
    d. Tax exemption

21. The _____ is a United States federal law enacted as an amendment to the Truth in Lending Act (codified at 15 U.S.C. § 1601 et seq.). Its purpose is to protect consumers from unfair billing practices and to provide a mechanism for addressing billing errors in 'open end' credit accounts, such as credit card or charge card accounts.
    a. Truth in Lending Act
    b. Fair Credit Reporting Act
    c. Fair Credit Billing Act
    d. Regulation Q

22. The _____ is a stock exchange based in New York City, New York. It is the largest stock exchange in the world by dollar value of its listed companies securities. As of October 2008, the combined capitalization of all domestic _____ listed companies was $10.1 trillion.
    a. 529 plan
    b. New York Stock Exchange
    c. 4-4-5 Calendar
    d. 7-Eleven

23. A _____, securities exchange or (in Europe) bourse is a corporation or mutual organization which provides 'trading' facilities for stock brokers and traders, to trade stocks and other securities. _____s also provide facilities for the issue and redemption of securities as well as other financial instruments and capital events including the payment of income and dividends. The securities traded on a _____ include: shares issued by companies, unit trusts and other pooled investment products and bonds.
    a. 4-4-5 Calendar
    b. 7-Eleven
    c. Stock Exchange
    d. 529 plan

24. The _____ is a United States law (codified at 15 U.S.C. § 1691 et seq.), enacted in 1974, that makes it unlawful for any creditor to discriminate against any applicant, with respect to any aspect of a credit transaction, on the basis of race, color, religion, national origin, sex, marital status, or age (provided the applicant has the capacity to contract); to the fact that all or part of the applicant's income derives from a public assistance program; or to the fact that the applicant has in good faith exercised any right under the Consumer Credit Protection Act. The law applies to any person who, in the ordinary course of business, regularly participates in a credit decision, including banks, retailers, bankcard companies, finance companies, and credit unions.
    a. A Random Walk Down Wall Street
    b. ABN Amro
    c. AAB
    d. Equal Credit Opportunity Act

25. A _____ is an institution, firm or individual who mediates between two or more parties in a financial context. Typically the first party is a provider of a product or service and the second party is a consumer or customer.

In the U.S., a _____ is typically an institution that facilitates the channelling of funds between lenders and borrowers indirectly.

    a. Financial intermediary
    b. Net asset value
    c. Mutual fund
    d. Savings and loan association

Chapter 18. Banking Regulation

26. The _____ of 1933 established the Federal Deposit Insurance Corporation (FDIC) in the United States and included banking reforms, some of which were designed to control speculation. Some provisions such as Regulation Q, which allowed the Federal Reserve to regulate interest rates in savings accounts, were repealed by the Depository Institutions Deregulation and Monetary Control Act of 1980. Provisions that prohibit a bank holding company from owning other financial companies were repealed on November 12, 1999, by the Gramm-Leach-Bliley Act.

a. 4-4-5 Calendar
b. 529 plan
c. 7-Eleven
d. Glass-Steagall Act

27. A _____ is a fungible, negotiable instrument representing financial value. They are broadly categorized into debt securities (such as banknotes, bonds and debentures), and equity securities; e.g., common stocks. The company or other entity issuing the _____ is called the issuer.

a. Security
b. Book entry
c. Securities lending
d. Tracking stock

28.

A _____ is a type of financial intermediary and a type of bank. Commercial banking is also known as business banking. It is a bank that provides checking accounts, savings accounts, and money market accounts and that accepts time deposits.

a. Commercial bank
b. 7-Eleven
c. 4-4-5 Calendar
d. 529 plan

29. _____ is the removal or simplification of government rules and regulations that constrain the operation of market forces. _____ does not mean elimination of laws against fraud, but eliminating or reducing government control of how business is done, thereby moving toward a more free market.

The stated rationale for '_____' is often that fewer and simpler regulations will lead to a raised level of competitiveness, therefore higher productivity, more efficiency and lower prices overall.

a. Supply shock
b. Value added
c. Demand shock
d. Deregulation

30. The _____ of 1991, passed during the Savings and loan crisis, strengthened the power of the Federal Deposit Insurance Corporation.

It allowed the FDIC to borrow directly from the Treasury department and mandated that the FDIC resolve failed banks using the least-costly method available. It also ordered the FDIC to assess insurance premiums according to risk and created new capital requirements.

a. Covenant
b. Fair Debt Collection Practices Act
c. Federal Deposit Insurance Corporation Improvement Act
d. National Securities Markets Improvement Act of 1996

31. _____ is an insurance-related term that describes a splitting or spreading of risk among multiple parties.

In the US insurance market, _____ is the joint assumption of risk between the insurer and the insured. In title insurance it also means the sharing of risks between two or more title insurance companies.

a. 4-4-5 Calendar
c. 7-Eleven
b. 529 plan
d. Coinsurance

32. In finance, a _____ is a debt security, in which the authorized issuer owes the holders a debt and, depending on the terms of the _____, is obliged to pay interest (the coupon) and/or to repay the principal at a later date, termed maturity.

Thus a _____ is a loan: the issuer is the borrower, the _____ holder is the lender, and the coupon is the interest. _____s provide the borrower with external funds to finance long-term investments, or, in the case of government _____s, to finance current expenditure.

a. Convertible bond
c. Catastrophe bonds
b. Puttable bond
d. Bond

33. In business and finance, a _____ (also referred to as equity _____) of stock means a _____ of ownership in a corporation (company.) In the plural, stocks is often used as a synonym for _____s especially in the United States, but it is less commonly used that way outside of North America.

In the United Kingdom, South Africa, and Australia, stock can also refer to completely different financial instruments such as government bonds or, less commonly, to all kinds of marketable securities.

a. Margin
c. Procter ' Gamble
b. Bucket shop
d. Share

34. In financial accounting, the term _____ is most commonly used to describe any part of shareholders' equity, except for basic share capital. Sometimes, the term is used instead of the term provision; such a use, however, is inconsistent with the terminology suggested by International Accounting Standards Board. For more information about provisions, see provision (accounting.)

a. Treasury stock
c. FIFO and LIFO accounting
b. Reserve
d. Closing entries

Chapter 19. Insurance Companies and Pension Funds

1. A _____ is a pool of assets forming an independent legal entity that are bought with the contributions to a pension plan for the exclusive purpose of financing pension plan benefits.

   _____s are important shareholders of listed and private companies. They are especially important to the stock market where large institutional investors like the Ontario Teachers' Pension Plan dominate.

   a. Leverage
   b. Limited liability company
   c. Leveraged buyout
   d. Pension fund

2. A _____ is an institution, firm or individual who mediates between two or more parties in a financial context. Typically the first party is a provider of a product or service and the second party is a consumer or customer.

   In the U.S., a _____ is typically an institution that facilitates the channelling of funds between lenders and borrowers indirectly.

   a. Net asset value
   b. Mutual fund
   c. Savings and loan association
   d. Financial intermediary

3. The _____ is the guaranteed payoff at which a person is 'indifferent' between accepting the guaranteed payoff and a higher but uncertain payoff. (It is the amount of the higher payout minus the risk premium).
   a. 529 plan
   b. 7-Eleven
   c. 4-4-5 Calendar
   d. Certainty equivalent

4. In business, _____ is the total assets minus total outside liabilities of an individual or a company. For a company, this is called shareholders' equity and may be referred to as book value. _____ is stated as at a particular point in time.
   a. Restructuring
   b. Moneylender
   c. Certified International Investment Analyst
   d. Net worth

5. Unemployment occurs when a person is available to work and currently seeking work, but the person is without work. The prevalence of unemployment is usually measured using the _____, which is defined as the percentage of those in the labor force who are unemployed. The _____ is also used in economic studies and economic indexes such as the United States' Conference Board's Index of Leading Indicators as a measure of the state of the macroeconomics.
   a. Unemployment rate
   b. ABN Amro
   c. AAB
   d. A Random Walk Down Wall Street

6. A _____ is a professionally managed type of collective investment scheme that pools money from many investors and invests it in stocks, bonds, short-term money market instruments, and/or other securities. The _____ will have a fund manager that trades the pooled money on a regular basis. Currently, the worldwide value of all _____s totals more than $26 trillion.

   Since 1940, there have been three basic types of investment companies in the United States: open-end funds, also known in the US as _____s; unit investment trusts (UITs); and closed-end funds.

   a. Trust company
   b. Financial intermediary
   c. Net asset value
   d. Mutual fund

7. In business and accounting, _____s are everything of value that is owned by a person or company. The balance sheet of a firm records the monetary value of the _____s owned by the firm. The two major _____ classes are tangible _____s and intangible _____s.
   a. EBITDA
   b. Income
   c. Accounts payable
   d. Asset

8. _____ is a type of permanent life insurance based on a cash value. That is, the policy is established with the insurer where premium payments above the cost of insurance are credited to the cash value. The cash value is credited each month with interest, and the policy is debited each month by a cost of insurance (COI) charge, and any other policy charges and fees which are drawn from the cash value if no premium payment is made that month.
   a. A Random Walk Down Wall Street
   b. ABN Amro
   c. AAB
   d. Universal life

9. _____ is a life insurance policy that remains in force for the insured's whole life and requires (in most cases) premiums to be paid every year into the policy.

All life insurance was originally term insurance. However, because term life insurance only pays a claim upon death within the stated term, most term insurance policy holders became upset over the idea that they could be paying premiums for 20 or 30 years and then wind up with nothing to show for it.

   a. Term life insurance
   b. 529 plan
   c. Whole life insurance
   d. 4-4-5 Calendar

10. A _____ is a bond issued by a national government denominated in the country's own currency. Bonds issued by national governments in foreign currencies are normally referred to as sovereign bonds. The first ever _____ was issued by the British government in 1693 to raise money to fund a war against France.
    a. Zero-coupon bond
    b. Collateralized debt obligations
    c. Municipal bond
    d. Government bond

11. In finance, a _____ is a debt security, in which the authorized issuer owes the holders a debt and, depending on the terms of the _____, is obliged to pay interest (the coupon) and/or to repay the principal at a later date, termed maturity.

Thus a _____ is a loan: the issuer is the borrower, the _____ holder is the lender, and the coupon is the interest. _____s provide the borrower with external funds to finance long-term investments, or, in the case of government _____s, to finance current expenditure.

   a. Puttable bond
   b. Bond
   c. Convertible bond
   d. Catastrophe bonds

12. _____ provides protection against most risks to property, such as fire, theft and some weather damage. This includes specialized forms of insurance such as fire insurance, flood insurance, earthquake insurance, home insurance or boiler insurance. Property is insured in two main ways - open perils and named perils.
    a. 529 plan
    b. 4-4-5 Calendar
    c. Lenders Mortgage Insurance
    d. Property insurance

Chapter 19. Insurance Companies and Pension Funds

13. A _____, reserve bank, or monetary authority is the entity responsible for the monetary policy of a country or of a group of member states. It is a bank that can lend money to other banks in times of need. Its primary responsibility is to maintain the stability of the national currency and money supply, but more active duties include controlling subsidized-loan interest rates, and acting as a lender of last resort to the banking sector during times of financial crisis (private banks often being integral to the national financial system.)

   a. 7-Eleven   b. 4-4-5 Calendar
   c. 529 plan   d. Central bank

14. In business and finance, a _____ (also referred to as equity _____) of stock means a _____ of ownership in a corporation (company.) In the plural, stocks is often used as a synonym for _____s especially in the United States, but it is less commonly used that way outside of North America.

In the United Kingdom, South Africa, and Australia, stock can also refer to completely different financial instruments such as government bonds or, less commonly, to all kinds of marketable securities.

   a. Bucket shop   b. Procter ' Gamble
   c. Margin   d. Share

15. In business, _____ is income that a company receives from its normal business activities, usually from the sale of goods and services to customers. Some companies also receive _____ from interest, dividends or royalties paid to them by other companies. _____ may refer to business income in general, or it may refer to the amount, in a monetary unit, received during a period of time, as in 'Last year, Company X had _____ of $32 million.'

In many countries, including the UK, _____ is referred to as turnover.

   a. Matching principle   b. Furniture, Fixtures and Equipment
   c. Revenue   d. Bottom line

16. In finance, _____ is the process of estimating the potential market value of a financial asset or liability. they can be done on assets (for example, investments in marketable securities such as stocks, options, business enterprises, or intangible assets such as patents and trademarks) or on liabilities (e.g., Bonds issued by a company.) _____s are required in many contexts including investment analysis, capital budgeting, merger and acquisition transactions, financial reporting, taxable events to determine the proper tax liability, and in litigation.

   a. Procter ' Gamble   b. Share
   c. Margin   d. Valuation

17. In financial accounting, _____s are precautions for which the amount or probability of occurrence are not known. Typical examples are _____s for warranty costs and _____ for taxes the term reserve is used instead of term _____; such a use, however, is inconsistent with the terminology suggested by International Accounting Standards Board.

   a. Momentum Accounting and Triple-Entry Bookkeeping   b. Petty cash
   c. Provision   d. Money measurement concept

18. _____ is an insurance-related term that describes a splitting or spreading of risk among multiple parties.

In the US insurance market, _____ is the joint assumption of risk between the insurer and the insured. In title insurance it also means the sharing of risks between two or more title insurance companies.

a. 529 plan
c. 4-4-5 Calendar
b. 7-Eleven
d. Coinsurance

19. A _____ is a fungible, negotiable instrument representing financial value. They are broadly categorized into debt securities (such as banknotes, bonds and debentures), and equity securities; e.g., common stocks. The company or other entity issuing the _____ is called the issuer.
a. Tracking stock
c. Securities lending
b. Book entry
d. Security

20. _____ mature in one year or less. Like zero-coupon bonds, they do not pay interest prior to maturity; instead they are sold at a discount of the par value to create a positive yield to maturity. Many regard _____ as the least risky investment available to U.S. investors.
a. Treasury securities
c. 4-4-5 Calendar
b. Treasury Inflation Protected Securities
d. Treasury bills

21. An _____ is a contract written by a seller that conveys to the buyer the right -- but not the obligation -- to buy (in the case of a call _____) or to sell (in the case of a put _____) a particular asset, such as a piece of property such as, among others, a futures contract. In return for granting the _____, the seller collects a payment (the premium) from the buyer.

For example, buying a call _____ provides the right to buy a specified quantity of a security at a set strike price at some time on or before expiration, while buying a put _____ provides the right to sell.

a. AT'T Mobility LLC
c. Annuity
b. Amortization
d. Option

22. _____ is the incidence or process of transferring ownership of a business, enterprise, agency or public service from the public sector (government) to the private sector (business.) In a broader sense, _____ refers to transfer of any government function to the private sector including governmental functions like revenue collection and law enforcement.

The term '_____' also has been used to describe two unrelated transactions. The first is a buyout, by the majority owner, of all shares of a public corporation or holding company's stock, privatizing a publicly traded stock. The second is a demutualization of a mutual organization or cooperative to form a joint stock company.

a. 7-Eleven
c. 529 plan
b. 4-4-5 Calendar
d. Privatization

23. The institution most often referenced by the word '_____' is a public or publicly traded _____, the shares of which are traded on a public stock exchange (e.g., the New York Stock Exchange or Nasdaq in the United States) where shares of stock of _____s are bought and sold by and to the general public. Most of the largest businesses in the world are publicly traded _____s. However, the majority of _____s are said to be closely held, privately held or close _____s, meaning that no ready market exists for the trading of shares.

Chapter 19. Insurance Companies and Pension Funds

a. Depository Trust Company
c. Protect
b. Federal Home Loan Mortgage Corporation
d. Corporation

24. The _____ of 1974 (Pub.L. 93-406, 88 Stat. 829, enacted September 2, 1974) is an American federal statute that establishes minimum standards for pension plans in private industry and provides for extensive rules on the federal income tax effects of transactions associated with employee benefit plans.
   a. Articles of Partnership
   c. Employee Retirement Income Security Act
   b. Expedited Funds Availability Act
   d. Express warranty

25. _____, refers to consumption opportunity gained by an entity within a specified time frame, which is generally expressed in monetary terms. However, for households and individuals, '_____ is the sum of all the wages, salaries, profits, interests payments, rents and other forms of earnings received... in a given period of time.' For firms, _____ generally refers to net-profit: what remains of revenue after expenses have been subtracted.
   a. Annual report
   c. OIBDA
   b. Accrual
   d. Income

26. An _____ is a retirement plan account that provides some tax advantages for retirement savings in the United States.
   a. ABN Amro
   c. A Random Walk Down Wall Street
   b. AAB
   d. Individual Retirement Arrangement

27. _____s are full-fledged pension plans for self-employed people in the United States. They are sometimes called HR10 plans and are not Individual Retirement Accounts (IRA.)

Since a _____ is a full-fledged pension, there is a Keogh for every employer-sponsored pension-plan design.

   a. 529 plan
   c. 7-Eleven
   b. 4-4-5 Calendar
   d. Keogh plan

28. _____, in bookkeeping, refers to assets, liabilities, income, and expenses recorded on individual pages of the so called book of final entry or ledger. Changes in _____ value are made by chronologically posting debit (DR) and credit (CR) entries to its page. Examples of _____s are cash, _____s receivable, mortgages, loans, land and buildings, common stock, sales, services provided, wages, and payroll overhead.
   a. Accretion
   c. Option
   b. Alpha
   d. Account

Chapter 20. Venture Capital Firms, Finance Companies, and Financial Conglomerates

1. _____ is a type of private equity capital typically provided to early-stage, high-potential, growth companies in the interest of generating a return through an eventual realization event such as an IPO or trade sale of the company. _____ investments are generally made as cash in exchange for shares in the invested company. It is typical for _____ investors to identify and back companies in high technology industries such as biotechnology and ICT.
   - a. Tail risk
   - b. Probability distribution
   - c. Venture capital
   - d. Treasury Inflation-Protected Securities

2. A _____ is a financial crisis that occurs when many banks suffer runs at the same time. A systemic banking crisis is one where all or almost all of the banking capital in a country is wiped out. The resulting chain of bankruptcies can cause a long economic recession. Much of the Great Depression's economic damage was caused directly by bank runs. The cost of cleaning up a systemic banking crisis can be huge, with fiscal costs averaging 13% of GDP and economic output losses averaging 20% of GDP for important crises from 1970 to 2007.
   - a. Banking panic
   - b. Probability of default
   - c. Deposit insurance
   - d. Credit bureau

3. The _____ is based on common law stemming from the 1830 Massachusetts court decision - Harvard College v. Armory, 9 Pick. (26 Mass.)
   - a. Rule 144A
   - b. SIPC
   - c. Williams Act
   - d. Prudent man rule

4. The phrase _____ according to the Organization for Economic Co-operation and Development, refers to 'creative work undertaken on a systematic basis in order to increase the stock of knowledge, including knowledge of (hu)man, culture and society, and the use of this stock of knowledge to devise new applications'.

   New product design and development is more than often a crucial factor in the survival of a company. In an industry that is fast changing, firms must continually revise their design and range of products. This is necessary due to continuous technology change and development as well as other competitors and the changing preference of customers.

   - a. 529 plan
   - b. 4-4-5 Calendar
   - c. 7-Eleven
   - d. Research and Development

5. A _____ is a professionally managed type of collective investment scheme that pools money from many investors and invests it in stocks, bonds, short-term money market instruments, and/or other securities. The _____ will have a fund manager that trades the pooled money on a regular basis. Currently, the worldwide value of all _____s totals more than $26 trillion.

   Since 1940, there have been three basic types of investment companies in the United States: open-end funds, also known in the US as _____s; unit investment trusts (UITs); and closed-end funds.

   - a. Financial intermediary
   - b. Net asset value
   - c. Trust company
   - d. Mutual fund

6. In financial accounting, a _____ or statement of financial position is a summary of a person's or organization's balances. Assets, liabilities and ownership equity are listed as of a specific date, such as the end of its financial year. A _____ is often described as a snapshot of a company's financial condition.

Chapter 20. Venture Capital Firms, Finance Companies, and Financial Conglomerates 145

a. Statement on Auditing Standards No. 70: Service Organizations
b. Financial statements
c. Balance sheet
d. Statement of retained earnings

7. _____ is the provision of resources (such as granting a loan) by one party to another party where that second party does not reimburse the first party immediately, thereby generating a debt, and instead arranges either to repay or return those resources (or material(s) of equal value) at a later date. The first party is called a creditor, also known as a lender, while the second party is called a debtor, also known as a borrower.

Movements of financial capital are normally dependent on either _____ or equity transfers.

a. Warrant
b. Clearing house
c. Comparable
d. Credit

8. In finance, the _____ is the global financial market for short-term borrowing and lending. It provides short-term liquidity funding for the global financial system. The _____ is where short-term obligations such as Treasury bills, commercial paper and bankers' acceptances are bought and sold.
a. Cramdown
b. Debt-for-equity swap
c. Money market
d. Consumer debt

9. In economics, business, and accounting, a _____ is the value of money that has been used up to produce something, and hence is not available for use anymore. In business, the _____ may be one of acquisition, in which case the amount of money expended to acquire it is counted as _____. In this case, money is the input that is gone in order to acquire the thing.
a. Sliding scale fees
b. Fixed costs
c. Marginal cost
d. Cost

10. _____ or financing is to provide capital (funds), which means money for a project, a person, a business or any other private or public institutions.

Those funds can be allocated for either short term or long term purposes. The health fund is a new way of _____ private healthcare centers.

a. Product life cycle
b. Synthetic CDO
c. Funding
d. Proxy fight

11. A _____ is a fungible, negotiable instrument representing financial value. They are broadly categorized into debt securities (such as banknotes, bonds and debentures), and equity securities; e.g., common stocks. The company or other entity issuing the _____ is called the issuer.
a. Securities lending
b. Book entry
c. Tracking stock
d. Security

12. In finance, _____ occurs when a debtor has not met its legal obligations according to the debt contract, e.g. it has not made a scheduled payment, or has violated a loan covenant (condition) of the debt contract. _____ may occur if the debtor is either unwilling or unable to pay their debt. This can occur with all debt obligations including bonds, mortgages, loans, and promissory notes.

Chapter 20. Venture Capital Firms, Finance Companies, and Financial Conglomerates

a. Default
b. Vendor finance
c. Credit crunch
d. Debt validation

13. _____ is the risk of loss due to a debtor's non-payment of a loan or other line of credit (either the principal or interest (coupon) or both)

Most lenders employ their own models (credit scorecards) to rank potential and existing customers according to risk, and then apply appropriate strategies. With products such as unsecured personal loans or mortgages, lenders charge a higher price for higher risk customers and vice versa. With revolving products such as credit cards and overdrafts, risk is controlled through careful setting of credit limits.

a. Transaction risk
b. Liquidity risk
c. Credit risk
d. Market risk

14. _____ is a measure of the ability of a debtor to pay their debts as and when they fall due. It is usually expressed as a ratio or a percentage of current liabilities.

For a corporation with a published balance sheet there are various ratios used to calculate a measure of liquidity.

a. Accounting liquidity
b. Operating leverage
c. Invested capital
d. Operating profit margin

15. _____ is a term used to explain a difference between two types of financial securities (e.g. stocks), that have all the same qualities except liquidity. For example:

_____ is a segment of a three-part theory that works to explain the behavior of yield curves for interest rates. The upwards-curving component of the interest yield can be explained by the _____.

a. 529 plan
b. 7-Eleven
c. 4-4-5 Calendar
d. Liquidity premium

16. _____ is that which is owed; usually referencing assets owed, but the term can cover other obligations. In the case of assets, _____ is a means of using future purchasing power in the present before a summation has been earned. Some companies and corporations use _____ as a part of their overall corporate finance strategy.

a. Partial Payment
b. Credit cycle
c. Debt
d. Cross-collateralization

17. _____, in bookkeeping, refers to assets, liabilities, income, and expenses recorded on individual pages of the so called book of final entry or ledger. Changes in _____ value are made by chronologically posting debit (DR) and credit (CR) entries to its page. Examples of _____ s are cash, _____ s receivable, mortgages, loans, land and buildings, common stock, sales, services provided, wages, and payroll overhead.

a. Option
b. Alpha
c. Accretion
d. Account

Chapter 20. Venture Capital Firms, Finance Companies, and Financial Conglomerates 147

18. _____ is one of a series of accounting transactions dealing with the billing of customers who owe money to a person, company or organization for goods and services that have been provided to the customer. In most business entities this is typically done by generating an invoice and mailing or electronically delivering it to the customer, who in turn must pay it within an established timeframe called credit or payment terms.

An example of a common payment term is Net 30, meaning payment is due in the amount of the invoice 30 days from the date of invoice.

  a. Income
  b. Accounting methods
  c. Impaired asset
  d. Accounts receivable

19. _____ is a financial transaction whereby a business sells its accounts receivable (i.e., invoices) at a discount. _____ differs from a bank loan in three main ways. First, the emphasis is on the value of the receivables (essentially a financial asset), not the firm's credit worthiness.

  a. Debt-for-equity swap
  b. Credit card balance transfer
  c. Financial Literacy Month
  d. Factoring

20. _____ is a process by which a firm can obtain the use of a certain fixed assets for which it must pay a series of contractual, periodic, tax deductable payments. The lessee is the receiver of the services or the assets under the lease contract and the lessor is the owner of the assets. The relationship between the tenant and the landlord is called a tenancy, and can be for a fixed or an indefinite period of time (called the term of the lease).

  a. Leasing
  b. Quiet period
  c. Foreign Corrupt Practices Act
  d. Royalties

21. _____ is the value of a homeowner's unencumbered interest in their property, i.e. the difference between the home's fair market value and the unpaid balance of the mortgage and any outstanding debt over the home. _____ increases as the mortgage is paid or as the property enjoys appreciation. This is sometimes called real property value in economics.

  a. REIT
  b. Liquidation value
  c. Real Estate Investment Trust
  d. Home equity

22. The institution most often referenced by the word '_____' is a public or publicly traded _____, the shares of which are traded on a public stock exchange (e.g., the New York Stock Exchange or Nasdaq in the United States) where shares of stock of _____s are bought and sold by and to the general public. Most of the largest businesses in the world are publicly traded _____s. However, the majority of _____s are said to be closely held, privately held or close _____s, meaning that no ready market exists for the trading of shares.

  a. Depository Trust Company
  b. Federal Home Loan Mortgage Corporation
  c. Protect
  d. Corporation

23. _____ is a legally declared inability or impairment of ability of an individual or organization to pay their creditors. Creditors may file a _____ petition against a debtor ('involuntary _____') in an effort to recoup a portion of what they are owed or initiate a restructuring. In the majority of cases, however, _____ is initiated by the debtor (a 'voluntary _____' that is filed by the bankrupt individual or organization.)

  a. Debt settlement
  b. 4-4-5 Calendar
  c. 529 plan
  d. Bankruptcy

Chapter 20. Venture Capital Firms, Finance Companies, and Financial Conglomerates

24. The _____, a component of the Federal Reserve System, is charged under United States law with overseeing the nation's open market operations. It is the Federal Reserve Committee that makes key decisions about interest rates and the growth jam of the United States money supply. It is the principal organ of United States national monetary policy.
   a. Fiscal policy
   b. Tax exemption
   c. Tax incidence
   d. Federal Open Market Committee

25. In business and accounting, _____s are everything of value that is owned by a person or company. The balance sheet of a firm records the monetary value of the _____s owned by the firm. The two major _____ classes are tangible _____s and intangible _____s.
   a. Income
   b. Accounts payable
   c. Asset
   d. EBITDA

26. In financial accounting, the term _____ is most commonly used to describe any part of shareholders' equity, except for basic share capital. Sometimes, the term is used instead of the term provision; such a use, however, is inconsistent with the terminology suggested by International Accounting Standards Board. For more information about provisions, see provision (accounting.)
   a. FIFO and LIFO accounting
   b. Closing entries
   c. Treasury stock
   d. Reserve

27. In United States banking, _____ is a marketing term for certain services offered primarily to larger business customers. It may be used to describe all bank accounts (such as checking accounts) provided to businesses of a certain size, but it is more often used to describe specific services such as cash concentration, zero balance accounting, and automated clearing house facilities. Sometimes, private banking customers are given _____ services.
   a. Global tactical asset allocation
   b. Cash management
   c. Capitalization rate
   d. Profitability index

28. _____, in microeconomics, are the cost advantages that a business obtains due to expansion. _____ may be utilized by any size firm expanding its scale of operation.
   a. Uniform Commercial Code
   b. Employee Retirement Income Security Act
   c. Articles of incorporation
   d. Economies of scale

Chapter 21. Investment Banks, Brokerage Firms, and Mutual Funds   149

1. In finance, a _____ is a debt security, in which the authorized issuer owes the holders a debt and, depending on the terms of the _____, is obliged to pay interest (the coupon) and/or to repay the principal at a later date, termed maturity.

Thus a _____ is a loan: the issuer is the borrower, the _____ holder is the lender, and the coupon is the interest. _____s provide the borrower with external funds to finance long-term investments, or, in the case of government _____s, to finance current expenditure.

a. Convertible bond
c. Puttable bond
b. Catastrophe bonds
d. Bond

2. The _____ is a financial market where participants buy and sell debt securities, usually in the form of bonds. As of 2006, the size of the international _____ is an estimated $45 trillion, of which the size of the outstanding U.S. _____ debt was $25.2 trillion.

Nearly all of the $923 billion average daily trading volume in the U.S. _____ takes place between broker-dealers and large institutions in a decentralized, over-the-counter market.

a. Fixed income
c. 529 plan
b. Bond market
d. 4-4-5 Calendar

3. In economics, a _____ is a mechanism that allows people to easily buy and sell (trade) financial securities (such as stocks and bonds), commodities (such as precious metals or agricultural goods), and other fungible items of value at low transaction costs and at prices that reflect the efficient-market hypothesis.

_____s have evolved significantly over several hundred years and are undergoing constant innovation to improve liquidity.

Both general markets (where many commodities are traded) and specialized markets (where only one commodity is traded) exist.

a. Delta hedging
c. Cost of carry
b. Secondary market
d. Financial market

4. The _____ is that part of the capital markets that deals with the issuance of new securities. Companies, governments or public sector institutions can obtain funding through the sale of a new stock or bond issue. This is typically done through a syndicate of securities dealers.

a. Primary market
c. Peer group analysis
b. Sector rotation
d. Volatility clustering

5. The _____ is the financial market where previously issued securities and financial instruments such as stock, bonds, options, and futures are bought and sold. The term '_____' is also used refer to the market for any used goods or assets, or an alternative use for an existing product or asset where the customer base is the second market

With primary issuances of securities or financial instruments, or the primary market, investors purchase these securities directly from issuers such as corporations issuing shares in an IPO or private placement, or directly from the federal government in the case of treasuries.

Chapter 21. Investment Banks, Brokerage Firms, and Mutual Funds

a. Financial market
b. Delta neutral
c. Performance attribution
d. Secondary market

6. A _____ is a fungible, negotiable instrument representing financial value. They are broadly categorized into debt securities (such as banknotes, bonds and debentures), and equity securities; e.g., common stocks. The company or other entity issuing the _____ is called the issuer.

a. Book entry
b. Securities lending
c. Tracking stock
d. Security

7. A _____ is a private or public market for the trading of company stock and derivatives of company stock at an agreed price; these are securities listed on a stock exchange as well as those only traded privately.

The size of the world _____ is estimated at about $36.6 trillion US at the beginning of October 2008 . The world derivatives market has been estimated at about $480 trillion face or nominal value, 12 times the size of the entire world economy.

a. Anton Gelonkin
b. Andrew Tobias
c. Adolph Coors
d. Stock market

8. The _____ of 1933 established the Federal Deposit Insurance Corporation (FDIC) in the United States and included banking reforms, some of which were designed to control speculation. Some provisions such as Regulation Q, which allowed the Federal Reserve to regulate interest rates in savings accounts, were repealed by the Depository Institutions Deregulation and Monetary Control Act of 1980. Provisions that prohibit a bank holding company from owning other financial companies were repealed on November 12, 1999, by the Gramm-Leach-Bliley Act.

a. 529 plan
b. 7-Eleven
c. 4-4-5 Calendar
d. Glass-Steagall Act

9.

A _____ is a type of financial intermediary and a type of bank. Commercial banking is also known as business banking. It is a bank that provides checking accounts, savings accounts, and money market accounts and that accepts time deposits.

a. 7-Eleven
b. 529 plan
c. Commercial bank
d. 4-4-5 Calendar

10. A _____ is a financial contract whose value is derived from the value of something else (known as the underlying.) The underlying on which a _____ is based can be an asset, weather conditions bonds or other forms of credit.

a. 4-4-5 Calendar
b. 7-Eleven
c. Derivative
d. 529 plan

11. _____, is when a company issues common stock or shares to the public for the first time. They are often issued by smaller, younger companies seeking capital to expand, but can also be done by large privately-owned companies looking to become publicly traded.

Chapter 21. Investment Banks, Brokerage Firms, and Mutual Funds   151

In an _____ the issuer may obtain the assistance of an underwriting firm, which helps it determine what type of security to issue (common or preferred), best offering price and time to bring it to market.

a. Interest
b. Asian Financial Crisis
c. Insolvency
d. Initial public offering

12. Congress enacted the _____, in the aftermath of the stock market crash of 1929 and during the ensuing Great Depression. It requires that any offer or sale of securities using the means and instrumentalities of interstate commerce be registered pursuant to the 1933 Act, unless an exemption from registration exists under the law.

a. Securities Act of 1933
b. 7-Eleven
c. 4-4-5 Calendar
d. 529 plan

13. The U.S. _____ is an independent agency of the United States government which holds primary responsibility for enforcing the federal securities laws and regulating the securities industry, the nation's stock and options exchanges, and other electronic securities markets. The SEC was created by section 4 of the SEC of 1934 (now codified as 15 U.S.C. § 78d and commonly referred to as the 1934 Act.)

a. Securities and Exchange Commission
b. 529 plan
c. 4-4-5 Calendar
d. 7-Eleven

14. A _____, reserve bank, or monetary authority is the entity responsible for the monetary policy of a country or of a group of member states. It is a bank that can lend money to other banks in times of need. Its primary responsibility is to maintain the stability of the national currency and money supply, but more active duties include controlling subsidized-loan interest rates, and acting as a lender of last resort to the banking sector during times of financial crisis (private banks often being integral to the national financial system.)

a. 7-Eleven
b. 529 plan
c. 4-4-5 Calendar
d. Central bank

15. In the United States, a _____ is an offering of securities that are not registered with the Securities and Exchange Commission (SEC.) Such offerings exploit an exemption offered by the Securities Act of 1933 that comes with several restrictions, including a prohibition against general solicitation. This exemption allows companies to avoid quarterly reporting requirements and many of the legal liabilities associated with the Sarbanes-Oxley Act.

a. 4-4-5 Calendar
b. 7-Eleven
c. 529 plan
d. Private placement

16. _____ is a term used for a number of concepts involving either the performance of an investigation of a business or person, or the performance of an act with a certain standard of care. It can be a legal obligation, but the term will more commonly apply to voluntary investigations. A common example of _____ in various industries is the process through which a potential acquirer evaluates a target company or its assets for acquisition.

a. Due diligence
b. Down payment
c. Bond indenture
d. Quiet period

17. The phrase _____ refers to the aspect of corporate strategy, corporate finance and management dealing with the buying, selling and combining of different companies that can aid, finance, or help a growing company in a given industry grow rapidly without having to create another business entity.

An acquisition, also known as a takeover, is the buying of one company (the 'target') by another. An acquisition may be friendly or hostile.

a. 7-Eleven
b. 4-4-5 Calendar
c. 529 plan
d. Mergers and acquisitions

18. A _____ is the highest price that a buyer (i.e., bidder) is willing to pay for a good. It is usually referred to simply as the 'bid.'

In bid and ask, the _____ stands in contrast to the ask price or 'offer', and the difference between the two is called the bid/ask spread.

An unsolicited bid or offer is when a person or company receives a bid even though they are not looking to sell.

a. Political risk
b. Mid price
c. Settlement date
d. Bid price

19. In finance, _____ refers to Monday, October 19, 1987, when stock markets around the world crashed, shedding a huge value in a very short time. The crash began in Hong Kong, spread west through international time zones to Europe, hitting the United States after other markets had already declined by a significant margin. The Dow Jones Industrial Average (DJIA) dropped by 508 points to 1738.74 (22.61%).

a. 529 plan
b. Black Monday
c. 4-4-5 Calendar
d. 7-Eleven

20. The _____ was a worldwide economic downturn starting in most places in 1929 and ending at different times in the 1930s or early 1940s for different countries. It was the largest and most important economic depression in the 20th century, and is used in the 21st century as an example of how far the world's economy can fall. The _____ originated in the United States; historians most often use as a starting date the stock market crash on October 29, 1929, known as Black Tuesday.

a. 529 plan
b. 7-Eleven
c. Great Depression
d. 4-4-5 Calendar

21. In finance, a _____ (non-investment grade bond, speculative grade bond or junk bond) is a bond that is rated below investment grade at the time of purchase. These bonds have a higher risk of default or other adverse credit events, but typically pay higher yields than better quality bonds in order to make them attractive to investors.

a. Volatility
b. Private equity
c. Sharpe ratio
d. High yield bond

22. A _____ is a buy or sell order to be executed by the broker immediately at current market prices. As long as there are willing sellers and buyers, _____s are filled.

A _____ is the simplest of the order types.

Chapter 21. Investment Banks, Brokerage Firms, and Mutual Funds 153

a. Trading curb
c. Stockholder

b. Block premium
d. Market order

23. A _____ is a sudden dramatic decline of stock prices across a significant cross-section of a stock market. Crashes are driven by panic as much as by underlying economic factors. They often follow speculative stock market bubbles.

a. 7-Eleven
c. 529 plan

b. 4-4-5 Calendar
d. Stock market crash

24. _____ is the provision of resources (such as granting a loan) by one party to another party where that second party does not reimburse the first party immediately, thereby generating a debt, and instead arranges either to repay or return those resources (or material(s) of equal value) at a later date. The first party is called a creditor, also known as a lender, while the second party is called a debtor, also known as a borrower.

Movements of financial capital are normally dependent on either _____ or equity transfers.

a. Comparable
c. Warrant

b. Credit
d. Clearing house

25. A _____ is an order to buy a security at no more (or sell at no less) than a specific price. This gives the customer some control over the price at which the trade is executed, but may prevent the order from being executed ('filled'.)

A buy _____ can only be executed by the broker at the limit price or lower.

a. Block premium
c. Limit order

b. Commercial mortgage-backed securities
d. Common stock

26. In finance, a _____ is collateral that the holder of a position in securities, options, or futures contracts has to deposit to cover the credit risk of his counterparty (most often his broker.) This risk can arise if the holder has done any of the following:

- borrowed cash from the counterparty to buy securities or options,
- sold securities or options short, or
- entered into a futures contract.

The collateral can be in the form of cash or securities, and it is deposited in a _____ account. On U.S. futures exchanges, '_____' was formally called performance bond.

_____ buying is buying securities with cash borrowed from a broker, using other securities as collateral.

a. Credit
c. Procter ' Gamble

b. Margin
d. Share

27. In business and finance, a _____ (also referred to as equity _____) of stock means a _____ of ownership in a corporation (company.) In the plural, stocks is often used as a synonym for _____s especially in the United States, but it is less commonly used that way outside of North America.

In the United Kingdom, South Africa, and Australia, stock can also refer to completely different financial instruments such as government bonds or, less commonly, to all kinds of marketable securities.

a. Margin
b. Bucket shop
c. Procter ' Gamble
d. Share

28. In United States banking, _____ is a marketing term for certain services offered primarily to larger business customers. It may be used to describe all bank accounts (such as checking accounts) provided to businesses of a certain size, but it is more often used to describe specific services such as cash concentration, zero balance accounting, and automated clearing house facilities. Sometimes, private banking customers are given _____ services.

a. Cash management
b. Capitalization rate
c. Global tactical asset allocation
d. Profitability index

29. _____, in bookkeeping, refers to assets, liabilities, income, and expenses recorded on individual pages of the so called book of final entry or ledger. Changes in _____ value are made by chronologically posting debit (DR) and credit (CR) entries to its page. Examples of _____s are cash, _____s receivable, mortgages, loans, land and buildings, common stock, sales, services provided, wages, and payroll overhead.

a. Option
b. Account
c. Alpha
d. Accretion

30. A '_____' is a 'Charge' that is paid to obtain the right to delay a payment. Essentially, the payer purchases the right to make a given payment in the future instead of in the Present. The '_____', or 'Charge' that must be paid to delay the payment, is simply the difference between what the payment amount would be if it were paid in the present and what the payment amount would be paid if it were paid in the future.

a. Value at risk
b. Risk aversion
c. Discount
d. Risk modeling

31. In the United States, the Financial Industry Regulatory Authority (FINRA) is a self-regulatory organization (SRO) under the Securities Exchange Act of 1934, successor to the _____, Inc.

FINRA is responsible for regulatory oversight of all securities firms that do business with the public; professional training, testing and licensing of registered persons; arbitration and mediation; market regulation by contract for The NASDAQ Stock Market, Inc., the American Stock Exchange LLC, and the International Securities Exchange, LLC; and industry utilities, such as Trade Reporting Facilities and other over-the-counter operations.

a. 7-Eleven
b. 529 plan
c. National Association of Securities Dealers
d. 4-4-5 Calendar

32. '_____' is a 1970 paper by the economist George Akerlof. It discusses information asymmetry, which occurs when the seller knows more about a product than the buyer. Akerlof, Michael Spence, and Joseph Stiglitz jointly received the Nobel Memorial Prize in Economic Sciences in 2001 for their research related to asymmetric information.

a. 529 plan
b. The Market for Lemons: Quality Uncertainty and the Market Mechanism
c. 7-Eleven
d. 4-4-5 Calendar

Chapter 21. Investment Banks, Brokerage Firms, and Mutual Funds 155

33. A _____ is a firm that quotes both a buy and a sell price in a financial instrument or commodity, hoping to make a profit on the bid/offer spread, or turn.

In foreign exchange trading, where most deals are conducted over-the-counter and are, therefore, completely virtual, the _____ sells to and buys from its clients. Hence, the client's loss and the spread is the _____ firm's profit, which gets thus compensated for the effort of providing liquidity in a competitive market.

a. 7-Eleven
b. 4-4-5 Calendar
c. 529 plan
d. Market maker

34. A _____ is a financial crisis that occurs when many banks suffer runs at the same time. A systemic banking crisis is one where all or almost all of the banking capital in a country is wiped out. The resulting chain of bankruptcies can cause a long economic recession. Much of the Great Depression's economic damage was caused directly by bank runs. The cost of cleaning up a systemic banking crisis can be huge, with fiscal costs averaging 13% of GDP and economic output losses averaging 20% of GDP for important crises from 1970 to 2007.

a. Deposit insurance
b. Credit bureau
c. Probability of default
d. Banking panic

35. The institution most often referenced by the word '_____' is a public or publicly traded _____, the shares of which are traded on a public stock exchange (e.g., the New York Stock Exchange or Nasdaq in the United States) where shares of stock of _____s are bought and sold by and to the general public. Most of the largest businesses in the world are publicly traded _____s. However, the majority of _____s are said to be closely held, privately held or close _____s, meaning that no ready market exists for the trading of shares.

a. Depository Trust Company
b. Corporation
c. Federal Home Loan Mortgage Corporation
d. Protect

36. A _____ is a professionally managed type of collective investment scheme that pools money from many investors and invests it in stocks, bonds, short-term money market instruments, and/or other securities. The _____ will have a fund manager that trades the pooled money on a regular basis. Currently, the worldwide value of all _____s totals more than $26 trillion.

Since 1940, there have been three basic types of investment companies in the United States: open-end funds, also known in the US as _____s; unit investment trusts (UITs); and closed-end funds.

a. Net asset value
b. Financial intermediary
c. Mutual fund
d. Trust company

37. The _____ is a federally mandated non-profit corporation in the United States that protects securities investors from harm if a broker-dealer company fails. Investors are not insured for any potential loss while invested in the market.

Congress created _____ in 1970 through the Securities Investor Protection Act (15 U.S.C.

a. Securities Investor Protection Corporation
b. SIPC
c. Rule 144A
d. Prudent man rule

Chapter 21. Investment Banks, Brokerage Firms, and Mutual Funds

38. _____ is that which is owed; usually referencing assets owed, but the term can cover other obligations. In the case of assets, _____ is a means of using future purchasing power in the present before a summation has been earned. Some companies and corporations use _____ as a part of their overall corporate finance strategy.
   a. Cross-collateralization
   b. Credit cycle
   c. Partial Payment
   d. Debt

39. An _____ or index tracker is a collective investment scheme (usually a mutual fund or exchange-traded fund) that aims to replicate the movements of an index of a specific financial market regardless of market conditions.

   Tracking can be achieved by trying to hold all of the securities in the index, in the same proportions as the index. Other methods include statistically sampling the market and holding 'representative' securities.

   a. AAB
   b. Investment company
   c. A Random Walk Down Wall Street
   d. Index fund

40. _____ is a term used to describe the value of an entity's assets less the value of its liabilities. The term is commonly used in relation to collective investment schemes. It may also be used as a synonym for the book value of a firm.
   a. Passive management
   b. Retail broker
   c. Net asset value
   d. Financial intermediary

41. In business and accounting, _____s are everything of value that is owned by a person or company. The balance sheet of a firm records the monetary value of the _____s owned by the firm. The two major _____ classes are tangible _____s and intangible _____s.
   a. EBITDA
   b. Accounts payable
   c. Income
   d. Asset

42. _____ are sometimes the same as net worth, or shareholders' equity - assets minus liabilities. The term _____ is commonly used with charities or not for profit entities. Although these entities don't make money, it is important to maintain reasonable reserves to help future growth.
   a. Cash conversion cycle
   b. Sharpe ratio
   c. Net assets
   d. Sustainable growth rate

43. In economic models, the _____ time frame assumes no fixed factors of production. Firms can enter or leave the marketplace, and the cost (and availability) of land, labor, raw materials, and capital goods can be assumed to vary. In contrast, in the short-run time frame, certain factors are assumed to be fixed, because there is not sufficient time for them to change.
   a. 4-4-5 Calendar
   b. 529 plan
   c. Short-run
   d. Long-run

44. An _____ is a company whose main business is holding securities of other companies purely for investment purposes. The _____ invests money on behalf of its shareholders who in turn share in the profits and losses.
   a. Investment Company
   b. A Random Walk Down Wall Street
   c. Unit investment trust
   d. AAB

Chapter 21. Investment Banks, Brokerage Firms, and Mutual Funds

45. The _____ of 1934 is a law governing the secondary trading of securities (stocks, bonds, and debentures) in the United States of America. The Act, 48 Stat. 881 (enacted June 6, 1934), codified at 15 U.S.C. §78a et seq., was a sweeping piece of legislation. The Act and related statutes form the basis of regulation of the financial markets and their participants in the United States.
   a. 529 plan
   b. Securities Exchange Act
   c. 7-Eleven
   d. 4-4-5 Calendar

46. In finance, a _____ is a position established in one market in an attempt to offset exposure to the price risk of an equal but opposite obligation or position in another market -- usually, but not always, in the context of one's commercial activity. Hedging is a strategy designed to minimize exposure to such business risks as a sharp contraction in demand for one's inventory, while still allowing the business to profit from producing and maintaining that inventory. A typical hedger might be a farmer with 2000 acres of unharvested wheat in the ground, who would rather tend his crop without the distraction of uncertain prices.
   a. 7-Eleven
   b. 529 plan
   c. 4-4-5 Calendar
   d. Hedge

47. A _____ is a private investment fund open to a limited range of investors that is permitted by regulators to undertake a wider range of activities than other investment funds and also pays a performance fee to its investment manager. Each fund will have its own strategy which determines the type of investments and the methods of investment it undertakes. _____s as a class invest in a broad range of investments extending over shares, debt, commodities and beyond.
   a. 529 plan
   b. 7-Eleven
   c. 4-4-5 Calendar
   d. Hedge fund

48. An _____ is a retirement plan account that provides some tax advantages for retirement savings in the United States.
   a. AAB
   b. A Random Walk Down Wall Street
   c. Individual Retirement Arrangement
   d. ABN Amro

49. The _____ , a component of the Federal Reserve System, is charged under United States law with overseeing the nation's open market operations. It is the Federal Reserve Committee that makes key decisions about interest rates and the growth jam of the United States money supply. It is the principal organ of United States national monetary policy.
   a. Tax exemption
   b. Tax incidence
   c. Fiscal policy
   d. Federal Open Market Committee

Chapter 22. Risk Management in Financial Institutions

1. _____ is the provision of resources (such as granting a loan) by one party to another party where that second party does not reimburse the first party immediately, thereby generating a debt, and instead arranges either to repay or return those resources (or material(s) of equal value) at a later date. The first party is called a creditor, also known as a lender, while the second party is called a debtor, also known as a borrower.

Movements of financial capital are normally dependent on either _____ or equity transfers.

a. Warrant
c. Comparable
b. Clearing house
d. Credit

2. _____ is the risk of loss due to a debtor's non-payment of a loan or other line of credit (either the principal or interest (coupon) or both)

Most lenders employ their own models (credit scorecards) to rank potential and existing customers according to risk, and then apply appropriate strategies. With products such as unsecured personal loans or mortgages, lenders charge a higher price for higher risk customers and vice versa. With revolving products such as credit cards and overdrafts, risk is controlled through careful setting of credit limits.

a. Transaction risk
c. Liquidity risk
b. Market risk
d. Credit risk

3. _____ is the discipline of identifying, monitoring and limiting risks. In some cases the acceptable risk may be near zero. Risks can come from accidents, natural causes and disasters as well as deliberate attacks from an adversary.

a. Risk management
c. 4-4-5 Calendar
b. Penny stock
d. FIFO

4. In business and accounting, _____s are everything of value that is owned by a person or company. The balance sheet of a firm records the monetary value of the _____s owned by the firm. The two major _____ classes are tangible _____s and intangible _____s.

a. Asset
c. EBITDA
b. Income
d. Accounts payable

5. In finance, _____ is the process of estimating the potential market value of a financial asset or liability. they can be done on assets (for example, investments in marketable securities such as stocks, options, business enterprises, or intangible assets such as patents and trademarks) or on liabilities (e.g., Bonds issued by a company.) _____s are required in many contexts including investment analysis, capital budgeting, merger and acquisition transactions, financial reporting, taxable events to determine the proper tax liability, and in litigation.

a. Valuation
c. Share
b. Margin
d. Procter ' Gamble

6. In economics and contract theory, _____ deals with the study of decisions in transactions where one party has more or better information than the other. This creates an imbalance of power in transactions which can sometimes cause the transactions to go awry. Examples of this problem are adverse selection and moral hazard.

a. AAB
c. A Random Walk Down Wall Street
b. ABN Amro
d. Information asymmetry

Chapter 22. Risk Management in Financial Institutions

7. In business, _____ is the total assets minus total outside liabilities of an individual or a company. For a company, this is called shareholders' equity and may be referred to as book value. _____ is stated as at a particular point in time.
   a. Restructuring
   b. Net worth
   c. Moneylender
   d. Certified International Investment Analyst

8. In economic models, the _____ time frame assumes no fixed factors of production. Firms can enter or leave the marketplace, and the cost (and availability) of land, labor, raw materials, and capital goods can be assumed to vary. In contrast, in the short-run time frame, certain factors are assumed to be fixed, because there is not sufficient time for them to change.
   a. Long-run
   b. Short-run
   c. 529 plan
   d. 4-4-5 Calendar

9. In lending agreements, _____ is a borrower's pledge of specific property to a lender, to secure repayment of a loan. The _____ serves as protection for a lender against a borrower's risk of default - that is, a borrower failing to pay the principal and interest under the terms of a loan obligation. If a borrower does default on a loan (due to insolvency or other event), that borrower forfeits (gives up) the property pledged as _____ *ollateral* - and the lender then becomes the owner of the _____.
   a. Nominal value
   b. Future-oriented
   c. Refinancing risk
   d. Collateral

10. _____, refers to consumption opportunity gained by an entity within a specified time frame, which is generally expressed in monetary terms. However, for households and individuals, '_____ is the sum of all the wages, salaries, profits, interests payments, rents and other forms of earnings received... in a given period of time.' For firms, _____ generally refers to net-profit: what remains of revenue after expenses have been subtracted.
    a. Accrual
    b. OIBDA
    c. Annual report
    d. Income

11. In finance, the _____ of a financial asset measures the sensitivity of the asset's price to interest rate movements, expressed as a number of years. The reason for expressing this sensitivity in years is that the time that will elapse until a cash flow is received allows more interest to accumulate. Therefore the price of an asset with long term cashflows has more interest rate sensitivity than an asset with cashflows in the near future.
    a. Yield to maturity
    b. Macaulay duration
    c. 4-4-5 Calendar
    d. Duration

12. The _____ is a financial and accounting term for the difference between the duration of assets and liabilities, and is typically used by banks, pension funds, or other financial institutions to measure their risk due to changes in the interest rate. This is one of the mismatches that can occur and are known as asset liability mismatches. Another way to define _____ is : it is the difference in the sensitivity of interest-yielding assets and the sensitivity of liabilities (of the organization) to a change in market interest rates (yields.)
    a. Debt cash flow
    b. Modern portfolio theory
    c. Net worth
    d. Duration gap

Chapter 23. Hedging with Financial Derivatives

1. The _____ was a worldwide economic downturn starting in most places in 1929 and ending at different times in the 1930s or early 1940s for different countries. It was the largest and most important economic depression in the 20th century, and is used in the 21st century as an example of how far the world's economy can fall. The _____ originated in the United States; historians most often use as a starting date the stock market crash on October 29, 1929, known as Black Tuesday.
   - a. Great Depression
   - b. 4-4-5 Calendar
   - c. 529 plan
   - d. 7-Eleven

2. In finance, a _____ in a security, such as a stock or a bond means the holder of the position owns the security and will profit if the price of the security goes up.

   Similarly, a _____ in a futures contract or similar derivative, means the holder of the position will profit if the price of the underlying security goes up. Going long is the more conventional practice of investing and is contrasted with going short

   - Short (finance)

   - a. Delta hedging
   - b. Central Securities Depository
   - c. Forward market
   - d. Long position

3. Days to Cover (DTC) is a numerical term that describes the relationship between the amount of shares in a given equity that have been short sold and the number of days of typical trading that it would require to 'cover' all _____ outstanding. For example, if there are ten million shares of XYZ Inc. that are currently short sold and the average daily volume of XYZ shares traded each day is one million, it would require ten days of trading for all _____ to be covered (10 million / 1 million.)
   - a. Cash budget
   - b. Guaranteed investment contracts
   - c. Short positions
   - d. Stock or scrip dividends

4. A _____ is a financial contract whose value is derived from the value of something else (known as the underlying.) The underlying on which a _____ is based can be an asset, weather conditions bonds or other forms of credit.
   - a. 4-4-5 Calendar
   - b. Derivative
   - c. 7-Eleven
   - d. 529 plan

5. A _____ is an agreement between two parties to buy or sell an asset at a specified point of time in the future. The price of the underlying instrument, in whatever form, is paid before control of the instrument changes. This is one of the many forms of buy/sell orders where the time of trade is not the time where the securities themselves are exchanged.
   - a. Derivatives markets
   - b. Forward contract
   - c. Constant maturity credit default swap
   - d. Loan Credit Default Swap Index

6. A _____ is an exchange of promises between two or more parties to do an act which is enforceable in a court of law. It is where an unqualified offer meets a qualified acceptance and the parties reach Consensus ad Idem. The parties must have the necessary capacity to _____ and the _____ must not be either trifling, indeterminate, impossible or illegal.
   - a. 529 plan
   - b. 4-4-5 Calendar
   - c. 7-Eleven
   - d. Contract

Chapter 23. Hedging with Financial Derivatives

7. In finance, _____ occurs when a debtor has not met its legal obligations according to the debt contract, e.g. it has not made a scheduled payment, or has violated a loan covenant (condition) of the debt contract. _____ may occur if the debtor is either unwilling or unable to pay their debt. This can occur with all debt obligations including bonds, mortgages, loans, and promissory notes.
   a. Debt validation
   b. Credit crunch
   c. Vendor finance
   d. Default

8. _____ is the risk of loss due to a debtor's non-payment of a loan or other line of credit (either the principal or interest (coupon) or both)

Most lenders employ their own models (credit scorecards) to rank potential and existing customers according to risk, and then apply appropriate strategies. With products such as unsecured personal loans or mortgages, lenders charge a higher price for higher risk customers and vice versa. With revolving products such as credit cards and overdrafts, risk is controlled through careful setting of credit limits.

   a. Liquidity risk
   b. Transaction risk
   c. Credit risk
   d. Market risk

9. _____ is a measure of the ability of a debtor to pay their debts as and when they fall due. It is usually expressed as a ratio or a percentage of current liabilities.

For a corporation with a published balance sheet there are various ratios used to calculate a measure of liquidity.

   a. Operating leverage
   b. Accounting liquidity
   c. Invested capital
   d. Operating profit margin

10. The _____ is the over-the-counter financial market in contracts for future delivery, so called forward contracts. Forward contracts are personalized between parties. The _____ is a general term used to describe the informal market by which these contracts are entered into.
   a. Forward market
   b. Limits to arbitrage
   c. Delta hedging
   d. Spot rate

11. _____ is that which is owed; usually referencing assets owed, but the term can cover other obligations. In the case of assets, _____ is a means of using future purchasing power in the present before a summation has been earned. Some companies and corporations use _____ as a part of their overall corporate finance strategy.
   a. Debt
   b. Cross-collateralization
   c. Partial Payment
   d. Credit cycle

12. A _____ is a futures contract on a short term interest rate (STIR.) Contracts vary, but are often defined on an interest rate index such as 3-month sterling or US dollar LIBOR.

They are traded across a wide range of currencies, including the G12 country currencies and many others.

   a. Real estate derivatives
   b. Financial future
   c. Notional amount
   d. Dual currency deposit

13. _____ are government bonds issued by the United States Department of the Treasury through the Bureau of the Public Debt. They are the debt financing instruments of the U.S. Federal government, and they are often referred to simply as Treasuries or Treasurys. There are four types of marketable _____: Treasury bills, Treasury notes, Treasury bonds, and Treasury Inflation Protected Securities (TIPS.)

   a. Treasury securities   b. Treasury Inflation-Protected Securities
   c. Treasury Inflation Protected Securities   d. 4-4-5 Calendar

14. In finance, a _____ is a debt security, in which the authorized issuer owes the holders a debt and, depending on the terms of the _____, is obliged to pay interest (the coupon) and/or to repay the principal at a later date, termed maturity.

Thus a _____ is a loan: the issuer is the borrower, the _____ holder is the lender, and the coupon is the interest. _____s provide the borrower with external funds to finance long-term investments, or, in the case of government _____s, to finance current expenditure.

   a. Catastrophe bonds   b. Puttable bond
   c. Convertible bond   d. Bond

15. In finance, a _____ is a standardized contract, to buy or sell a specified commodity of standardized quality at a certain date in the future, at a market determined price (the futures price.)

The price is determined by the instantaneous equilibrium between the forces of supply and demand among competing buy and sell orders on the exchange at the time of the purchase or sale of the contract.

In many cases, the items may be such non-traditional 'commodities' as foreign currencies, commercial or government paper [e.g., bonds], or 'baskets' of corporate equity ['stock indices'] or other financial instruments.

   a. Financial future   b. Repurchase agreement
   c. Heston model   d. Futures contract

16. In the original and simplified sense, _____ were things of value, of uniform quality, that were produced in large quantities by many different producers; the items from each different producer are considered equivalent. It is the contract and this underlying standard that define the commodity, not any quality inherent in the product.

_____ exchanges include:

- Chicago Board of Trade
- Kansas City Board of Trade
- Euronext.liffe
- Kuala Lumpur Futures Exchange
- Bhatinda Om ' Oil Exchange
- London Metal Exchange
- New York Mercantile Exchange
- Multi Commodity Exchange
- Dalian Commodity Exchange

Markets for trading _____ can be very efficient, particularly if the division into pools matches demand segments. These markets will quickly respond to changes in supply and demand to find an equilibrium price and quantity.

a. 529 plan
b. 7-Eleven
c. 4-4-5 Calendar
d. Commodities

17. In economics and finance, _____ is the practice of taking advantage of a price differential between two or more markets: striking a combination of matching deals that capitalize upon the imbalance, the profit being the difference between the market prices. When used by academics, an _____ is a transaction that involves no negative cash flow at any probabilistic or temporal state and a positive cash flow in at least one state; in simple terms, a risk-free profit.
a. Initial margin
b. Arbitrage
c. Efficient-market hypothesis
d. Issuer

18. The _____ is an American financial and commodity derivative exchange based in Chicago. The _____ was founded in 1898 as the Chicago Butter and Egg Board. Originally, the exchange was a non-profit organization.
a. Chicago Mercantile Exchange
b. Gamelan Council
c. Public Company Accounting Oversight Board
d. Financial Crimes Enforcement Network

19. A _____ is something for which there is demand, but which is supplied without qualitative differentiation across a market. It is a product that is the same no matter who produces it, such as petroleum, notebook paper, or milk. In other words, copper is copper.
a. 4-4-5 Calendar
b. 529 plan
c. 7-Eleven
d. Commodity

20. A _____ is a central financial exchange where people can trade standardized futures contracts; that is, a contract to buy specific quantities of a commodity or financial instrument at a specified price with delivery set at a specified time in the future.

Though the origins of futures trading can supposedly be traced to Ancient Greek or Phoenician times, the first modern organized _____ began in 1710 at the Dojima Rice Exchange in Osaka, Japan.

The United States followed in the early 1800s.

a. 7-Eleven
b. 529 plan
c. 4-4-5 Calendar
d. Futures Exchange

21. In finance, a _____ is a position established in one market in an attempt to offset exposure to the price risk of an equal but opposite obligation or position in another market -- usually, but not always, in the context of one's commercial activity. Hedging is a strategy designed to minimize exposure to such business risks as a sharp contraction in demand for one's inventory, while still allowing the business to profit from producing and maintaining that inventory. A typical hedger might be a farmer with 2000 acres of unharvested wheat in the ground, who would rather tend his crop without the distraction of uncertain prices.

a. 529 plan
b. 4-4-5 Calendar
c. 7-Eleven
d. Hedge

22. In the global money market, _____ is an unsecured promissory note with a fixed maturity of one to 270 days. _____ is a money-market security issued (sold) by large banks and corporations to get money to meet short term debt obligations (for example, payroll), and is only backed by an issuing bank or corporation's promise to pay the face amount on the maturity date specified on the note. Since it is not backed by collateral, only firms with excellent credit ratings from a recognized rating agency will be able to sell their _____ at a reasonable price.

a. Financial distress
b. Book building
c. Trade-off theory
d. Commercial paper

23. _____s are deposits denominated in United States dollars at banks outside the United States, and thus are not under the jurisdiction of the Federal Reserve. Consequently, such deposits are subject to much less regulation than similar deposits within the United States, allowing for higher margins. There is nothing 'European' about _____ deposits; a US dollar-denominated deposit in Tokyo or Caracas would likewise be deemed _____ deposits.

a. AAB
b. ABN Amro
c. A Random Walk Down Wall Street
d. Eurodollar

24. The _____ started life on September 30, 1982, to take advantage of the removal of currency controls in the UK in 1979. The exchange modelled itself after the Chicago Board of Trade and the Chicago Mercantile Exchange. It initially offered futures contracts and options linked to short term interest rates.

a. London International Financial Futures Exchange
b. 4-4-5 Calendar
c. 7-Eleven
d. 529 plan

25. _____ denotes the total number of derivative contracts, like futures and options, that are currently active on a specific underlying security, having specific terms.

Namely, the total contracts for a specific strike price and expiration date, that have been traded, but have not yet expired, have not yet been closed through a closing transaction, or have not yet been terminated via early exercise. A closing transaction occurs when a counterparty that longs the contract sells, or, conversely, when a counterparty that shorts the contract buys.

a. Open interest
b. Equity derivative
c. Equity swap
d. International Swaps and Derivatives Association

26. A _____, securities exchange or (in Europe) bourse is a corporation or mutual organization which provides 'trading' facilities for stock brokers and traders, to trade stocks and other securities. _____s also provide facilities for the issue and redemption of securities as well as other financial instruments and capital events including the payment of income and dividends. The securities traded on a _____ include: shares issued by companies, unit trusts and other pooled investment products and bonds.
   a. 4-4-5 Calendar
   b. 529 plan
   c. Stock Exchange
   d. 7-Eleven

27. _____ is a fee paid on borrowed assets. It is the price paid for the use of borrowed money, or, money earned by deposited funds. Assets that are sometimes lent with _____ include money, shares, consumer goods through hire purchase, major assets such as aircraft, and even entire factories in finance lease arrangements.
   a. Insolvency
   b. A Random Walk Down Wall Street
   c. AAB
   d. Interest

28. A _____ is a fungible, negotiable instrument representing financial value. They are broadly categorized into debt securities (such as banknotes, bonds and debentures), and equity securities; e.g., common stocks. The company or other entity issuing the _____ is called the issuer.
   a. Securities lending
   b. Security
   c. Book entry
   d. Tracking stock

29. In finance, a _____ is collateral that the holder of a position in securities, options, or futures contracts has to deposit to cover the credit risk of his counterparty (most often his broker.) This risk can arise if the holder has done any of the following:

   - borrowed cash from the counterparty to buy securities or options,
   - sold securities or options short, or
   - entered into a futures contract.

The collateral can be in the form of cash or securities, and it is deposited in a _____ account. On U.S. futures exchanges, '_____' was formally called performance bond.

_____ buying is buying securities with cash borrowed from a broker, using other securities as collateral.

   a. Margin
   b. Procter ' Gamble
   c. Share
   d. Credit

30. _____ or fair value accounting refers to the accounting standards of assigning a value to a position held in a financial instrument based on the current fair market price for the instrument or similar instruments. Fair value accounting has been a part of US Generally Accepted Accounting Principles (GAAP) since the early 1990s. The use of fair value measurements has increased steadily over the past decade, primarily in response to investor demand for relevant and timely financial statements that will aid in making better informed decisions.

a. 529 plan
b. Mark-to-market
c. 4-4-5 Calendar
d. 7-Eleven

31. In finance, the _____ between two currencies specifies how much one currency is worth in terms of the other. For example an _____ of 102 Japanese yen to the United States dollar means that JPY 102 is worth the same as USD 1. The foreign exchange market is one of the largest markets in the world.
   a. AAB
   b. A Random Walk Down Wall Street
   c. ABN Amro
   d. Exchange rate

32. When companies conduct business across borders, they must deal in foreign currencies. Companies must exchange foreign currencies for home currencies when dealing with receivables, and vice versa for payables. This is done at the current exchange rate between the two countries. _____ is the risk that the exchange rate will change unfavorably before the currency is exchanged.
   a. Lower of cost or market rule
   b. 529 plan
   c. Foreign exchange risk
   d. 4-4-5 Calendar

33. The institution most often referenced by the word '_____' is a public or publicly traded _____, the shares of which are traded on a public stock exchange (e.g., the New York Stock Exchange or Nasdaq in the United States) where shares of stock of _____s are bought and sold by and to the general public. Most of the largest businesses in the world are publicly traded _____s. However, the majority of _____s are said to be closely held, privately held or close _____s, meaning that no ready market exists for the trading of shares.
   a. Depository Trust Company
   b. Corporation
   c. Federal Home Loan Mortgage Corporation
   d. Protect

34. A _____ is a method of measuring a section of the stock market. Many indices are cited by news or financial services firms and are used to benchmark the performance of portfolios such as mutual funds.
   a. Stop order
   b. Program trading
   c. Trading curb
   d. Stock market index

35. A _____ is a private or public market for the trading of company stock and derivatives of company stock at an agreed price; these are securities listed on a stock exchange as well as those only traded privately.

The size of the world _____ is estimated at about $36.6 trillion US at the beginning of October 2008 . The world derivatives market has been estimated at about $480 trillion face or nominal value, 12 times the size of the entire world economy.

   a. Adolph Coors
   b. Andrew Tobias
   c. Anton Gelonkin
   d. Stock market

Chapter 23. Hedging with Financial Derivatives

36. _____ is the risk that the value of an investment will decrease due to moves in market factors. The five standard _____ factors are:

- Equity risk, the risk that stock prices will change.
- Interest rate risk, the risk that interest rates will change.
- Currency risk, the risk that foreign exchange rates will change.
- Commodity risk, the risk that commodity prices (e.g. grains, metals) will change.

As with other forms of risk, _____ may be measured in a number of ways. Traditionally, this is done using a Value at Risk methodology. Value at risk is well established as a risk management technique, but it contains a number of limiting assumptions that constrain its accuracy.

a. Currency risk
c. Market risk

b. Tracking error
d. Transaction risk

37. _____ is the difference between price and the costs of bringing to market whatever it is that is accounted as an enterprise (whether by harvest, extraction, manufacture, or purchase) in terms of the component costs of delivered goods and/or services and any operating or other expenses.

A key difficulty in measuring profit is in defining costs. Pure economic monetary profits can be zero or negative even in competitive equilibrium when accounted monetized costs exceed monetized price.

a. Economic profit
c. AAB

b. Accounting profit
d. A Random Walk Down Wall Street

38. In finance, _____ refers to Monday, October 19, 1987, when stock markets around the world crashed, shedding a huge value in a very short time. The crash began in Hong Kong, spread west through international time zones to Europe, hitting the United States after other markets had already declined by a significant margin. The Dow Jones Industrial Average (DJIA) dropped by 508 points to 1738.74 (22.61%).

a. 529 plan
c. 4-4-5 Calendar

b. 7-Eleven
d. Black Monday

39. _____ is a method of hedging a portfolio of stocks against the market risk by short selling stock index futures.

This hedging technique is frequently used by institutional investors when the market direction is uncertain or volatile. Short selling index futures can offset any downturns, but it also hinders any gains.

a. Freight derivative
c. Delivery month

b. Portfolio insurance
d. PAUG

40. _____ is casually defined as the use of computers in stock markets to engage in arbitrage and portfolio insurance strategies. However, the New York Stock Exchange (NYSE) defines the term as 'a wide range of portfolio trading strategies involving the purchase or sale of 15 or more stocks having a total market value of $1 million or more' without any direct reference to the use of computers. The word 'program' can be interpreted in its earlier, more general meaning of a defined and pre-arranged sequence of steps, rather than specifically a computer program.

a. Wash sale
c. Share price
b. Program trading
d. Stop order

41. A _____ is a sudden dramatic decline of stock prices across a significant cross-section of a stock market. Crashes are driven by panic as much as by underlying economic factors. They often follow speculative stock market bubbles.
  a. 7-Eleven
  c. 4-4-5 Calendar
  b. Stock market crash
  d. 529 plan

42. In options, the _____ is a key variable in a derivatives contract between two parties. Where the contract requires delivery of the underlying instrument, the trade will be at the _____, regardless of the spot price (market price) of the underlying instrument at that time.

Definition - The fixed price at which the owner of an option can purchase, in the case of a call in the case of a put, the underlying security or commodity.

  a. Moneyness
  c. Naked put
  b. Strike price
  d. Swaption

43. An _____ is a contract written by a seller that conveys to the buyer the right -- but not the obligation -- to buy (in the case of a call _____) or to sell (in the case of a put _____) a particular asset, such as a piece of property such as, among others, a futures contract. In return for granting the _____, the seller collects a payment (the premium) from the buyer.

For example, buying a call _____ provides the right to buy a specified quantity of a security at a set strike price at some time on or before expiration, while buying a put _____ provides the right to sell.

  a. AT'T Mobility LLC
  c. Annuity
  b. Amortization
  d. Option

44. The _____ is the price the buyer of the options contract pays for the right to buy or sell a security at a specified price in the future.
  a. AAB
  c. ABN Amro
  b. A Random Walk Down Wall Street
  d. Option premium

45. A _____ is a financial contract between two parties, the buyer and the seller of this type of option. Often it is simply labeled a 'call'. The buyer of the option has the right, but not the obligation to buy an agreed quantity of a particular commodity or financial instrument (the underlying instrument) from the seller of the option at a certain time (the expiration date) for a certain price (the strike price.)
  a. Bear spread
  c. Call option
  b. Bull spread
  d. Bear call spread

46. A _____ is a financial contract between two parties, the seller (writer) and the buyer of the option. The put allows its buyer the right but not the obligation to sell a commodity or financial instrument (the underlying instrument) to the writer (seller) of the option at a certain time for a certain price (the strike price.) The writer (seller) has the obligation to purchase the underlying asset at that strike price, if the buyer exercises the option.

Chapter 23. Hedging with Financial Derivatives

a. Bear spread
c. Bear call spread
b. Put option
d. Debit spread

47. The U.S. _____ is an independent agency of the United States government which holds primary responsibility for enforcing the federal securities laws and regulating the securities industry, the nation's stock and options exchanges, and other electronic securities markets. The SEC was created by section 4 of the SEC of 1934 (now codified as 15 U.S.C. Â§ 78d and commonly referred to as the 1934 Act.)
a. 7-Eleven
c. 4-4-5 Calendar
b. Securities and Exchange Commission
d. 529 plan

48. A _____ is a foreign exchange agreement between two parties to exchange principal and fixed rate interest payments on a loan in one currency for principal and fixed rate interest payments on an equal (regarding net present value) loan in another currency. They are motivated by comparative advantage.
a. Currency swap
c. Foreign exchange market
b. Forex swap
d. Currency pair

49. In finance, a _____ is a derivative in which two counterparties agree to exchange one stream of cash flows against another stream. These streams are called the legs of the _____.

The cash flows are calculated over a notional principal amount, which is usually not exchanged between counterparties.

a. Swap
c. Volatility swap
b. Volatility arbitrage
d. Local volatility

50. A _____ is an institution, firm or individual who mediates between two or more parties in a financial context. Typically the first party is a provider of a product or service and the second party is a consumer or customer.

In the U.S., a _____ is typically an institution that facilitates the channelling of funds between lenders and borrowers indirectly.

a. Mutual fund
c. Net asset value
b. Savings and loan association
d. Financial intermediary

51. _____ is a legally declared inability or impairment of ability of an individual or organization to pay their creditors. Creditors may file a _____ petition against a debtor ('involuntary _____') in an effort to recoup a portion of what they are owed or initiate a restructuring. In the majority of cases, however, _____ is initiated by the debtor (a 'voluntary _____' that is filed by the bankrupt individual or organization.)
a. Bankruptcy
c. 4-4-5 Calendar
b. Debt settlement
d. 529 plan

52. In political science and economics, the _____ or agency dilemma treats the difficulties that arise under conditions of incomplete and asymmetric information when a principal hires an agent. Various mechanisms may be used to try to align the interests of the agent with those of the principal, such as piece rates/commissions, profit sharing, efficiency wages, performance measurement (including financial statements), the agent posting a bond, or fear of firing. The _____ is found in most employer/employee relationships, for example, when stockholders hire top executives of corporations.

    a. 7-Eleven   b. 529 plan
    c. Principal-agent problem   d. 4-4-5 Calendar

53. _____ is the provision of resources (such as granting a loan) by one party to another party where that second party does not reimburse the first party immediately, thereby generating a debt, and instead arranges either to repay or return those resources (or material(s) of equal value) at a later date. The first party is called a creditor, also known as a lender, while the second party is called a debtor, also known as a borrower.

Movements of financial capital are normally dependent on either _____ or equity transfers.

    a. Clearing house   b. Comparable
    c. Warrant   d. Credit

ANSWER KEY

Chapter 1
1. d   2. d   3. d   4. a   5. d   6. d   7. d   8. d   9. b   10. d
11. a   12. d   13. d   14. c   15. d   16. c   17. d   18. d   19. d   20. a
21. d   22. a   23. d   24. d   25. d   26. d

Chapter 2
1. d   2. c   3. a   4. b   5. d   6. a   7. a   8. c   9. a   10. b
11. d   12. d   13. d   14. a   15. b   16. d   17. d   18. d   19. d   20. c
21. d   22. b   23. c   24. c   25. d   26. c   27. d   28. b   29. a   30. c
31. a   32. a   33. c   34. d   35. d   36. b   37. d   38. d   39. d   40. c
41. d   42. c   43. c   44. d   45. a   46. b   47. d   48. a   49. d   50. d
51. c   52. b   53. b   54. d   55. d   56. d   57. d

Chapter 3
1. d   2. c   3. d   4. a   5. d   6. d   7. b   8. d   9. c   10. c
11. d   12. d   13. d   14. d   15. d   16. d   17. d   18. b   19. d   20. b
21. c   22. d   23. d   24. d   25. c   26. a   27. d   28. d   29. d   30. d
31. d   32. d   33. d   34. a   35. a   36. b

Chapter 4
1. a   2. d   3. d   4. b   5. a   6. d   7. d   8. b   9. d   10. d
11. b   12. a   13. b   14. c   15. d   16. d   17. a   18. c   19. c   20. d
21. a   22. b   23. a   24. d   25. d   26. d   27. c   28. c   29. d   30. d
31. d   32. c   33. c

Chapter 5
1. c   2. b   3. d   4. c   5. a   6. d   7. a   8. c   9. d   10. c
11. d   12. b   13. d   14. b   15. b   16. a   17. a   18. a   19. b   20. d
21. b   22. a   23. b   24. d   25. d   26. a   27. d   28. c   29. d   30. d
31. d   32. d   33. c   34. d   35. a

Chapter 6
1. c   2. d   3. a   4. d   5. c   6. c   7. c   8. d   9. c   10. d
11. b   12. b   13. d   14. c   15. b   16. a   17. b   18. d   19. d   20. d
21. d   22. d

Chapter 7
1. b   2. d   3. d   4. d   5. d   6. a   7. d   8. c   9. d   10. d
11. d   12. b   13. c   14. d   15. d   16. d   17. d   18. c   19. d   20. d
21. a   22. d   23. b   24. d   25. d   26. b   27. a   28. a   29. b   30. c
31. d   32. a   33. b   34. a   35. d   36. b   37. b   38. c   39. b   40. a
41. b   42. d   43. c   44. d   45. d

Chapter 8

1. b	2. d	3. a	4. d	5. d	6. d	7. c	8. c	9. d	10. b
11. a	12. b	13. d	14. d	15. b	16. c	17. d	18. a	19. d	20. a
21. b	22. d	23. c	24. b	25. a	26. d	27. b	28. d	29. d	30. b
31. b	32. d	33. d	34. a	35. c	36. a	37. d	38. b	39. c	40. d
41. d	42. a	43. a							

Chapter 9

1. d	2. c	3. c	4. d	5. d	6. b	7. b	8. c	9. d	10. a
11. b	12. d	13. b	14. c	15. a	16. d	17. d	18. b	19. d	20. d
21. d	22. c	23. c	24. c	25. a	26. d	27. a	28. b	29. d	30. d
31. d	32. b	33. b	34. d	35. a	36. d	37. a	38. b	39. b	40. a
41. d	42. d	43. a	44. c	45. d	46. a	47. d	48. d	49. a	50. d
51. b	52. c	53. d	54. b	55. a	56. a	57. c	58. d	59. c	60. d
61. d	62. a	63. b	64. d						

Chapter 10

1. d	2. d	3. d	4. d	5. b	6. b	7. d	8. d	9. b	10. d
11. d	12. a	13. d	14. d	15. d	16. a	17. d	18. d	19. a	20. b
21. c	22. d	23. b	24. b	25. c	26. b	27. b	28. d		

Chapter 11

1. d	2. d	3. b	4. d	5. d	6. d	7. d	8. d	9. d	10. d
11. b	12. d	13. a	14. c	15. d	16. b	17. a	18. d	19. a	20. d
21. b	22. d	23. d	24. c	25. d	26. d	27. b	28. b	29. d	30. b
31. b	32. d	33. d	34. d	35. d	36. d	37. a	38. d	39. d	40. d
41. c	42. b	43. b	44. a	45. d	46. b	47. d	48. d		

Chapter 12

1. b	2. d	3. c	4. a	5. a	6. d	7. a	8. d	9. a	10. a
11. d	12. c	13. d	14. b	15. c	16. a	17. d			

Chapter 13

1. d	2. c	3. b	4. a	5. c	6. a	7. a	8. d	9. b	10. a
11. d	12. c	13. d	14. d	15. d	16. d	17. d	18. b	19. d	20. d
21. b	22. c	23. d	24. c	25. b	26. d	27. d	28. b	29. d	30. a
31. d	32. d	33. d	34. d	35. a	36. d	37. d	38. d	39. d	40. b

ANSWER KEY

Chapter 14

1. d	2. d	3. b	4. d	5. a	6. b	7. c	8. d	9. c	10. a
11. d	12. d	13. b	14. d	15. b	16. d	17. c	18. d	19. d	20. b
21. a	22. a	23. c	24. c	25. a	26. d	27. d	28. d	29. b	30. c
31. b	32. c	33. a	34. a	35. d	36. b	37. d	38. a	39. d	40. d
41. a	42. d	43. d	44. d	45. d	46. c	47. d	48. d	49. d	50. d
51. b	52. d	53. d							

Chapter 15

1. b	2. d	3. d	4. d	5. c	6. c	7. b	8. d	9. d	10. d
11. b	12. a	13. b	14. b	15. d	16. d	17. a	18. b	19. d	20. d
21. d	22. d	23. c	24. a	25. a	26. a	27. a	28. d	29. c	30. d
31. c	32. d	33. a	34. d	35. d	36. c	37. c	38. d	39. b	40. c
41. d	42. c	43. b	44. d	45. d	46. a	47. c	48. d	49. c	50. d
51. d	52. d	53. d	54. b	55. d					

Chapter 16

1. c	2. a	3. c	4. c	5. d	6. a	7. c	8. a	9. b	10. a
11. b	12. a	13. c	14. c	15. c	16. a	17. d	18. b	19. a	20. d
21. b	22. d	23. b	24. b	25. d	26. d	27. b	28. b	29. d	30. a
31. a	32. c	33. a	34. b	35. b	36. b				

Chapter 17

1. c	2. d	3. a	4. d	5. a	6. d	7. d	8. d	9. a	10. c
11. b	12. d	13. c	14. a	15. d	16. d	17. d	18. b	19. d	20. d
21. d									

Chapter 18

1. c	2. d	3. d	4. b	5. a	6. a	7. d	8. d	9. d	10. a
11. d	12. c	13. c	14. b	15. d	16. a	17. c	18. d	19. b	20. c
21. c	22. b	23. c	24. d	25. a	26. d	27. a	28. a	29. d	30. c
31. d	32. d	33. d	34. b						

Chapter 19

1. d	2. d	3. d	4. d	5. a	6. d	7. d	8. d	9. c	10. d
11. b	12. d	13. d	14. d	15. c	16. d	17. c	18. d	19. d	20. d
21. d	22. d	23. d	24. c	25. d	26. d	27. d	28. d		

Chapter 20

1. c	2. a	3. d	4. d	5. d	6. c	7. d	8. c	9. d	10. c
11. d	12. a	13. c	14. a	15. d	16. c	17. d	18. d	19. d	20. a
21. d	22. d	23. d	24. d	25. c	26. d	27. b	28. d		

Chapter 21

1. d	2. b	3. d	4. a	5. d	6. d	7. d	8. d	9. c	10. c
11. d	12. a	13. a	14. d	15. d	16. a	17. d	18. d	19. b	20. c
21. d	22. d	23. d	24. b	25. c	26. b	27. d	28. a	29. b	30. c
31. c	32. b	33. d	34. d	35. b	36. c	37. a	38. d	39. d	40. c
41. d	42. c	43. d	44. a	45. b	46. d	47. d	48. c	49. d	

Chapter 22

| 1. d | 2. d | 3. a | 4. a | 5. a | 6. d | 7. b | 8. a | 9. d | 10. d |
| 11. d | 12. d | | | | | | | | |

Chapter 23

1. a	2. d	3. c	4. b	5. b	6. d	7. d	8. c	9. b	10. a
11. a	12. b	13. a	14. d	15. d	16. d	17. b	18. a	19. d	20. d
21. d	22. d	23. d	24. a	25. a	26. c	27. d	28. b	29. a	30. b
31. d	32. c	33. b	34. d	35. d	36. c	37. b	38. d	39. b	40. b
41. b	42. b	43. d	44. d	45. c	46. b	47. b	48. a	49. a	50. d
51. a	52. c	53. d							

www.ingramcontent.com/pod-product-compliance
Lightning Source LLC
Chambersburg PA
CBHW082203230426
43672CB00015B/2880